‖‖‖‖ W9-COZ-391

10/27/23

Hi,
Chapter 5 of this book is titled:
"The Stories Behind Touchdown
Jesus." I did A LOT of research for
this book here in Hesburgh Library,

Everybody Knows
a Salesman Can't
Write a Book

Sitting right here on the 11th floor,
near all the books about the
era of WWII in Europe.

Please feel free to take this copy to
read ... keep ... share ... whatever ...

I hope you enjoy reading it as

Bill Whiteside

much as I enjoyed writing it.

Bill Whiteside

BWHITESIDE3@GMAIL.COM

Perfectly Adequate Press
Lancaster, Pennsylvania

Copyright © 2022 by Bill Whiteside.

All rights reserved.

No part of this publication may be reproduced, distributed, or transmitted physically, electronically or by any other means, without the prior written permission of the publisher, except in the case of brief quotations embodied in critical reviews and certain other noncommercial uses permitted by copyright laws.

Publisher contact: bill.whiteside@perfectlytruestory.com

As of the time of initial publication, the Internet addresses displayed in this book link to or refer to existing websites on the Internet. Neither the publisher nor the author assumes any responsibility for errors or for changes that occur after publication. Neither Perfectly Adequate Press nor the author are responsible for, and should not be deemed to endorse or recommend, any website other than the author's perfectly-truestory.com site.

LIBRARY OF CONGRESS CATALOGING-IN-PUBLICATION DATA
Names: Whiteside, Bill, author,
Title: Everybody Knows a Salesman Can't Write a Book / Bill Whiteside
Description: First Edition. | Lancaster: Perfectly Adequate Press, [2022]
Includes bibliographical references and index.
Identifiers: LCCN 2022913639 (print)
ISBN 9798986660707 (hardcover) | ISBN 9798986660714 (trade paperback) | ISBN 9798986660721 (eBook}

Front Cover photograph of Chartwell (Winston Churchill's country residence) by Barbara Whiteside
Author photograph by Barbara Whiteside
Cover design by Fayyaz Ahmed (dezinir.99)
https://99designs.com/profiles/2311985

To my parents – Eileen and Bill Whiteside,
my wife Barbara,
our children Billy and Brittany,
their spouses Daneen and Steve,
and to Britt and Steve's son Liam.

Thank you for the comfort of a close family,
the blessings of your confidence and encouragement,
the unforgettable adventures that we've shared and will
never stop celebrating,
your love that brightens every day,
and all of the smiles still to come.

Contents

Introduction

During the course of writing my second book, I decided to start writing my first.

My family, some co-workers, and a few friends know all about that second book. None of them knew I was writing this book. For the longest time *I* didn't know I was writing this book.

My second book grew from a lifelong fascination with Winston Churchill. After reading a half-dozen biographies, I noticed that every author briefly mentioned Churchill's pivotal role in a deadly clash between the British and French navies early in World War II. Since Churchill was an unabashed Francophile, and since Britain and France had battled against Germany as allies only two weeks prior to that incident, there had to be more to the story.

That one-sided bombardment in the small port of Mers-el-Kébir on the coast of Algeria ended with the Royal Navy killing more French seamen than the Germans killed during the entire war. The more I learned about this story, the more determined I became to learn why Churchill turned against his former allies and why Britain and France risked war against one another in July 1940. As I researched and learned more about the clashes of personalities, priorities, trust, and honor in the months and minutes leading up to the incident, it became a story I just had to write.

Of course, I had to jump a couple of hurdles along the way. I have a fulltime job. I'm a software salesman and, significantly, not a professional writer or a pedigreed historian.

Fortunately, I run my own small business and control my schedule. I could always make time for research and writing - early in the day, late at night, and often squeezing in a few sentences and paragraphs on planes and trains on my way to customers and prospects.

As for writing ... although my writing ability has added value to every job I've ever had, I'm not blind to the reality that writing a book about a significant event in history is many degrees of magnitude more challenging than writing a paper on how to improve forecast accuracy. The only way to become a better writer was to keep writing. And so I did, contributing papers and e-books for work, posting dozens of articles on a wide range of subjects online, and – as it turned out – writing this book; all part of an ongoing writing-improvement process that I do not expect to ever end.

The field research for my book was a regular source of astonishment and adventure. I was pleasantly surprised – shocked, actually - when the archivists of Winston Churchill's and Franklin D. Roosevelt's private papers allowed a software salesman to rustle through their priceless documents. I attended a reading by a Pulitzer-Prize-winning historian who then was kind enough to share how he organized and prioritized his massive compilation of research materials. I made a pilgrimage to a remote site outside of Paris at which "the greatest dishonor of all time" had taken place – or so Adolf Hitler claimed. I learned how to find the facts that helped make my story sparkle.

My book was coming together... but the pace of my progress was frustratingly slow. I still spent much more time with my nose buried in dusty old diaries and with my eyes glued to digitized archives of 80-year-old newspapers than I spent writing. The input that I still had to digest was a flood and my output was just a trickle.

To stimulate my imagination and to exercise some writing muscles, I wrote a piece about my pilgrimage to Compiegne, a small town one hour north of Paris. Germany and France signed their armistice agreement in a recently-requisitioned private rail car there at the end of World War I. Twenty-two years later, when Germany overwhelmed France after just six weeks of serious fighting in the early days of World War II, Hitler humiliated the French by insisting they sign an armistice in that same rail car – after his henchmen rolled it through a freshly chiseled hole in the front wall of the museum in which it had rested in quiet repose for the previous decade. Although I thought I knew all about Compiegne's history, my visit also exposed me to a couple of soul-wrenching revelations about the Holocaust. The story of that trip stretched my imagination and sharpened my writing.

Of all the different experiences in the new research and writing side of my life, the most fascinating was my three-day immersion in the papers of Winston Churchill in the Churchill Archives at the University of Cambridge. In addition to Churchill's papers, I also read the letters, diaries, and other documents in the donated collections of British admirals, generals, and statesmen who directly impacted the story I was writing. Wrapped around the time I spent literally holding history in my hands, I meandered from one edge of the majestic campus to the other at the beginning and end of each of my three workdays in the archives. And so the centuries-old grandeur of Cambridge added to the magic of that experience. The story of my time at Cambridge became another advanced writing exercise.

I've turned myself into a dogged researcher, and I wanted to enrich my story by exploring as many useful historical resources as possible. Most of those resources are the products of other writers. After finding one especially interesting book about the German hierarchy, but then learning the remarkable tale of that book's disreputable Holocaust-denying author, I could not resist writing about him ... after first purging his material from my notes.

Those pieces were a joy to write, and those stories begat more stories. I wrote about used books, old words, how I taught myself to read French, and how I made steady progress with my research and writing once I applied lessons from my business career and found a way to meaningfully quantify my progress. As those stories came together, I realized that I just might be writing a book about how I wrote my book.

I had met the journalist and author Paul Reid at a conference of the International Churchill Society in Charleston, South Carolina a number of years ago. At that time, he was in the process of wrapping up a book that he had not originally planned to write.

Many years before, Reid had befriended William Manchester, who had published the first two volumes of his *Last Lion* trilogy on the life of Winston Churchill. After Manchester suffered two strokes and acknowledged that his failing health would prevent him from completing the final volume in the trilogy, he asked Reid to take over his project. Paul Reid subsequently shared with me that his immediate reaction was "a confused look," to which Manchester responded: "I want you to finish the book, to write it." When Reid – a newspaperman at heart and experience – hesitated, Manchester encouraged him by suggesting: "A book is nothing more than a collection of stories. You've written stories your entire career." The final volume in the trilogy was published as a collaboration between Manchester and Reid, and it has become an acclaimed entry in the Churchill canon (and it is, of course, much more than a collection of stories).

For a time, this collection of stories was a personal project, something that I thought I might share with just a small circle of friends and family.

This dangerously unfocused and uncharacteristically limited ambition changed very suddenly one day while I was listening to an audiobook on my way to a software demo to a women's underwear company in northern New Jersey. About 90 minutes into the audio version of *Perennial Seller*, Ryan Holiday, who was reading his own book, grabbed my attention with a question:

"Who is this thing for?"

Let me first tell you who *Perennial Seller* is for. Ryan Holiday writes about the making and the marketing of work that lasts. *Perennial Seller* is not just about books and it's not just for writers. It's for creative types - writers, musicians, computer programmers, architects – anyone who has given over their life to a creative project.

It's not just about the creative process either. Ryan Holiday preaches the creator's essential role in the marketing of his or her material. *Perennial Seller* is more of an inspirational guide than it is an instructional manual. It inspired me to start caring more about shaping my stories into a work with wider appeal. It also got me thinking more seriously about how to find and reach the audience most likely to welcome this book. I realized that in writing a collection of individually aimless and too-loosely-related stories for a small and scattered group of readers, I was writing a book that might not appeal to anyone at all.

One of my favorite Winston Churchill stories tells of a dinner at which he sent back a disappointing dessert, damning the concoction with: "Take away this pudding, it has no theme." As I set about the task of stirring a theme into my pudding, I rewrote individual stories, rearranged the sequence in which some chapters appeared, and found several interesting strands of continuity that I could weave from beginning to end.

As I rewrote and rewrote and rewrote this book, I kept another quote from Ryan Holiday in mind, a piece of advice that an editor had passed on to him. "It's not what a book is, it's what a book does." Holiday adds: "Just as we should ask 'Who is this for?' we must also ask, 'What does this do?' … How will it improve the lives of the people who buy it?"

So, what is this book, who is it for, what does it do, and … will it really improve your life?

This is a narrative non-fiction book about the writing of a narrative non-fiction book. It is an account of one software salesman's crusade to research and write a book while working full time. It tells of how surprisingly simple it was to gain access to unique collections of invaluable primary research materials, how I learned to wrangle tens of thousands of accumulated bits of research into a coherent story, how I fought through periodic bouts of imposter syndrome, and much more.

This book is for anyone who dreams of turning a creative idea into commercial reality, and especially for anyone who carries the weight of self-doubt - as in "Allow a software salesman to browse through Winston Churchill's papers, are you kidding me?" or "Just who do you think you are to think you can write a book?" This book is for anyone with an interest in history, including how it is made and how it is written.

This book is pollinated with stories that most people have never heard about Winston Churchill and dozens of the admirals, generals, diplomats, statesmen, and one deranged French mistress – not Churchill's – whose actions made history in 1939 and 1940.

My goal is to inspire you to action with these stories of how I found my own way through a series of continuously unfolding challenges and apprehensions while I learned how to research and write a book. I hope you will see yourself in my stories.

Will this book change your life? Despite a trusted colleague telling me I was not cut out for sales (he was right at the time), I eventually built a small but very successful business around my ability to sell software. At our peak, my business helped support the families of nine other colleagues – just as their talent and dedication helped support me. Together we sold $60 million in software and services during my 30-year career. My "secret" was that I do not meet most people's stereotypical expectations of a salesman. I'm humble, I'm honest (as are all of the best salesmen and women) and I'm very genuine. In that vein of being honest and genuine, while the process of writing two books at one time has certainly changed my life, I have to tell you: No... Come on, of course reading my book will not change your life.

What will change your life in more good ways than you can possibly imagine will be when you write that first sentence, when the first colors brighten your canvas, or when you press "Record" and start playing ... and then keep at it and at it and at it.

Remember, actions count. Every step in the process – starting when the product of your imagination begins to take shape, and then as it is continually refined, and finally when it is exposed it to an audience that is rooting for your success – brings incredibly rewarding levels of satisfaction.

I want this book to inform, inspire, enlighten, and entertain. I hope you will put these stories and lessons about curiosity, determination, confidence, keeping score, and persistence to work for you.

CHAPTER 1

This Is Not That Book

I've had this wild notion that I could write a book. I've written for all kinds of reasons for as long as I could hold a pencil. There's a story I'd like to share. It's a true story, about a significant incident from early in World War II, a story that most people have never heard. I believe my story will not just interest and surprise you; it will also inspire you. I've exhaustively researched all the heroes and villains, as well as the events and the atmosphere in the run-up to this incident from multiple perspectives. I'm confident in my ability to paint this story with the depth, the drama, the color, all of the personality, and the intrigue that it deserves.

This is not that book, however. That book comes next.

That book tells the story of a controversial and catastrophic event in the early days of World War II, during Winston Churchill's second month as Great Britain's Prime Minister.

That story – of how Churchill ordered the destruction of much of the French fleet just two weeks after France and Great Britain ended their wartime alliance - is briefly mentioned in almost every Churchill biography. It's typically addressed in a few paragraphs; occasionally it gets several pages. Andrew Roberts tells the story across two of the 982 pages in his definitive *Churchill: Walking with Destiny*. Paul Reid covers the buildup, the carnage, and the aftermath in six of the 1,053 pages in

Defender of the Realm, 1940-1965. Given the scope of those two books, that's appropriate detail. But there is much more to this story than is typically written.

That book is much more than just a simple retelling of history. It's also a tale of uncommon character and conviction, and a parable for those in power – in government and business - today.

Most biographies are written by authors who laud their subjects, and that's especially appropriate anytime anyone writes about Winston Churchill. William F. Buckley stated: "For as long as heroes are written about, Winston Churchill will be written about."

Most Churchill books convey the impression that his actions against the French fleet in July 1940 were justified, perhaps even necessary. I initially believed Churchill's decision to decimate the French fleet was one of his finest moments. That conviction inspired me to write my book. In that vein, I was disappointed when I learned about the bitter opposition of Britain's senior naval officers to Churchill's order to fire upon their former comrades, and I rejoiced when I read about the boisterous and unanimous cheers of approval in the House of Commons when Churchill reported the results of his decision the day after the shots were fired.

But as my research exposed me to more of the details, I began to question my original premise. The process of researching and writing that book changed my perspective multiple times in multiple directions. If you dig deeply into the motivations, decisions, actions, and personalities from the years, months, weeks, hours and even the minutes leading up to the clash between the French and British navies on July 3, 1940, well ... you just might be inspired to write a book to share the entire story.

I'm a software salesman. I've never written a book before. I've never done the research, visited a presidential library, or the Army War College. I've never immersed myself in the Churchill Archives at the University of Cambridge. I've never taught myself to read French, and I've certainly never before planted my feet in the precise spot in a remarkably calm French forest where Adolf Hitler reflected before imposing his devious armistice terms on France. I've never needed a color-coded spreadsheet to organize the books and articles that I've researched. I've never held the personal correspondence of Winston Churchill, Franklin D. Roosevelt, Admiral Sir James Somerville, and other diplomats, aides, and officers. I've never had to deal with those "Just who do you think you are ...?" moments of self-doubt. I've never had a Pulitzer-Prize-winning author tell me about "the greatest invention since the plow." I've never made a list of the most loathsome characters I've encountered in my research, nor have I ever written about the admirals, ambassadors, interpreters, journalists, and other fascinating personalities with whom I wish I could have enjoyed a pint of beer. I never truly studied how to write, nor so earnestly practiced and refined my writing.

Those efforts included countless twists, wrinkles, revelations, and moments of astonishment.

That's this book.

CHAPTER 2

What Do I Don't Have?

In the beginning all I had were a few books about the life of Winston Churchill.

Books like Jon Meacham's *Franklin and Winston*, Roy Jenkins', *Churchill, A Biography*, and William Manchester's *The Last Lion: Winston Spencer Churchill, Alone, 1932-1940* were scattered across various shelves and bookcases in different rooms around our house.

My group of Churchill books (which was too small to call a collection) was casual, random, and sparse. When I embarked on my book project, it was clear that my personal library would not take me very far. So, for the first time since grade school, I acquired a library card, and began spending time at our local public library in downtown Lancaster, Pennsylvania.

I borrowed and read an armful of books every couple of weeks. I breezed through the history and biography sections in just a few months. Lancaster's library was a nice surprise, and the books that I borrowed significantly broadened the foundation of my knowledge. But I live in a fairly small town and the local library's collection clearly was not as far-reaching as I would need to research the story I was interested in writing about.

My software sales job requires quite a bit of travel, and I started wandering into used bookstores in Pittsburgh, Boston, St. Louis, Portsmouth, New Orleans and a few other towns along the way.

Since I was early in the information-gathering process and had not yet built up my resources, and since just about every new discovery was potentially useful, I found something new and interesting in just about every bookstore I entered.

To this day I don't notice the small bell that hangs on the front door of every used bookstore ... until it jingles and startles me as I open the door. An overly keen or an over-worked and droopy-eyed proprietor usually sits just off to the side at a book-strewn table or desk. If he's not reading a book, he's punching away at an adding machine. Some nod and say hello. Some ask if you have a specific interest they can help you with. Some just quietly keep their heads down as if to say: "I won't bother you if you don't bother me."

The used book essence, with varying degrees of dust, must, and nostalgia is always in the air. I don't think I'd be comfortable in a brightly lit used bookstore: I don't believe I've ever seen one. In the best used bookstores, every shelf is densely filled. I even encountered some shelves that were packed two-deep, as if to reward only the most tenacious researchers. The aisles between shelves tend to be very narrow. With the poor lighting and the narrow aisles, it's a special challenge to read the titles of the books on the bottom shelves that face you, even when you lean back and practically sit on the shelves behind you. It's heaven I'm telling you.

If you buy more books than you can carry in your hands, the store will hopefully, but not necessarily, have a stash of random shopping bags or a helpful cardboard box or two. If you're on a serious book quest, it's not a bad idea to bring your own bag.

I never went into a used bookstore looking for a specific title. Instead, I asked: Where can I find your World War II books? Do you have a section on French History? Can you point me toward the biographies? From there, each bookstore was its own unique source of occasional fascination amid long periods of mindless tedium.

Fortunately, my interests were confined to a fairly small number of topical sections, and I usually did not have to wander down too many aisles: World War II, British History, French History, Biographies, and Naval History pretty much covered it.

As my personal library grew, one small milestone was passed when I wondered: "Hey, do I already have this book?" I will admit to a few accidental duplicates in what has now grown into a true collection.

A number of years ago, when she was about kindergarten-age, I asked our daughter Brittany what she wanted for her birthday. After a moment of scrunch-faced contemplation, Britt replied: "What do I don't have?" I was at the point where I needed a system to help me regularly quantify what do I don't have, as well as what do I do have in my collection.

Thus began my color-coded spreadsheet. I listed the books that I had, plus the books that I wanted to find. A bit later, as my research continued to evolve and expand, I needed to track which books I owned but had not yet read, which books I had read and had not yet highlighted and transcribed, and those from which I had squeezed every bit of interesting information and could finally tuck away.

I'm a proponent of data visualization and the value of visual cues, and so of course I included a color-coded scheme. Here's what I use:

Blue:　　Books I want to find

Green:　Books I've acquired but have not yet read

Red: Books I've read and highlighted but have not yet transcribed

Black: Books I've read and transcribed and have finally tucked away.

There used to be several used bookstores on East Carson Street in Pittsburgh, Pennsylvania. As I sifted through the shelves at City Books one afternoon, I discovered an inventory that included a rare bounty of war tales and biographies ... *HMS Hood - Pride of the Royal Navy*, the two-volume *Memoirs of Cordell Hull*, a copy of William L. Shirer's *This is Berlin*, and a number of shelves randomly seeded with comparable beauties. But several titles seemed just a bit too familiar. By this time, I had a fairly robust color-coded spreadsheet, but I did not always carry a printed copy with me. This was one of those days when I entered a bookstore empty handed.

I carried three books toward the front of the store and told the proprietor that I intended to purchase those books, as well as a few more. But I needed to run to my car to get my laptop to check my book list to see if I already owned any of those titles. When I returned, I asked if I could leave my laptop open on a table near her perch at the front of the store, along with the books I was accumulating. She smiled wryly and said that would be OK.

After about my fourth ramble from her store's cavernous rows of shelves with a small stack of books, as I surveyed my spreadsheet she laughed and said, "Oh my, you really do have a list!" While some shoppers look for a specific book or a specific author, she told me that mine was the first list she had encountered. It was a good day for both of us.

Well maybe it was a better day for the proprietor. I was only interested in Volume 1 of Cordell Hull's memoirs, but she would only sell the complete two-volume set.

Since my list – as well as the hope-to-find, need-to-read, have-read, and transcribed-and-done status of the books on my list – changes almost weekly, I do not always carry a printed copy of the spreadsheet with me. But if I sense an opportunity to visit a bookstore or a library, I make it a point to print and pack a rainbow-colored copy. That spreadsheet now runs to over 800 rows, or 18 single-spaced printed pages.

I'm never quite sure if my color-coded list delights or frightens the proprietors of used bookstores, but it always seems to be a surprise. After many hours in too many dark and narrow aisles to count, my book collection, along with my perpetual list of books that I do, don't, and would like to have, is now anything but casual, random or sparse.

CHAPTER 3

Ben Coutts' Obituary and the Statue with the Blood Red Hands

I sometimes wondered if the story that seemed so important to me would matter at all to anyone else. There is no question that the British assault on the French fleet at Mers-el-Kébir and the death of 1,297 Frenchmen shocked the world on that one day in history and in the days that immediately followed. Newspapers from all corners of the world blared the news in banner headlines.

The *New York Times*:
BRITISH SEIZE OR SINK BULK OF FRENCH FLEET;
RESISTING UNITS DEFEATED IN FURIOUS BATTLE

In Britain, *The Daily Telegraph:*
NAVY TAKES OR SINKS
FRENCH WARSHIPS
Big Part of Her Fleet
Now in Our Hands

In Paris, *Le Matin* :
L'ODIEUSE AGRESSION DE L'ANGLETTERRE
CONTRE LA FLOTTE FRANCAISE A L'ANCRE
SOULEVE L'INDIGNATION MONDIALE

The Odious Aggression of England
Against the French Fleet at Anchor
Raises World Indignation

Even the *Intelligencer Journal* in small, faraway Lancaster, Pennsylvania:
BRITAIN SEIZES FRENCH NAVY IN BATTLE
Sink or Damage All That Refused British Offers

But this clash between former allies in a small harbor in Algeria was just one episode in a World War that raged for more than five years. There were much bigger battles with many more casualties and far deeper consequence across that time. Did Britain's assault on the French fleet in the harbor at Mers-el-Kébir near Oran, and the deaths of those 1,297 Frenchmen have any lasting significance?

One slight indication of its lingering impact emerged unexpectedly in the obituary of a Scottish war veteran who died in 2004 at the age of 87. Ben Coutts, a proud Scotsman, "a huge man seldom seen out of kilt" had worked as a shepherd and a groom. He managed farms and bred livestock in his native Scotland. Coutts was seriously wounded early in World War II, and he later earned more than a wee bit of renown across the United Kingdom as an author and broadcaster. His long obituary in *The Daily Telegraph* includes remarkable details about his tribulations in the war.

Ben Coutts was a 24-year-old sergeant-major with the Surrey and Sussex Yeomanry when he sailed to North Africa to fight the Germans in 1941. Not long after he landed, Coutts' face was sliced by a jagged piece of shrapnel during a German assault on the British garrison at Tobruk. The deep, horrific wound all but obliterated his nose.

En route to Alexandria and the promise of better care, the hospital ship carrying the still comatose Coutts was bombed and strafed by the Luftwaffe. The ship did not sink, but that was just a portent of what was to come.

After Coutts endured 10 plastic surgery procedures over the next year, he sailed for home aboard the RMS *Laconia*, a Cunard liner that had been converted to a troopship. Just before 10:30 on the night of September 12, 1942, the *Laconia* was torpedoed by a German U-boat, U-156. Passengers, crew members, soldiers, convalescing patients and 1,800 Italian prisoners of war cascaded over the sides and struggled for survival in the nighttime sea. Of the 4,532 souls who had been stuffed aboard the ship, Coutts was one of 1,668 who survived the *Laconia's* sinking, finding his way first to the tenuous safety of a flimsy raft, and then to a lifeboat.

The captain of U-156 was so horrified by the silhouettes of so many people flailing for their lives in the moonlit water that he broadcast an appeal for rescue ships and promised not to fire on those ships as long as his U-boat was not attacked.

After five days of helpless drifting, Coutts and his fellow lifeboat passengers were rescued by *La Gloire*, a cruiser in the Vichy French Navy. (France was split into two sections after its leaders signed an armistice agreement with Germany. An occupied zone was under German Control. A free zone, which was nominally led by a French government, was headquartered in the spa town of Vichy).

Ben Coutts' obituary described the Vichy hospitality aboard *La Gloire*:

> The French sailors, Coutts remembered, treated them with wonderful kindness; their officers, with memories of the destruction of the French fleet at Mers-el-Kébir in mind, did not. As Coutts, unable to walk, crawled from his berth to the heads, a French officer kicked him violently on the backside. Thereafter, Coutts decided to urinate where he lay.

Understandably, with the passage of just two years since the shots had been fired and the French sailors were laid to rest, the British assault on Mers-el-Kébir was still a raw wound for many in France in 1942.

In the immediate aftermath of the deaths of almost 1,300 of his men at Mers-el-Kébir in July 1940, Francois Darlan – France's Admiral of the Fleet - pressed for a declaration of war against Great Britain. The Anglophobic admiral was angry, bitter, and – surpassing all other emotions – he felt a sharp sense of personal betrayal. Just a few weeks earlier Darlan had given his solemn word to Winston Churchill and to his peers and friends in the Royal Navy that Germany would not take possession of a single French ship under any circumstances. The French would scuttle their ships rather than submit to German seizure.

"I've been betrayed by my brothers in arms," Darlan cried with disgust. "They did not believe in my word." Darlan argued for retribution – specifically for the bombing of the British naval base at Gibraltar, home to the British squadron that had attacked his ships. When France's new leader, 84-year-old Marshal Philippe Pétain expressed support for the bombing of Gibraltar, former president Pierre Laval cautioned: "We have just lost one war. Are we about to start and lose another?"

In the end, a small squadron of French planes made a weak, symbolic bombing run at Gibraltar two days after the British attack. Eight bombs were dropped; all fell into the sea. France never struck back at Britain in earnest. Just as Churchill was convinced of the need to throttle the French Navy in order to save France, the French leaders understood that a British triumph over Germany was their only path to freedom. Although he openly questioned the resolve and the military resources of Britain, Marshal Pétain understood that Britain's survival was France's only hope for liberation.

If Admiral Darlan was angered and insulted by Churchill's action, Adolf Hitler was astonished. After conquering Austria, Czechoslovakia, Poland, Denmark, Luxembourg, Holland, Belgium, and France, he was astonished by Churchill's attack on his former ally. Although leaders of other nations had resisted German attacks, none had lashed back with such vengeance.

As the author Michael Bloch relates, when France fell, German Foreign Minister Joachim von Ribbentrop convinced Hitler that "England was beaten, and it was only a question of time before she would finally admit her defeat" Hitler instructed his generals to prepare plans for Operation Sea Lion, a water-borne invasion of Britain. As his generals drafted plans for the invasion, Hitler also considered a peaceful alternative: a set of generous surrender terms (at least from the German perspective) that would avoid a costly battle.

The British attack at Mers-el-Kébir impressed Hitler that not only would Churchill's Britain never surrender, she fight with belligerence. Instead of invading by sea, Hitler attempted to weaken Britain from the air. The Battle of Britain raged in the skies above Britain for more than three months, but Germany never launched an assault against the shores of Churchill's island nation.

In a diary entry in early July 1940, Gian Galeazzo Ciano, Italy's freewheeling wartime Foreign Minister and son-in-law of Benito Mussolini, captured the world's reaction as well as anyone: "For the moment it proves that the fighting spirit of His British Majesty's fleet is quite alive, and still has the aggressive ruthlessness of the captains and pirates of the seventeenth century."

In *Roosevelt and Hopkins, An Intimate History*, Robert Sherwood writes that the attack at Mers-el-Kébir "served forcibly to underscore Churchill's defiant assurance that 'we will fight them in the streets' and 'never surrender'." Churchill's refusal to accept anything less than the elimination of the core of the French fleet from battle also calmed FDR's concerns that Churchill might one day be forced to cede control of the Royal Navy to Germany. It was now inconceivable that Churchill would ever allow any part of his Navy to fall into Hitler's hands. Roosevelt was reassured that Churchill would, indeed, never give in.

In Great Britain the news of the July 3 clash was announced at 3 a.m. on July 4, 1940. Churchill described the action to the House of Commons later that day. He had been Prime Minister for less than two months, and to that point, the opposition Labour Party had been tepid at best in their demonstrated support for his leadership. To a packed, hushed, and horrified Commons, Churchill began: "It is with sincere sorrow that I must now announce to the House the measures which we have felt bound to take in order to prevent the French Fleet from falling into German hands."

He noted "I fear the loss of life among the French and in the harbour must have been heavy, as we were compelled to use a severe measure of force and several immense explosions were heard."

Churchill concluded: "I leave the judgment of our action, with confidence, to Parliament. I leave it to the nation, and I leave it to the United States. I leave it to the world and history."

As Churchill ended his speech and took his seat on the Treasury bench, the MPs unexpectedly rose and cheered as one, without respect to party. Soviet Ambassador, Ivan Maisky who was seated in the visitors' gallery, noted the "loud, powerful and unanimous ovation" that lasted several minutes. As the ovation soared, "Churchill lowered his head and tears ran down his cheeks." He was, for the first time, embraced by all Members of Parliament.

An editorial in London's *Daily Express* proclaimed:

Churchill has once more shown himself as a rough, tough leader of our brave fighting men. He has shown that England, which was thought so old and staid and respectable, still has the smash-and-grab fighting spirit of Drake and Raleigh and Marlborough.

We rejoice in the realism which is not afraid to offend a potential enemy, which makes no pretence that the Bordeaux Government is our friend.

In this war we had been too kind and considerate. We tried to appease Italy. We turned the other cheek and looked the other way when we were insulted.

Now we face all our enemies boldly.

Perceptions of Winston Churchill in France remain mixed to this day. After France capitulated to Germany in 1940, most French leaders expected Germany to waste little time in beating Britain into submission. Abandoned to fight alone, Churchill's Britain took on Germany against nearly impossible odds in those early days of the war. In the end Britain helped liberate France from German tyranny. When Charles de Gaulle marched down the Avenue des Champs-Elysees in newly liberated Paris on November 11, 1944, Winston Churchill marched at his side.

However, for some in France, bitter memories of the action at Mers-el-Kébir have festered from generation to generation. Fifty-nine years after Churchill's decision to attack the French fleet, a fresh reminder of those harsh sentiments unexpectedly appeared in Paris.

You will not find many statues of foreigners in France's capital. Only two Britons are honored: Winston Churchill and King Edward VII (son of Queen Victoria and great grandfather of Queen Elizabeth II). Churchill's ten-foot-tall bronze statue watches over Avenue Winston Churchill, one block from the Champs-Elysees and one block from the River Seine. The $400,000 cost of the statue was generously funded by contributions from the French public.

This bronze likeness of France's most resolute ally leans forward in confident stride, walking stick in hand, lips pursed, a hint of triumph in his narrowed eyes. This was Winston Churchill as he marched down France's most sacred boulevard alongside General Charles de Gaulle just three months after the Allies liberated Paris from the Germans.

The statue was desecrated during the night of November 2, 1999 with the crudely painted indictment: "Mers-el-Kébir, 1300 killed." Churchill's sculpted hands were daubed in blood red paint as a further indication of the vandal's contempt.

More than half a century after Churchill's decision to assail the French fleet, some in France still resented his remorseless action. I understand those emotions, just as I understand those who question the necessity of Churchill's decision and the motives that drove it. It took the research and writing of a book for me to work through my own questions.

Some doubts still linger, but I do know this: The attack on the French fleet at Mers-el-Kébir was Britain's most belligerent act to that time, the most tangible expression of Churchill's commitment to fight to protect the interests of Great Britain. Without Churchill's confidence, tenacity, and willingness to engage the enemy, there would have been no sustained defense against Germany through 1940 and 1941 when Britain and her Dominion nations fought alone. If Britain had not survived through that perilous time there would have been no Allied invasion at Normandy, and there would have been no victorious march down the Champs-Elysees.

Churchill had no misgivings or regrets about his decision to attack the French ships. As he later wrote: "… no act was ever more necessary for the life of Britain and for all that depended on it."

As I've researched the conflict from every side, and as I've learned the stories of those who still question Churchill's action, I've confirmed that the story that is so important to me still holds its lasting significance to many others after all these years.

CHAPTER 4

A Most Disreputable Source

I knew I had the seed of a great story. But I also knew there were a frightening number of details that I still had to learn or confirm. As I fleshed out my research, I wanted to be sure that I found and incorporated information from all the *right* historical sources. Since every nonfiction book worthy of its prefix ends with a bibliography or a list of sources in its back pages, that was the obvious answer to the question of where I should look for the best sources.

Even I will admit that a long list of obscure history books can lose its charm rather quickly. But I have to tell you, there are those occasional moments of wondrous revelation when you find a fresh crop of new books and papers to pursue on glittery topics like the French Admiralty in 1940 or the incongruous personalities in Churchill's War Cabinet. In addition, there is that welcome sense of comfort when a newfound author rewards your hesitant trust by sprinkling her bibliography with works from writers whom you have learned to rely upon.

William L. Shirer, John Lukacs, William Manchester, Paul Reid, Arthur J. Marder, John Colville, Alistair Horne, General Sir Edward Louis Spears, and Sir Martin Gilbert were among the authors who I grew to respect as trusted pathfinders to truth, reliable guides to the unique details that helped enrich and differentiate the story I was writing. Especially when I was early in my research, I relied upon their guidance to help ensure that I did not overlook potentially relevant jewels of history and did not haphazardly embrace dubious information as truth. Through a combination of bibliographical guidance and ad hoc lucky finds in bookstores and book sales, the cache of resources for my story steadily grew.

Early in my quest for information about the war, David Irving was an author who impressed me as a bountiful source of historical detail, seasoned with irresistible anecdotes. He has written two-dozen books, several of which were cited by authors I respect. He first appeared on my radar when I saw his book *Hitler's War* cited as a source in another interesting book, Michael Bloch's biography of German Foreign Minister Joachim von Ribbentrop.

I bought two of Irving's books from online booksellers and read one of them. *Hitler's War* provided crystalline insights into the motivations and actions of some of the men most responsible for the war's buildup and detonation. Irving's writing is swift-paced and livened with fly-on-the-wall detail and first-person dialog. I was thoroughly drawn in after reading just a few pages, and I captured several dozen pages of notes. However, I never opened my other David Irving book - *Churchill's War* - for reasons you will soon understand.

My curiosity has few limits and it naturally extended into the works and lives of the growing universe of authors who were helping to educate me. Upon finishing *Hitler's War* and just about to begin *Churchill's War*, I looked into the life and other writings of David Irving. My Google search immediately introduced me to a shitstorm of Holocaust denial, anti-Semitism, reverence for Adolf Hitler, a profound distaste for Winston Churchill, and a landmark libel trial in Great Britain in which Irving sued the American historian who accused him of being a Holocaust denier.

The story of that trial was even made into a movie. Titled *Denial*, it stars Rachel Weisz, Tom Wilkinson, and Timothy Spall (aka Peter Pettigrew, aka Wormtail in the Harry Potter movies; he plays David Irving in *Denial*). The film tells the true story of historian Deborah Lipstadt and her successful defense against Irving's libel suit after she labeled him a Holocaust denier in her book *Denying the Holocaust*.

Irving denied being a denier and sued Lipstadt in the U.K., where the burden of proof in a libel case is on the defendant. Irving lost and was compelled to pay the trial costs of Lipstadt's publisher, Penguin Books. That $3 million obligation helped drive David Irving into bankruptcy.

Deborah Lipstadt's defense was supported by testimony from several expert witnesses who were authorities on the Holocaust. Richard J. Evans, Professor of Modern History at the University of Cambridge, and the author of a highly regarded trilogy about the Third Reich, played a critical role in toppling Irving's credibility. (After I learned this story, I added two of the three books in Evans' *Third Reich Trilogy* to my color-coded book list; the third covered a time period well after my focused interest).

Evans' testimony damned Irving's work with unequivocal vehemence:

> Not one of his books, speeches, or articles, not one paragraph, not one sentence in any of them, can be taken on trust as an accurate representation of its historical subject. All of them are completely worthless as history, because

Irving cannot be trusted anywhere, in any of them, to give
a reliable account of what he is talking or writing about.

It could not have been more clear that David Irving had zero
credibility, and was not a source that merited even the smallest
degree of my time or my trust.

I type all my notes into a series of Microsoft Word files.
Sometimes this is a good thing; other times it makes me question
my efficiency. In this case it was an especially good thing, making it easy to find and purge the notes I had taken from *Hitler's
War*. I was also tempted to toss my two David Irving books in
the garbage, but I decided to keep them as reminders of potentially toxic sources.

I want my book to be interesting and credible. I will be OK
with critiques of my word choices and sentence structures.
(Well … mildly OK). I will be horrified if anyone credibly questions my accuracy. To that end, as I sketched out the story of
the clash of the British and French navies in July of 1940, and as
I filtered and absorbed bits of information about sailors and soldiers, diplomats, and prime ministers, I carefully vetted my
sources for authenticity and reliability.

CHAPTER 5

The Stories Behind Touchdown Jesus

I n the spring of 1963, people I did not know began to stop by our house to drop off boxes crammed with serious-looking books. By Memorial Day, our two-car garage was more than half-filled with cartons of all sizes. I would have been 8 years old then. I was already an enthusiastic reader, and of course I poked through those boxes.

I had my father's OK to poach any books that caught my interest. But those cartons overflowing with bulky books for serious students of law, science, theology, French and British history, engineering, philosophy, math, and other fuzzy subjects were so far removed from the Tom Swift, Abe Lincoln, and Pony Express books that I read in those days that I left the collection slightly disturbed but still complete.

As it turned out, our garage was just a temporary way station for those books that held such fleeting interest. One final stranger arrived in early summer, packed the books into a large van, and carted them off to their ultimate destination – the new library at the University of Notre Dame in South Bend, Indiana.

Notre Dame had outgrown its old library, and there were plenty of shelves to fill in its replacement. Notre Dame's old building which had opened in 1917, was named in memory of Father Auguste Lemonnier, who was Notre Dame's president back when Ulysses Grant was America's President. 475,000 books strained the shelves in the formidable stone neoclassical building that still overlooks St. Mary's Lake on the western edge of the campus. Neither the collection nor the Lemonnier Library building was large enough to keep up with the interests of Notre Dame's expanding student body and faculty. Nor were they equal to the grand aspirations of the university's president.

Father Theodore Hesburgh was Notre Dame's president in 1963. He would serve in that role from 1952 to 1987. During the thirty-five years of Father Ted's stewardship Notre Dame's student body grew by more than 90% and the University's endowment grew almost forty-fold, from $9 million to $350 million. Under Father Hesburgh's leadership, an all-male school welcomed co-education. A football power gained prominence for the quality of the education it provided. Father Hesburgh's very public activism included his passionate involvement in America's civil rights movement. A world-class library was funded, built, and stocked. As coaches and quarterbacks came and went, Father Hesburgh was the face of Notre Dame to the world for one-third of the twentieth century.

More books, better books, and a bigger place to house them – a building large enough to hold more than a million books - were among the world class aspirations in mind when Father Hesburgh announced a fund-raising campaign for a new library in 1958. Ground was broken in the summer of 1961, and the striking new 14-story Memorial Library opened on September 18, 1963.

In August of that year, the 475,000 books from the old library were packed by student volunteers into thousands of Carling Black Label beer cases, rolled out the front door of Lemonnier on a makeshift roller-coaster-like conveyor, trucked to the opposite side of the campus, unpacked, and methodically shelved in the new building. With so many shelves still bare in the new library, the school's Board of Trustees approved special funding for the purchase of new books to update and fill in the library's collection. Notre Dame also solicited its vast network of alumni and friends for additional book donations.

The Fighting Irish alumni (a clan that included my father) heeded the call for "books of all special fields regardless of age." A university alumni publication announced a call to "book collectors who could be persuaded to donate their collections," as well as alumni in the legal field whose clients might be inclined to donate their collections "and take advantage of the tax angle." A steady stream of books has flowed to Notre Dame ever since. A very small portion of those donated books passed through our garage in the Philadelphia suburbs.

Notre Dame's new library building was initially a rather plain twelve-story tower atop a broad two-story base. The tower had few windows and was designed with a greater focus on ready access to the books inside than to its outward appearance. Father Hesburgh like to joke that the tall rectangular structure on the flat Indiana terrain inspired visions of a grain elevator.

A trip to Mexico provided Father Hesburgh with the inspiration for a striking enhancement to the building's design, one that changed the character of the building and Notre Dame's campus. The façade of the Central Library at the Universidad Nacional Autonoma de Mexico is completely wrapped in colorful iconography. Guided by that inspiration, Father Hesburgh suggested a colorful mosaic design for the face of Notre Dame's library, with imagery appropriate to a Catholic university, perhaps depicting saints and scholars through history. Notre Dame's president wanted the new library to be more than a research and educational resource. It would also play a striking role in the personality and topography of the campus.

The $8 million budget for the construction of the new library was augmented by a $200,000 donation from Mr. and Mrs. Howard V. Phalin for the design and construction of a façade that brought Father Hesburgh's vision to life. The artist Millard Sheets produced a massive work of art comprising 324 panels with 6,700 separate pieces of stone in 171 finishes, sourced from 16 countries, depicting Jesus Christ surrounded by icons of history and the early church. The kaleidoscopic 9,112 square foot mosaic was formally unveiled and dedicated on May 7, 1964, Ascension Thursday in the liturgical calendar, eight months after the library opened its doors.

The ten-story image of Jesus Christ now hovers over a shallow black reflecting pool. Just past the pool is a broad lawn, crisscrossed by a network of vertical and diagonal sidewalks. Head down any of those sidewalks, cross a narrow road, and you will find yourself standing at the main gate of Notre Dame's football stadium. The mosaic can be seen from many of the seats in the stadium.

In the mosaic, Jesus' arms are raised above his head in the sign of blessing. Inside the football stadium, of course, a similar gesture signifies a touchdown. Not surprisingly, the mosaic assumed a quick identity as Touchdown Jesus. To many, this unintended mashup of football and religion perfectly defines Notre Dame. With its striking design and its core location – just east of the golden domed Administration building and just north of Notre Dame Stadium - the library is one of the best known and most photographed buildings on the campus. It practically begs to be included in selfies. (Yes. Guilty).

By 1972 the library housed one million books. Today it holds more than three million volumes. After retiring as Notre Dame's president in 1987, Father Hesburgh worked from a small office on the 13th floor of the library (there are no superstitions about floor numbers at this Catholic university) and he remained a steady presence on Notre Dame's campus. The building – which he jokingly noted was called "Ted's Mahal" by some students - was formally rechristened Hesburgh Library in the year that he retired. Father Hesburgh died in 2015 at the age of 97.

The Touchdown Jesus mosaic has a formal name: The Word of Life. This image of Jesus, arms raised, perhaps about to preach, was inspired by a passage from the first book of John. The first few lines from that passage are familiar to many:

In the beginning was the Word:
the Word was with God
and the Word was God.

Although Winston Churchill had moments of reverence, he was not religious, and was not even an occasional churchgoer. Churchill once jested: "I could hardly be called a pillar of the Church, I am more in the manner of a buttress, for I support it from the outside."

Nonetheless, as I write a book about a leader who was a lone voice against bitter evil for the better part of a decade, I find myself especially taken with the relevance of the closing lines of that passage from the first book of John:

a light that shines in the dark,
a light that darkness could not overpower.

John 1:1-5

I was a member of Notre Dame's incoming freshmen class in the fall of 1972.

The campus was not an unfamiliar place. Our father, a former Notre Dame quarterback, had taken my brother Mike and me out for a football game several years earlier, and Mike and I attended a week-long hockey camp the summer after my junior year of high school. I eventually played on the junior varsity hockey team for three years.

My freshman year was the year that Notre Dame went co-ed. The incoming class of about 2,000 freshmen included 125 women. An additional 265 upperclasswomen transferred in that same year. Shy, skinny me, with scraggly hair and bad skin went four years without a single on-campus date.

By my first Fall at Notre Dame, the Hesburgh Library was almost 10 years old and was stocked with more than one million books. Although it was a vibrant student hub, I rarely visited the library during my four years at ND. I tried studying in the library a few times, but I was convinced that I needed music playing in the background in order to concentrate and study effectively. The library was just too quiet and most of my studying was done in my room, with a Doobie Brothers, Steely Dan, or Peter Frampton album blaring. On those rare occasions when I absolutely needed a book for a class, I fetched it from the library and returned to my dormitory room (during my first 2 years), my off-campus apartment (junior year) or my farther off-campus house (senior year).

I headed to college with the idea that I would major in English, but I did little during my first two years to prepare myself for any particular field of study. Even though I retained my interest in English, I did not focus very finely during those first two relatively free-range years. In addition to Notre Dame's mandatory theology and philosophy classes, I took a completely unfocussed liberal arts schedule that included Russian History, Introduction to Jazz, Social Psychology, and Introduction to Theater. I somehow managed to take only two actual English classes – Satire and Practical Literature Criticism – neither of which did a damn thing to advance my writing. I just liked to write. Or, rather, I liked the idea of writing, since I never took a college writing class. Nor did I write all that much.

Notre Dame offered several student-run publications, including a daily newspaper – The *Observer* - and a monthly literary magazine – The *Scholastic*. The *Observer* in particular would have provided an invaluable opportunity to practice and hone my writing while learning the craft of journalism. But aside from the papers required for my classes, I never wrote a thing. I'm sure I was intimidated by the idea of anyone reading and critiquing what I wrote.

Unlike one of my roommates who was laser-focused on medical school, and a couple of others who saw accounting careers in their future, I really had no idea what I wanted to do after graduation. During a conversation with my father over Christmas break in my sophomore year, he suggested that my two best options for putting an English degree to work would be either to teach English or to become a lawyer (like him).

Since neither path held any interest to me, we agreed that some form of business degree made the most sense. I was not inflamed by any specific concentration – Accounting, Finance, Marketing, etc. - so I went with the simplest and most general option – Business Management. One drastic consequence of my complete avoidance of business classes during my first two years was that I now had to squeeze 60 credit hours – roughly 20 business courses – into my final two years.

And so I graduated with a degree in Business Management and lucked into a career in marketing and sales: 10 years marketing Mrs. Paul's venerable fish sticks and onion rings, four years marketing ice cream after our move to Lancaster County, Pennsylvania, and 30 years in my own business, selling software from the comfortable sanctuary of a home office.

After graduating in 1976, aside from dashing in to use its convenient and little-known basement restrooms during occasional football weekend visits, I did not return to Notre Dame's library for more than thirty years.

When I began researching British, French, and naval history from the 1930s and 40s, I had a vague hope that Notre Dame's library could be a potentially helpful resource. My first visit to Hesburgh Library in the guise of a researcher took place late one Saturday night after a football game. I had returned for the weekend with my dad, my daughter Brittany and a couple of Britt's University of Pittsburgh roommates, and we watched Pitt beat Notre Dame in quadruple overtime. In the back of my mind – OK, way towards the front of my mind - I was curious about the quality and variety of books that the Hesburgh Library might possibly offer to a project like mine.

After the others settled back in our hotel after a postgame dinner and a clash of celebration and rationalization, I headed back to campus and visited the library at about 10:30 that Saturday night. The library is open 24 hours a day through much of the school year. It was fairly empty and very quiet the football-Saturday night of my visit.

As a test, I was curious if I could find books either written by or written about two reasonably obscure wartime figures:

Major-General Sir Edward Louis Spears of Great Britain and France's Admiral Jean Louis Xavier Francois Darlan.

Spears was a World War I veteran, a Member of Parliament, and a confidant of Winston Churchill. Churchill asked Spears – who spoke fluent French without an accent – to be his personal liaison to French Premier Paul Reynaud in the crucial early days after Hitler's Germany invaded France in World War II. Spears later took on the challenge of shepherding General Charles de Gaulle's often prickly liaison with Britain's armed forces and government.

Darlan was Admiral of the Fleet and Commander in Chief of the French Navy in 1940. French seamen were intensely loyal to Darlan, and he had the power to either submit the French fleet to German control or direct it to sail to Britain, America, or independent freedom.

I already owned both volumes of Spears' *Assignment to Catastrophe*, a very engaging account of the fall of France at the beginning of World War II. Both of those books were in Notre Dame's collection. So were Spears' two books about his experiences in the First World War, his two books about later stages of the Second World War, and a book *about* Spears that I had not been aware of. The Hesburgh Library collection even included a memoir and several novels by Spears' first wife, Mary Borden.

As for Darlan, the library had seven titles, including a wellworn paperback copy of a biography written by Alain Darlan, the Admiral's son, published in French.

I paid just peripheral attention that night to the books on surrounding shelves. They appeared to be stocked with the stories of soldiers, sailors, ambassadors, and statesmen. (As I would later learn, they are). In my short time among the stacks during my late-night reconnaissance visit, it was apparent that the Hesburgh Library could become a valuable research tool.

I live about 600 miles from Notre Dame's campus in South Bend, Indiana. If I get to Notre Dame twice a year, that's a lot, so in my next trip and subsequent visits, I did my best to efficiently read and capture as much as possible about the period, the people, and the events I was researching. Most of my visits were for two days and I made each day as long as I was physically able, typically from about 9 AM to about midnight. I learned to pre-search the library's website before each visit. The site lists the Dewey Decimal number for every book in its collection, and also directs you to the floor on which the book can be found.

In my time at the Hesburgh Library, I developed a serious crush on the organizing principles of the Dewey Decimal System. I prepped for each visit with an online search for the specific locations of a number of books of interest. The Dewey Decimal System served as a GPS, providing me the coordinates for those books. I would then scour the nearby shelves for the related books that might also be of interest and assistance.

Most of the books I read were on the library's 11th floor. The shelves and the carrels on the 11th floor are old, worn, austere, efficient, and rarely in use during my visits. The 11th floor quickly felt like home. Each of my visits typically included a short detour to the 10th floor for a book or two. The décor there is newer, with polished communal tables, comfortable chairs and electric outlets and USB ports galore. It's a much more popular place of study for Notre Dame's current crop of students, and I imagine this is the floor that campus guides show to prospective students and their parents while I camp out on 11 in senior-alum mode. The only times I felt like a trespasser in the library were during my quick forays to the 10th floor.

The friends and colleagues of mine who knew about my library pilgrimages sometimes asked why I went all the way to Notre Dame instead of the well-stocked municipal and college libraries in Philadelphia, New York, New Haven, and Boston – cities to which I regularly traveled for work. An undeniable measure of my preference for Notre Dame is the simple fact that the Notre Dame campus is still a magical place for me, an environment in which I always feel at home. More important, the Hesburgh Library has proven to be a deep and rich resource with – thanks to the vision of Father Hesburgh and donations of so many friends and alumni – a broad and incredibly eclectic collection of old and new books about the period and the people of interest to me.

For someone in search of so many books that were written in the 1940s and 50s, a library that was infused from its predecessor in 1963 and enriched by the donation of so many personal book collections from that same era is about as good as it gets. With three million books now in Hesburgh library, it's improbable that any of the books that I've researched were among the books that were temporarily parked in those cartons in my family's garage. Still, I like the thought that they might have been.

CHAPTER 6

Bookeye

*C*hips: The Diaries of Sir Henry Channon was exactly the sort of book I hoped to find at Notre Dame. Chips Channon was an American-born Member of Britain's Parliament. He was chatty and sophisticated, he knew all the right people, and his daily impressions and written recollections were unfiltered.

On top of the intimate insights they typically provide, diaries are especially helpful when a writer's focus is on a specific range of dates – from September 1939 to July 1940 in my case. Channon's public career spanned that period, and his diary added rich detail to the stories of Britain's principal government figures of the day.

For example, his June 3, 1940 entry both lauded and skewered Lord Halifax, Britain's Foreign Minister who had been the preference of Channon, King George VI, and many others over Winston Churchill for Prime Minister when Neville Chamberlain resigned less than a month before. After genuflecting at Halifax's "extraordinary character," "high principles," "engaging charm" and his "grand manner," (which, from everything else I've read, sounded like a perfect sketch of Halifax), Channon twisted back to disparage the otherwise proper British Lord's "snobbishness," "eel-like qualities" and "sublime treachery." That day's entry closed with: "He is insinuating, but unlovable." And Channon absolutely revered Halifax!

Chips was the first book I pulled from the 11th floor shelves at Notre Dame's Hesburgh Library on my first day of committed research. It was a Sunday in February. The library was relatively empty and quite hushed when I arrived shortly before 9:00 AM. I had set up camp in a deserted carrel – they were all deserted at that time on the 11th floor – comfortably provisioned with my iPod, coffee, bottled water, peppermint lifesavers, and a backpack carrying pens, a notebook, and several pads of Post-it Notes. As I skimmed through the diary of this reliably caustic Member of Parliament, I staked my interest in each entry worth capturing with a small yellow Post-it Note. It took about 25 minutes for me to work my way through Chips.

The next book I grabbed was *End of the Affair: The Collapse of the Anglo-French Alliance, 1939-40* by Eleanor M. Gates. *Affair* presented a much bigger gleaning challenge. The entire book – all 648 pages – appeared to be seeded with morsels of relevance and interest. I spent the next 90 minutes doing my best to skim and detect the most valuable nuggets of information. I used – and eventually re-used – quite a few Post-it Notes during this project.

By noon I had a short stack of books blooming with oddly spaced yellow foliage.

Next … well, I was not sure. I had not given much thought to how I would capture and retain such a mass of information - easily several-hundred pages of potential interest. This was a profoundly serious hurdle, a major productivity challenge. My unbridled excitement after discovering such a rich vein of source material turned to panic at the challenge of how to harness that much information.

My first thought was to begin taking hand-written notes in the spiral notebook that I had packed. But not only is my penmanship a catastrophe, I could not imagine being able to capture and digest the material from much more than one book per day, especially in my early days when most facts and stories were unspoiled ground in my research. After scribbling a few notes from Chips Channon's diary entries, I quickly gave up on that idea.

It was clear that I would have to find a photocopier, and was resigned to rolling up exorbitant charges, dimes, and quarters at a time. I expected to lug ridiculous piles of paper back to my hotel and then home in my suitcase.

There were no copiers on the 11th floor, and I assumed they would be in a central location, most likely on the ground floor. They were.

But before I made my first photocopy, I noticed several devices that looked like tabletop scanners. They were.

Notre Dame's library has four of these devices, called Bookeye scanners. Rather than print copies, the Bookeyes let you scan individual pages or two-page spreads. Just lay a book flat, pages facing up, and tap "Scan" on the touchscreen. After about two seconds, turn the page, repeat, and on and on and on. If you're interested in 16 pages in a book, you can scan those 16 pages. When you're done, the Bookeye saves those 16 pages in a single PDF file that you can save to a thumb-drive (there's a USB port in each Bookeye) or, if you have an email account at ND – email to yourself.

During each scanning session, I would save the relevant pages from each book in a separate PDF, and eventually head home with dozens of files with hundreds of pages on a thumb-drive in my pocket for future review at the time and place that was convenient for me. That convenient place was, of course, my home office.

I roughly figure that Bookeye scanners made me at least 40 times more productive than if I had written my notes by hand, and perhaps 10 times more productive than if I had used a photocopier.

I was tentative Bookeye user at first – scanning and saving the interesting pages from a small book – and then scurrying back up to the 11th floor to pick my next book. I gradually eased into a more efficient routine. I would mine the shelves for books of interest and skim through them at my carrel. (I would also stick a Post-it Note on the last shelf I visited so I could resume my search from the place where I left off. If nothing else comes from my book project, at least I've boosted 3M's revenues).

When I had a stack of books that could easily be carried without appearing obnoxious – sometimes two books, sometimes six books, depending on their size and the number of pages that had caught my attention – I would ride back down to the first floor and begin scanning at the Bookeye. I was always concerned and very conscious of potentially hogging a valuable resource, but I was surprised there was not more demand for time on the Bookeyes during my visits. I never had the impression that I was holding up other potential users, and I never had to wait to use one of the four Bookeyes.

The Bookeye is a product of Digital Library Systems Group in Boca Raton Florida. Bookeye scanners do not come cheaply. DLSG offers a variety of scanners, with a multitude of different features. Their products can cost from $5,000 to more than $20,000.

Notre Dame does not charge to use their Bookeye scanners. The Bookeye scanner is, to me, the most wondrous invention since the microwave oven. I would have gladly paid for the convenience and productivity that the Hesburgh Library's Bookeye scanners added to my visits.

Did I violate the spirit - and perhaps even the letter - of copyright law with my use of the library's Bookeye scanners? Perhaps so, but I'm not sure. I am certainly open to criticism. Here are the degrees of rationalization that I've worked through:

If I had opened the library's copy of *Chips: The Diaries of Sir Henry Channon* and transcribed an interesting sentence or a paragraph by hand, I would have had no qualms.

If I had photocopied pages 255 and 256 (where I found Chips Channon's comments about Lord Halifax), I would have felt only a bit more culpable.

Since Bookeye scanners let you efficiently copy pages instead of paragraphs, I ended up scanning 39 pages from *Chips* ..., with the idea that I would read through and harvest the most useful information when I returned home. This, admittedly, gave me pause, but it did not stop me.

In all three examples, I copied excerpts of copyrighted material. Different tools enabled me to copy different quantities of that material.

No matter what tool I used to collect the personal observations and experiences of Chips Channon – a pencil, a photocopier, or a Bookeye scanner – I must still request permission from the copyright owner if I eventually decide to incorporate that material into my book, and, of course, cite that original work as the source of my quotes. (I requested – and received – quite a few permissions for the material that I've used in this book).

One last point ... the books on the shelves on the 11th floor of the Hesburgh Library are, for the most part, old. Most of the books that I skimmed at my carrel were published fifty, sixty, seventy, or more years ago and are now out of print. Without exception, whenever I discovered a book that was clearly new and available to purchase, I purchased a copy.

CHAPTER 7

FDR Library: Hyde Park, NY

My attempt to write a book crossed from the land of whims and diversions into the world of serious projects about halfway through my first day in the archives at the Franklin D. Roosevelt Presidential Library and Museum in Hyde Park, NY.

The FDR Library houses the presidential and personal papers of President Franklin D Roosevelt along with the archives of 200 or so of his contemporaries. Anyone can visit their neighborhood public library, but ... well, as it turns out, anyone can visit the FDR library as well.

Before travelling to Hyde Park, it pays to visit the library's website (www.fdrlibrary.org) and fill out their simple, one-page Researcher Application in advance. This helps ensure a quick, productive start to your visit, and in return for handing over a completed application along with a photo ID upon arrival, you will receive a Researcher Identification card in return. I unabashedly admit to the childlike wonder brought about by the simple, wallet-size piece of blue cardboard that was handed to me when I completed the registration process at Hyde Park. I felt like an honored member of an exclusive club ... one that absolutely anyone can join.

The FDR Library's simple and non-exclusionary process and protocols for holding, reading, and photographing the letters, telegrams, memos, and other private papers of President Roosevelt and his contemporaries helped smooth my entry into the world of primary sources.

My wife and I drove to a hotel near Hyde Park the night before our visit. We live about four hours away, and I wanted to spend a full day in the archives. While I was busy in the library, Barbara toured Springwood, the Roosevelts' estate. FDR was born at Springwood, and it served as the "Summer White House" during the four terms of his presidency. Prominent visitors included Winston Churchill, King George VI, and Queen Elizabeth (the Queen Mum version). FDR and Eleanor Roosevelt are buried on the grounds, as is Fala, FDR's legendary Scottish Terrier. I was so absorbed in my research in the library that I never made it into the Roosevelts' home.

The FDR Presidential Library and Museum is a multi-purpose building on the Roosevelt estate. In addition to the Roosevelt archives, the building houses a museum, a gift shop, and a small cafeteria. The outside walls of the building are constructed from the same Hudson Valley fieldstone used to build the wall that marks the property's boundary on Albany Post Road. The library fits comfortably into the local terrain.

We arrived early and I was at the door a few minutes before the library's 9:00 AM opening time. No advance reservation is required (or even possible). Since I had followed the library's guidance to complete the Researcher Application in advance, I was knighted as a researcher after just a few quick verification and registration tasks. Only one other researcher was in the library as I got down to work, and during the course of the day, I never noticed more than five fellow researchers at work in the library at any one time.

I settled in with a rote awareness of the process for accessing the library's historical materials. Small slips of paper are provided on which you are instructed to write down the specific collections of documents that you wish to review. When you hand your list to an archivist, she then discreetly disappears into the labyrinth of the archives.

The archived materials are stored in sturdy brown cardboard boxes, each about the size of a cakebox, with a large, snug-fitting flap on one end. Some boxes hold the materials related to a specific individual or event. Many boxes hold the materials relevant to a specific date span. The archivist on duty helped me fine-tune my requests to the specific collections with documents related to the parties most relevant to my research. William Bullitt... Joseph P. Kennedy... Admiral Darlan.... You may request up to seven boxes of materials at any one time.

The Roosevelt archives run on a curiously rigid schedule. The staff will "pull" your selected boxes of research materials at four designated times during the day: at 9:15, 11:00, 2:00, and 3:45. One exception to this schedule is the staff's willingness to do a one-time "courtesy pull" for first-time researchers who arrive between these windows. If you quickly work your way through the materials that were pulled for you, or if you find that the materials you requested were not as relevant as you had hoped, you must bide your time until the next pull time.

The reading room is a bright, efficient, fairly spartan working space, with sixteen large tables in two parallel rows, comfortable chairs, and thoughtfully placed electric outlets by each table. As I waited for the arrival of my first set of documents, I killed time skimming through a few of the books that lined the library's walls – mostly about President Roosevelt, the Second World War, and political life in the first half of the twentieth century.

About ten minutes after she disappeared, the archivist wheeled out a cart that stood about waist-high, with two shelves, carrying seven boxes, five on the top shelf, two on the bottom. After a brief burst of "oh man, I'm really doing this" exhilaration, I settled into work.

The first box that I opened held a half-dozen solid cardboard folders. Each folder contained anywhere from a few sheets of paper to a half-inch thick collection of letters, telegrams, newspaper clippings, and memos. One of the first documents that captured my interest was a December 21, 1938 letter to FDR from Lord Lothian (aka Philip Kerr). Lothian (which is how he signed his typed letter, and how he was generally known) was a British aristocrat who would eventually be appointed Great Britain's ambassador to the U.S. in June 1939. In this short letter, he mentioned a planned visit to Washington in the last days of 1938 and requested a meeting to "have a talk with you about the present world situation."

Roosevelt wrote this, in pencil, in the upper left corner of the letter: "Mac, I'll be glad to see him for a few minutes. Give him 15 minute appt when he arrives." I swear I could "hear" FDR's patrician voice, garbled just slightly by the cigarette holder between his teeth, in that hand-written note.

I have never been a paragon of concentration or efficiency, and the tendency to let my mind stray worked against me at times during the research phase of my project. If a story seemed interesting, I would keep reading well beyond the point that its relevance to my book ended. If an idea really intrigued me, I would pursue it, even if it had no direct relevance to the story I was writing. A case in point: although it was not directly related to my research, I was drawn in by the correspondence between Alain Darlan and both FDR and Eleanor Roosevelt. Darlan's father, Jean Francois Xavier Darlan, was Admiral of the Fleet, the leader of France's navy, and, potentially, the villain in my other book. The younger Darlan was stricken by polio in 1942 when he was twenty-seven years old. FDR generously and compassionately arranged for him to be treated at Warm Springs, Georgia, where FDR himself convalesced, and where he would pass away in 1945.

I found a series of letters between both Roosevelts and the admiral's son, including this 1947 note from Alain Darlan to Eleanor Roosevelt:

All over the world people will remember the friend they lost two years ago. Personally, I shall never forget his kindness and generosity for me.

The FDR Library allows – in fact, they encourage – researchers to use digital cameras to capture images of the documents relevant to their interest. The old flip phone I used at the time had a camera that was just horrible, so we bought a small Nikon digital camera a couple of days before our trip. I charged the camera's battery and took several test pictures after checking into our hotel the night before our visit.

In part because there is not much traffic in, out or within the reading room, the atmosphere is quiet and sedate, which was appropriate for me and my new brotherhood of serious-looking researchers and readers. Silence was assumed but not mandated. Visual harmony was taken for granted as well, and while photography was promoted, flash-free shots were expected.

As I paged through the papers in the first box that I opened, it did not take me long to identify several picture-worthy items, including Lord Lothian's letter annotated with FDR's hand-written note.

I set the letter squarely on the table in front of me, zoomed in precisely, and then ... first a bright flash, then a very loud beep. In reality the beep probably was not all that loud, but in that quiet reading room, it might as well have been an air raid siren. I hurriedly closed the folder on my table and literally ran to the hallway, whispering "sorry ... sorry ... sorry" and making slight hand waves to the librarian and fellow researchers that I passed, their heads suddenly raised. I wasted about 15 minutes of potential research time, but I eventually figured how to control the camera's flash and how to mute its surprising array of selectable noises.

My day in the archives at Hyde Park was educational, productive, and perfectly exhilarating. In addition to the historical documents, I could not resist the touristy impulse to take several pictures of the carts and boxes in which the documents were delivered. Thinking back, it's a wonder I didn't beg the kind and very helpful librarians and archivists to pose for selfies with me. I took 58 pictures that day, which, by the standards of future visits to the FDR library and other archives, was paltry.

My first experience in the world of primary sources was enlightening in so many ways. For instance, I learned:

(1) In an April 18, 1940 letter to Assistant Secretary of State R. Walton Moore, William Bullitt, the U.S. Ambassador to France wrote: "The French General Staff expects an attack by Germany on the western front before the first of May, and is inclined to believe that both the Netherlands and Belgium will be attacked as well as France."

Germany's attack on the Netherlands, Belgium and – ultimately – France, was launched 22 days later, on May 10. The Allies' strikingly inadequate preparation, despite their informed anticipation of an inevitable German assault, is still baffling and maddening more than three-quarters of a century later.

(2) Winston Churchill became Britain's Prime Minister on May 10, 1940 - on the same day that Germany invaded Belgium and The Netherlands. Just five days later, after his first meeting with Churchill in his new role (they were previously well acquainted), Joseph Kennedy, U.S. Ambassador to Great Britain, conveyed Churchill's unshakable resolve in a cable to Secretary of State Cordell Hull. Kennedy – despite his defeatist mindset – was convinced that no matter what fate befell Britain and France in their fight against Germany, Churchill was resolute that: "... England will never give up as long as he remains a power in public life even if England is burnt to the ground. ... the government will move to Canada and take the fleet and fight on."

(3) U.S. Ambassador William Bullitt was a passionate Francophile and a candid, chatty correspondent. Bullitt often bypassed the State Department, and wrote directly to Roosevelt, and his free-wheeling communications captured the spirit and the distinctions of life in France as the war came to a boil. In that same April 18, 1940 letter to R. Walton Moore, Bullitt noted that the chief obstacle to a better working relationship between France's Prime Minister Paul Reynaud and his predecessor Edouard Daladier was the clash between their mistresses: "... the

lady love of each hates the lady love of the other, and from your experience as an old roué, you know that venom distilled in a horizontal position is always fatal." Have I mentioned that my focus tends to wander? Bullitt's communications were routinely a joy to read.

(4) I learned that you do not have to be a tenured academic or a dedicated historian to gain access to rich, firsthand sources of information. As I would continue to learn during the course of my research, all it takes to gain access to the Holy Grail of history – the personal papers of the men and women who created it - is the determination to do so, the willingness to follow simple instructions. and the confidence to get over the "who am I to trespass in these archives" moments of self-doubt. I still think of myself as a software salesman, so I am both relieved and delighted every time an unpedigreed researcher like me is welcomed by archivists who go out of their way to be helpful and encouraging. It took me a while to appreciate that the very reason for most archives' existence is to preserve and provide access to the priceless materials of their contributing sources. Those bits of paper are there for us to examine, absorb, interpret, and share the stories they tell.

(5) The sensation that you feel when you discover a quote or a story in an archive that you have never seen in a published source is incomparable.

I also learned a valuable lesson about capturing and re-reading a large quantity of historical material. All of the documents that I reviewed (some of which were carbon copies or photocopies) were more than 70 years old. Many were faded, and some handwriting was barely legible. After returning home and reviewing the photographed documents on my PC, one nice benefit was the ability to zoom in to decipher the details in any hard-to-read document.

It was encouraging to read later that my process for capturing the images of historical documents was remarkably similar to the one followed by Erik Larson, the successful author of narrative nonfiction best-sellers like *Devil in the White City*, *Dead Wake*, and of course *The Splendid and the Vile*, his tale of Winston Churchill's inspirational leadership in the first year of the war. Shortly after publication of *Dead Wake*, his gripping tale about the sinking of the Lusitania in 1915, Larson shared a blog post on his website about how he relies on his digital camera to snap pictures of historical documents that he is then able to review at his own time, pace, and location.

Larson notes: "I parachute into an archive, along with my trusty digital camera." That approach also speeds the sifting process. "I don't read all the way through each document I come across - only enough to gauge that it might be useful down the line." He photographs the documents that appear to be interesting and later reviews these photo-captured documents on his computer. "This is far more cost-effective than holing up in, say, the National Archives of the UK, in London, for months at a time, reading every word of every document, while spending pots of money on hotels, meals and martinis."

It's always reassuring when I learn that I'm on a good path.

I visited the FDR library again two years later to fill in some of the gaps in my research. By then I knew how to better prepare in advance - by making an on-line search of the available materials and arriving with a printed list of my targeted collections. That helped me focus my search and ensured that I filled my day with documents that were most relevant to my interests and needs. I also had an iPhone by then, which enabled more efficient and surreptitious photography.

Here is one last point about the FDR Library, as well as my future visits to the Churchill Archives at Cambridge University and to other archive sites: The servicemen, diplomats, and politicians in the story that I'm writing about have been dead for decades. Fortunately, their stories were captured in newspapers, magazines, diaries, books, and even newsreels. The stories told in history books are distilled and sometimes even distorted. Books are generally considered to be secondary sources (unless they're first-person accounts).

Letters, diaries, telegrams, personal papers, and other first-person accounts are considered primary sources. Primary sources get you closer to the raw, unvarnished, real-time truth. (Of course, it is not uncommon for authors and diarists to shade the truth – even about their own lives and exploits - so discernment and skepticism are essential traits for researchers and authors of history). Secondary sources – typically books - generally rely on primary sources. A book is someone else's interpretation of the truth.

Primary sources provide opportunities for unique perspective and fresh insights. They are the Holy Grail for historical researchers.

It was important to me personally, and also very important to the originality and credibility of my book that I dig deeply into primary sources. My field trip to the Roosevelt library was my first engagement with primary sources, and, personally, a significant advance in the quality of my research.

CHAPTER 8

Inscrutably Inscribed

This was written inside the front cover of one of the used books that I bought:

> To My Beloved Husband
> On our Third Christmas
> Together
> Love,
> Your Nan
> December 25, 1969

I do not know Nan, but I was instantly touched to learn of this still-burning affection for her beloved husband after three Christmases together.

What moved me even more was the gift that she inscribed in blue ink in her neat, precise handwriting: the diary of a Soviet Union Ambassador from the early days of World War II. What could possibly be more romantic for a couple's third Christmas together?

Memoirs of a Soviet Ambassador, The War: 1939-43 imparts the experiences and perspective of Ivan Mikhailovich Maisky, the Soviet Union's Ambassador to the United Kingdom during the buildup and initial years of World War II. Maisky was fluent in English, sociable, cunning, and well-connected. He was on good terms with Winston Churchill, Anthony Eden, Lord Beaverbrook, and most other British luminaries. His diaries provide unique perspective on the events and the people driving the events at that critical time.

OK, so Nan's husband and I might be the only two people in the world who would have been charmed to receive the Maisky diaries as a Christmas or anniversary gift. I hope he was charmed.

The world of used books can be interesting, surprising, charming, and occasionally startling. As with the life of Forest Gump and those boxes of chocolates, you never know what you're gonna get.

Sometimes you turn a page and find an inscription that just perfectly fits the book as well as the writer and the recipient. This simple note, jotted inside *De Gaulle, The Rebel 1890-1944*, by Jean Lacouture, was doubly warming. Perhaps because it accompanied the biography of an especially dour man, this very brief note made me smile when I first read it, and I smiled again as I typed this:

December 25, 1990

Daddy,
Joyeaux Noel!
Love,
Susan

My favorite inscription was written inside a book I purchased for $2.00 at the Lancaster Library's annual used book sale.

George Seldes was a journalist and foreign correspondent. I had never heard of him before I saw his memoir *Witness to a*

Century: Encounters With the Noted, the Notorious, and the Three SOBs on the long table of used history books at the library sale. Given the title and the timespan that his book covered, I thought it might include a few interesting and useful anecdotes, and I bought it without even skimming its pages. I was wrong. As it turned out, there was not a single story in *Witness* ... that contributed to the book I was writing. But that was perfectly alright. The payoff to my $2.00 investment was the inscription penned on the first page, and it was priceless.

Honey
The title of this
book makes me wish
that we could spend the next
century together, without Arthur, of course.
    I Love You,
        Joe

CHAPTER 9

Mug Shots

B y the time I finally realized you are never too old to start reading about wizards, six of the seven volumes in the Harry Potter series had been published. By then I had a fan's acquaintance with the main characters after watching the first couple of movies filmed on the campus of Hogwarts School of Witchcraft and Wizardry.

Like the rest of the Muggle world, I was taken in by J. K. Rowling's craft and imagination, as mesmerized as any pre-teen. While her tales of potions and incantations, Quidditch matches, and the Ministry of Magic were engrossing on paper, her accounts of Professor Severus Snape's evil intrigues were animated by my ability to visualize Alan Rickman's ominous scowl, sinister hair and swirling black cassock. Knowing that Harry Potter and Hermione Granger bore such strong resemblance to Daniel Radcliffe and Emma Watson added significant degrees of empathy and charm to the time I spent reading about their exploits.

In contrast to the fictional young wizards in J.K. Rowling's brilliantly imagined world, the venerable officers and statesmen in my book are very real. However, few of them are household names, and fewer still are household faces.

No cues are required to conjure up mental images of Winston Churchill or Adolf Hitler – Churchill with a clenched cigar or a twinkling smile, Hitler with his stern gaze, ridiculous haircut, and toothbrush mustache. As I wrote about lesser-known characters, though – such as Admiral Francois Darlan and Premier Paul Reynaud of France, or Admiral James Somerville and General Sir Edward Louis Spears of Britain - I had to get to know them myself before I could effectively depict them for other readers.

Even after reading thousands of pages of research, I still did not have the sense that I really knew some of the people I was writing about until I found their pictures. I cared about my characters in different ways once I could visualize them. I found that tagging faces to their names and exploits added an essential dimension to my ability to capture them in words.

Of course, I used Google Images to search for their pictures. I selected one picture for each figure and pasted each photograph into a separate PowerPoint slide. I like PowerPoint because its draggable slide format makes it so easy to rearrange the pictures in any sequence – alphabetically by last name in my case.

Now that I know them better, I would like you to meet a few of my guys.

Jean Louis Xavier Francois Darlan

Admiral of the Fleet and Commander in Chief of the French Navy

Admiral Darlan held the fate of the French fleet in his hands. His officers and sailors were unconditionally loyal and would have followed any order authenticated with his secret "Xavier 377" signature ... whether he commanded them to surrender to Germany, join with Britain, flee to America, scuttle their ships, or pursue any other action that he directed. As France crumbled towards an armistice with Germany, Winston Churchill and Franklin Roosevelt applied relentless pressure on Darlan to align the French fleet with Great Britain's. His family history (particularly the death of his great-grandfather in the sea battle against Britain at Trafalgar) helped inspire the Anglophobia that Darlan routinely denied. His piercing eyes are indicative of his iron will, deadly serious demeanor, and lavish sense of honor.

Admiral James Fownes Somerville
Commander of Britain's Force H, at Mers-el-Kébir

One year after a forced retirement from the Royal Navy due to a suspected case of tuberculosis, James Somerville revived his career by means of his personal initiative, and worked his way back into active duty, (although he officially remained on the Navy's Inactive List until the last months of the war).

Somerville's vigor was routinely on display. When his ships were not at sea, Somerville began many days by rowing his 16-foot skiff throughout the harbor where his ships were anchored.

Somerville played a largely unsung role in the miraculously successful evacuation of the British Expeditionary Force from Dunkirk, thus saving Britain's army to fight on. His next assignment was to subdue key elements of the French fleet before they could be seized by Germany, using mortal force against his recent allies if necessary. Just days after France signed an armistice with Germany, Winston Churchill is said to have cabled Admiral Somerville: "You are charged with one of the most disagreeable tasks that a British Admiral has ever been faced with."

In the showdown with the French ships at Mers-el-Kébir, Somerville issued the ultimatum: "I must with profound regret require you to sink your ships within six hours." Sometimes referred to as "Naughty James" for his impish sense of humor and scatological vocabulary – a fellow officer claimed "he could pour forth the language of a fisherman."

Paul Reynaud

Winston Churchill's counterpart as Premier of France

Paul Reynaud was a long-standing friend of Winston Churchill, and like Churchill, was an unheeded voice against Nazi Germany's creeping expansion of evil during the 1930s. As was typical during the nonstop rotation of France's governments, Reynaud had previously served in multiple ministerial posts, including Minister of Finance (twice), Minister of the Colonies, and Minister of Justice (twice). Reynaud had been France's Premier for just two months when, on one monumentally historic day, Germany invaded Western Europe and Churchill was asked to serve as Britain's Prime Minister.

Reynaud was Winston Churchill's counterpart while France endured a horrendous assault by Wehrmacht forces. He also had to contend with an ineffective senior officer corps, a government pocked with defeatists, and a treacherous mistress with fascist and defeatist leanings. Reynaud resigned before he was able to fulfill his final commitment to Churchill: to hand 400 captured Luftwaffe pilots to Britain.

Writers often mentioned Reynaud's diminutive status (he was 5 feet, 3 inches tall) and, in a phrase from those times, made note of his "Oriental features."

Major-General Sir Edward Louis Spears
(Seated to the right, next to General Charles de Gaulle)
Winston Churchill's Liaison to the French Government

Fluent in French, with experience as British liaison to the French Army in World War I, Spears was asked by Churchill to serve as his direct liaison with Premier Paul Reynaud. When France withdrew from the fighting, and France's General Charles de Gaulle fled to the safety of Britain, Spears worked closely with him as liaison to de Gaulle's Free French movement. As was the case with most of de Gaulle's relationships, theirs was continuously prickly and contentious. Before that, Spears and Britain's Ambassador Sir Ronald Campbell had been pesky and outspoken sideline observers of the French Cabinet's deliberations leading up to their armistice with Germany.

Spears was a superb writer and had a wondrous and often snide ability to sketch his contemporaries at his typewriter. For example, here is how he described Joseph Vuillemin, Chief of Staff of the French Air Force: "...his bovine blue eyes had the same expression of rather hostile bewilderment to be observed in oxen as the trains go by." His books are valued resources for their detail and imagination. Spears plays a small role in my other book, but, more important, he was a trusted source of first-hand information and an absolute delight to read. Plus, I really like Spears, and this is one of my favorite pictures.

As you will read later, to my surprise and delight my archival research uncovered an unknown story about Spears that adds a fascinating twist to this book.

I regularly flip through my slides for a refreshed view of my subjects, and often jump to the photo of whomever I happen to be writing about. I have, at times, even taped printed copies of their pictures on the wall that I face while sitting at my computer.

The ability to attach faces to the names and stories of these sailors, soldiers, and statesmen helped ground and energize my writing. In addition, so many elements in the photographs from that period – the heavy texture of neatly pressed military uniforms, the expertly tailored and accessorized civilian suits, the dangling cigarettes, and decanted wine, even the black and whiteness of the pictures – helped transport me to the era when the ambitions, fears, and prejudices of these complicated men collided to create the story I decided to write.

CHAPTER 10

Words of Extinction

M ost of the books and magazines and newspapers and letters that I read for my research were written in the nineteen-forties or fifties. In the time I spent in the company of those historical accounts I would often be charmed, transfixed, and transported by words that have since faded from general usage.

I read words and phrases that we don't (or at least I don't) so commonly see or hear today, words like plenipotentiary, plebiscite, condoled, fair copy, and wagon lit. I also came across "new" words like aeroplane that had not yet matured into their current usage or spelling.

A quick aside: When you query Google for the meaning of a word, in addition to multiple definitions (which are provided to Google by Oxford Languages), Google also provides synonyms, and, in many cases, a chart that shows the trends for the usage of the word across decades and centuries. Usage trends for "plenipotentiary" and "plebiscite" over the past 220 years are shown on the next page. For a word nerd who is focused on a small slice of history, it was fascinating to see how the word "plebiscite" spiked in the years leading up to 1940.

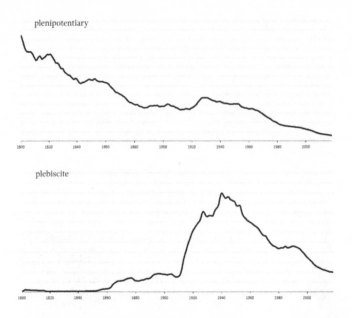

There were other words that we commonly use today, but which appeared in slightly different form back then, some rendered with hyphens – like: co-operate - and a few newly abbreviated nouns such as: 'planes, and 'phone, apostrophized in their days of fragile early usage.

I even came across a few mysterious references to time. Did 6.5 p.m. mean 6:30 or 6:50? I guessed 6:30. But then I encountered a reference to 12.7 and another to 8.9 a.m., and still have no idea what they signified on the clock.

Barton Swaim's review of John Simpson's book *The Word Detective* in the Wall Street Journal noted that one of the goals of the Oxford English Dictionary was to provide "a biography of each word." In addition to supplying every known definition for every word from "a" to "zyxt," the OED also sought to provide "as nearly as possible the date of its birth or first known appearance."

I sometimes wonder if the books that I read provided the last known appearance of some words.

CHAPTER 11

The Churchill Archives Centre: Cambridge

My three-day immersion in historical letters, telegrams, diaries, and manuscripts at the Churchill Archives Centre at the University of Cambridge made the deepest and longest-lasting impression out of all the visits during my research and writing journey.

The Churchill Centre's website provides a simple set of guidelines for "readers" – their term for visitors. Prospective readers must complete a one-page Reader Application Form. When you check in on-site you must also provide two forms of ID along with your completed form, one with a photograph. Appointments are recommended but not required. It's that simple. Once again, I was astonished at how welcoming the guardians of historical treasures were to a pedestrian like me.

The rules for the reading room – where you work with archive materials - are short and simple, with a couple of interesting twists.

Of course, you may not bring food or drink into the room, nor can you bring bags, coats, briefcases, or backpacks. It's OK to have a laptop, and if you need a place to stow your bag or your coat, there's a row of lockers outside the reading room where you can store your goods for a £1 refundable deposit.

In consideration of the priceless historical value of the archive materials, only yellow-paper may be used for note-taking - to provide contrast and help prevent any accidental or intentional misappropriation of those papers. In addition, pens are banned; if you intend to write out your notes, you must do so in pencil. If you arrive unprovisioned, pencils and yellow A4 pads can be purchased at the Archives Centre.

Visitors are encouraged to use their cameras or smart phones to photograph as many documents as they would like. The website mentions a £1 daily courtesy fee for the use of such devices, but I was only charged on the first day of my visit.

My first direct contact with the Churchill Archives Centre was an email that I sent three months before our trip. I mentioned my interest in "researching the destruction of the French Fleet at Mers-el-Kébir on July 3, 1940, including events leading up to the battle, the battle itself, and the aftermath of the battle."

I also noted that I wished to review the following collections:

- Cabinet Office
- Churchill – Winston Spencer
- Colville, Sir John Rupert
- Godfrey, Admiral John Henry
- Pound, Admiral of the Fleet Sir Dudley Pickman
- Roskill, Captain Stephen Wentworth
- Somerville, Admiral Sir James Fownes
- Spears, Major-General Sir Edward Louis

An Archives Assistant replied to my email in less than 24 hours. Her note included helpful reminders about pencils, yellow notepaper, and the £1 daily camera fee. Not only did she provide a link to the Archives' general online catalog, she also did a bit of pre-search for me and added a personal link that she created for "my search for "French fleet" between June and July 1941." OK, her search was off by one year, but her intent was delightful and much appreciated. I was excited and charmed and still just slightly intimidated by the prospect of a software salesman immersing himself in Winston Churchill's papers.

With one significant exception – which you will learn about soon – I was all set, registered for the three days I planned to spend on the Cambridge campus.

After an eight-day London-centered vacation, my wife Barbara and I departed King's Cross station for the one-hour train ride to Cambridge. A short taxi ride brought us to our hotel, which was just on the outskirts of the college. A 45-minute meander helped me find the best path for the next three mornings' 25-minute walks to Churchill College.

Barbara and I walked along worn sidewalks and pebbled roads each evening as we explored the campus. We found Cambridge to be a completely astounding and absolutely magical place. While London is a mix of the old and new, where much of the old is safely on display, Cambridge is a mix of the old and the ancient, and everything is put to use.

A stroll through Cambridge conjures up a sense of crossing the grounds of Hogwarts School of Witchcraft and Wizardry. We passed castles and cathedrals (in reality classrooms, libraries, dormitories and chapels) at every turn. Ancient windows, misshapen from time, in great stone walls overlooked broad greens and cobbled roads.

Stroll onto Trumpington Street, and you will find Ede and Ravenscroft, purveyors of high-end garments. They are also, as a sign at the bottom of the shop's main window wondrously declares, "Robemakers." I stopped at a coffee shop each morning on my way to the Archives. As I waited in the coffee queue one day, I listened to three Cambridge students who were just outside, drilling each other in Latin grammar. It sounded to me as if they were prepping for a Spells and Incantations final.

The University of Cambridge comprises 31 individual colleges (Trinity, Christ, King's, etc.). Churchill College is relatively new – it was established in 1960 – and it is the home of the Churchill Archives Centre. In addition to serving as the repository for Winston Churchill's papers, the archives also house the papers of approximately 600 other political and military figures of significance – several of whom play a role in my story, and whose papers I also intended to read.

The Churchill Library is the most out-of-place looking building that I noticed in Cambridge. The building's façade reminds me of a charming old-fashioned radiator. But of course, it's what's inside the building that matters. And that is the stuff of history, wonder, adventure, and fascination.

The Churchill Archives are open from 9 AM to 5 PM, Monday to Friday, and are closed on weekends. I arrived promptly at 9:00 and left as the archives closed on all three of my days in Cambridge.

I stashed my backpack in a locker each morning, and carried my laptop, yellow legal pad, iPhone, and shirt-pocket-full of sharpened pencils into the bright, quiet reading room. The reading room was not an excessively busy place. During the month of my visit, the Archives hosted 80 total visitors. Since I was there three days, I counted as three of those visitors. During that year, 559 other people visited the archives. A total of 8,985 files were reviewed during those twelve months. I probably accounted for about two percent of those file requests.

The archives staff was quietly observant and very efficient. I checked in, hoping to meet the archives assistant who had been so helpful by email. She was not working that morning but the staff was expecting me. They had a copy of my registration form, and as soon as I showed my photo ID, I was able to get to work.

The reading room is small and intimate. Four large wooden tables are joined together to form one very large communal workspace. I plugged in my laptop (so I could take some notes in Word and record a complete list of the materials that I viewed in Excel) and got right to work. Four people could have worked there very comfortably, but there was never more than one other person at "my" table.

The Churchill Archives, like the FDR Presidential Library, houses "collections." A collection typically consists of the accumulated letters, telegrams, speeches, diaries, and other papers of an eminent personality. The core of the Churchill Centre's holdings of course is its collection of Winston Churchill's papers. The archives also hold the papers of 600 or so figures, spanning the full range of eminence from Margaret Thatcher to names that are barely familiar even to Churchill devotees. That full range includes his contemporaries Leo Amery, Robert Vansittart and General Sir Edward Louis Spears.

The materials are safely tucked away from direct public access. A Reader may not fetch his own research documents. Instead, the highly agreeable and efficient archive staff will "pull" the material that you request ... as long as it's available for public review. There are some parts of some collections that may only be viewed upon the granting of specific permission. I needed this permission for one personal and private batch of documents – which is a story that I will share in the next chapter. The Churchill Centre suggests that prospective Readers send an email in advance of their visits, listing their subject matters of interest, in part to ensure adequate time to seek the necessary permissions to view restricted documents.

Unlike the FDR Library, the Churchill Archives has no schedule for the pulling of archive materials. You simply write the code for the next folder that you would like to read on a small slip of paper and hand it to the archivist behind the counter in the reading room. She will disappear into the back for perhaps a minute and return with anything from a small folder to a medium-size box.

The process includes one touch of charming practicality that, in my experience, is unique to the Churchill Archives. The folders are gently secured by loosely tied silk ribbons. Readers are instructed not to re-tie the wide, slightly-worn ribbons when they are done with a folder. Instead, the archivist at the counter will re-tie the ribbon for you, after taking a gently inquisitive look inside each returned bundle of papers. I arrived prepared with a long list of the collections and folders that I was interested in, so my interactions with the assistants were very efficient.

I knew the sequence of events and the critical details of my story before making the trip to Cambridge. I had studied the key players in some depth, and I had a good sense of whose papers would provide the most interesting and valuable content.

I was most anxious to see the papers of Admiral James Somerville. His archived papers – which had been donated by his son, Commander James Somerville - span 14 folders, organized by chronological category. The first folder I requested - coded "SMVL 7" - was titled "Force H."

Force H was the British naval squadron consisting of 17 ships that Admiral Somerville commanded at Mers-el-Kébir on July 3, 1940. Somerville's papers revealed his personal anguish before and after his ships shelled the French squadron that was anchored at the French colonial port.

Admiral Somerville's papers also filled in details of his life, personality, and character. I found transcripts of several "Weekly Review of the War" broadcasts that he made on the BBC. They were conversational chats from the early days of the war, intended to explain the war's recent doings and their significance in layman's terms ... albeit from the perspective of a knighted Admiral. His folders also included fan letters and critiques from everyday British citizens.

Two other especially rich collections in which I was immersed for hours were those of Somerville's ultimate boss, First Sea Lord and Admiral of the Fleet Sir Dudley Pound, and Major-General Sir Edward Louis Spears, who was Winston Churchill's personal liaison to the French Government and French military in the early months of World War II.

There were unexpected and eclectic findings along the way. Certainly, it was no surprise to find much about the challenges of working with the hyper-sensitive and always grumpy Charles de Gaulle in Spears' papers. However, the hand-written postcards from George Bernard Shaw and the riotously entertaining correspondence between Spears and M.P. Harold Nicolson were fascinating diversions.

Before my visit to Cambridge, I had a high-level understanding of the path that led the British and French navies toward their clash at Mers-el-Kébir. I had a decent outline of the forest of facts in mind and could also make out a number of trees. In my time in the archives, I swooped into the forest and saw not only trees, but individual branches and even twigs of detail.

I was quickly and deeply immersed in the naval rivalries, diplomatic tensions, and Parliamentary fuss of 1940. I viewed papers of admirals, generals, Members of Parliament, and other statesmen. Surprisingly, I did not pick up a letter that Winston Churchill had personally signed until my third day in the Reading Room. It was an unexpected find in one of General Spears' folders. I swear I felt a very slight breeze from the gentle flap of angels' wings as harps glistened in the background when I held that letter.

Out of the hundreds of Churchill-era books that I've read, my absolute favorite is *The Fringes of Power*, the personal diary of John Colville, Churchill's private secretary.

I knew that Colville's original diaries were in the archives, and, on my final day, I wrote "CLVL 1/3," on one of the small slips of paper. This was the code for the third of ten individual manuscript books that comprise Colville's diaries. I had not expected to be taken by a wave of emotion when I viewed the actual hand-written diary, but I was. No doubt, the rather formal and elegant presentation of the diary contributed to that sensation. An archivist carried a medium-size cardboard box – it could have held a family bible - to the table where I was working. She eased the box open, carefully took out the diary and laid it open on a red velvet pillow - a "purpose made bookrest" as I was to learn. She opened the diary to a random page and gently settled the open pages with a short cut of beaded cotton cord – my first exposure to "archive weights."

The original two-inch thick book that Colville purchased was a lined notebook, not a calendared diary with dated pages. This book had a black, leather-like cover, with a partially ripped cheap paper label pasted to the front cover. The label, in Colville's writing, read:

Diary 1940
Part II: July 1 – October 31st

Colville began each new day's entry just below the last line of the previous day's account. To start, he wrote and underlined the day of the week and the date. It was sometimes a challenge to read Colville's black-inked handwriting. It was never anything other than a delight. I had read many of those same words before but seeing them in the author's own hand was a remarkable experience. It was also tangibly enlightening. When Colville published *The Fringes of Power*, he omitted some of the minor – but still interesting – details that appear in his handwritten diaries.

It is a challenge to put into words just how exhilarating – and even somewhat emotional – the experience was of turning the actual pages on which Colville had personally jotted his daily observations and experiences. I thought of twenty-five-year-old John Colville, pen literally in hand, considering and casually capturing each day's events and conversations while at the beck and call of Winston Churchill at a time when the world was on fire.

Three days in Cambridge had seemed just about right when we planned our trip to the U.K. … but I until our time at Cambridge neared the end, I wasn't really sure if I had planned too much or too little time. As it turned out, my three-day research visit was just about perfect.

Each day in the archives went by quickly. I ended the first two days wishing the archives would stay open for a few more hours. By late afternoon of my third day, I had plundered the collections that seemed most relevant to my work. I'm sure I could have remained productive if we stayed for another couple of days, but I was satisfied with the details I had harvested.

The papers in the Churchill Archives provided unique and very personal insights that added incredibly rich dimension to my research. To borrow a phrase from Rick Atkinson, the Churchill Archives are a trove of "facts that tease coherence and intimacy from the past." I returned home with pages of typed and penciled notes, and an iPhone that bulged with more than 700 pictures of historical documents.

At five o'clock on that final afternoon I thanked the Archives' staff, collected my backpack from my locker, and started back towards our hotel. Barbara met me along the way at a pub called The Mitre. After fish & chips (OK, I might have had a burger with my chips), I raised a pint to Winston Churchill, to the Churchill Archives, and to Cambridge. Barbara and I walked the rest of the way back to our hotel, on a cobbled path that took us past the Robemakers at Ede and Ravenscroft on Trumpington Street one final time.

CHAPTER 12

Perfectly Adequate

My project reached new thresholds of significance and terror when I first interacted with the staff of The Churchill Archives Centre at Churchill College at the University of Cambridge.

The prospect of me doing research at Cambridge – the thought of my untenured and unworthy hands digging through the personal papers of Winston Churchill and dozens of his contemporaries - engendered several of my recurring "just who do you think you are?" moments of imposter syndrome. The very idea of a career-long peddler of fish sticks, ice cream and software handling priceless historical documents – some of which had been read, written, or signed by Winston Churchill - just seemed to beg for someone in authority to declare "Oh no, no, no dear boy; this just will not do."

As it turned out, the Churchill Centre's archive staff could not possibly have been more welcoming, knowledgeable, delightful, charming, or helpful.

When an archives assistant replied to the initial email in which I listed the collections of papers I hoped to review, her prompt reply, which began: "Dear Bill (if I may)" was equal parts charming, to the point, and helpful.

She did, however, alert me to one minor roadblock. One of the collections I requested contained the papers of Admiral

James Somerville. Somerville commanded the British fleet that partially demolished the French Fleet at Mers-el-Kébir. The collection was available for public review "except for Section 3 (correspondence) of the Somerville papers." That section included private correspondence between Admiral Somerville, his wife, and other family members – in other words: potentially the good stuff. Access to those papers could only be explicitly granted by the Admiral's grandson, Christopher Somerville. My new friend at Cambridge very kindly mentioned: "We will be happy to forward a letter or email requesting permission."

I drafted a letter to Christopher Somerville, politely requesting permission to view his grandfather's private, restricted papers. Not entirely confident in the phrasing of my request, I forwarded it to the archivist for her to review and edit as she thought necessary. She quickly replied: "I have just forwarded your letter to Mr. Somerville (which was perfectly adequate)."

In about two weeks' time, I received a gracious email from Christopher Somerville in which he very kindly granted me a conditional OK to wander through his grandfather's restricted private papers.

You should find plenty to interest you in my grandfather's papers - I hope your researches are successful.

I appreciate your sensitivity over quoting this personal and private correspondence, and would be very glad to have a sight of any material you'd like to include in your book, so that I can just cast an eye over it on behalf of the Somerville family.

Would you please very kindly send me a copy of the book when it comes out?

And of course I will.

CHAPTER 13

Writing Practice

D r. Atul Gawande, a practicing surgeon at Brigham and Women's Hospital in Boston, is the author of four books and dozens of articles that have appeared in the *New York Times*, the *New Yorker*, and other periodicals. A clear and imaginative writer who covers an eclectic variety of healthcare topics, Dr. Gawande enriches his books and articles with lessons from NASCAR pit crews, Cheesecake Factory restaurants, personal tennis coaching, Van Halen concerts, and pre-flight checklists (just to list a few examples). It is no wonder that he appeals to a large and diverse following that extends well beyond the world of medicine.

He is one of my favorite writers. If I had to recommend just one Atul Gawande piece, it would not be one of his books, and it would not be one of his articles. Instead, I would point you to the commencement address that he delivered to the Harvard Medical School's Class of 2005. In an address titled "5 Rules," Dr. Gawande offered this advice to his alma mater's graduating class:

1. Ask an unscripted question
2. Don't whine
3. Count something
4. Write something
5. Change

Although his address was written for - and delivered to - an audience of brilliant medical minds, Dr. Gawande's 5 Rules would have equal relevance in a personal development seminar or a sales training class. All five rules have helped me become more effective in my business. "Write something" was, of course, a call to action that I was eager to follow.

Dr. Gawande discussed his evolution as a writer in an interview with the *New York Times*. He started small with articles on Slate.com during the years of his residency. Slate was an ideal platform for a new writer "because it enabled me to fly under the radar."

As I ran my business and as I worked to sell our software, I knew that I needed to start somewhere with my writing. I knew I would also need to stretch and regularly exercise my writing muscles. I love a quote that I saw in Dr. Philip Tetlock's book *Superforecasting*: "We learn new skills by doing. We improve those skills by doing more."

I began to write papers and blog posts in support of my work as a software salesman. I also sought opportunities to speak at trade shows and to conduct online webinars. The primary objective of my early writing projects was to attract attention to our company and our software, but I also wanted to regularly follow Atul Gawande's "write something" precept and to improve my writing skills by doing more.

There was a time when my writing appeared in hundreds of thousands of homes across America. Despite the fact that I did not eat seafood, I had a knack for describing the crispy batter and mild flavor of our company's fish sticks and fish fillets in mouth-watering prose. In truth, my employer – Mrs. Paul's

Kitchens – saved money by having me write the descriptive copy on the back of our packages. I was never reviewed in the *New York Times*, but my work was widely circulated in home and supermarket freezers.

My first paid writing project was a software manual. After 10 years at Mrs. Paul's, I moved to Lancaster, Pennsylvania to work as director of marketing for a 99-year-old family-owned dairy. I bought a software package to help forecast our ice cream sales and optimize our inventory levels in a business with seasonal peaks and valleys. The software company – Demand Solutions – was fairly new and it had no sales force. After using the software for three years and evangelizing its capabilities to other businesses, I approached Steve Johnston, Demand Solution's founder, with the suggestion that he hire me as his sales force. Steve didn't like my idea; he did not want to add to his overhead. However, he said it would be OK if I started a business to sell his software, and as I embarked on my own business in my first attempt to sell *anything*, Steve provided these words of encouragement "... but you're a complete idiot if you try."

With my income solely dependent on commissions from the sales I wasn't making along with the training fees from the companies I wasn't selling to, I proved Steve right for the next two years. But I believed in myself and in Steve's product. I stuck it out and built a successful business that I ran for three decades.

Steve did a lot of things right, but as a one-man software startup, he did a lot of things, period. He loved the intellectual challenge of writing code, but he hated the tedium of documenting how users should put his code into practice. I became the biggest whiner about the quality of our user manual. (This was years before I read Atul Gawande's second rule). Eventually, Steve challenged me: "If you're so smart, you write it," and he softened the challenge with an offer to pay me $10,000 to write a guide to the features and functionality in his software. That was at the time when I was not making much money. That was Steve.

I wanted my manual to be better than any software reference ever written. In addition to providing clear direction for how to select a specific forecasting formula (for example), I also sprinkled in jocular tips for why users should do some things, and why they should not do other things (like select a specific forecasting formula). Steve was happy with the end result, and my documentation was embraced by our user community and the company's growing independent sales force. (I was the guinea pig for the independent sales model that Steve quickly embraced. There were eventually dozens of versions of me around the world).

If there is such a thing as an engaging set of instructions for how to generate forecasts, create product family subtotals, and measure forecast accuracy, I delivered. Although the software has evolved significantly since I wrote the manual for the DOS version of Steve's software, I'm proud that fragments of my writing live on in the software's latest online documentation and Help files.

My small company (there have been anywhere between two and ten of us at any one time) works with several hundred businesses that range in size from tens of millions to several billion dollars in annual revenue. The software that we sell helps them project their future sales as well as ensure that they have just enough – but not too much – inventory in place to manage their supply chains and support their sales.

A challenge faced by many of the individual managers that we work with is how to comprehend sales, supply, and inventory data for tens of thousands of different items. The ability to manage by exception, to focus on their most important items, is vital.

Of course, someone smarter than me had already developed an effective approach for managing what matters. Around 1890, Vilfredo Pareto, who was born in Paris and raised in Italy, noted that 80% of the land in Italy was owned by 20% of the population and – according to legend – that 20% of the pea pods in his garden accounted for 80% of the peas that he harvested.

Businesses with large numbers of products frequently apply Pareto Analysis to identify the relatively small number of products that account for the significant majority of their sales. They objectively identify the 20% of items or 20% of customers that account for about 80% of their sales and focus a higher level of time and attention on those most critical and profitable slices of their business.

Many prospective customers were not aware that our software enabled users to apply Pareto Analysis to prioritize and manage by exception, so I wrote a paper and delivered a webinar with one of my characteristically long titles: "Manage What Matters: The Pareto Principle, ABC Analysis and How to Manage by Exception" to help attract potential customers to our website. As you might imagine, the 80/20 rule is about as dry a topic as one could possibly find. But while researching that paper, I learned that the life of Vilfredo Pareto was quite a bit more interesting than his principle.

In 1889, at the age of 41, Pareto married a 29-year-old Russian maid, Allessandrina Bakunin. After less than three years together, she ran away with the family's cook and a share of the family's valuables. In time, Pareto's academic reputation was such that the Italian tyrant Benito Mussolini falsely claimed to have taken one of Pareto's courses at the University of

Lausanne. After Allesandrina left him, Pareto fell in love with Jane Regis – who was 30 years younger than him. Because divorce was not legal in Italy (it was not legalized until 1970), they could not marry, at least not in Italy. In the aftermath of World War I, the architects of peace carved the Free State of Fiume out of Austro-Hungary. This small state existed for only five years, and Pareto made the best of its brief sovereignty by becoming a citizen of Fiume in 1923 solely for the purpose of divorcing Allesandrina and marrying Jane. The Paretos acquired 18 Angora cats over time and named their house Villa Angora. Vilfredo died later in the year that he married Jane. In the end, Vilfredo Pareto's story was a love story.

I incorporated Pareto's story into my paper and presentations. While doing research for the paper I also learned that something close to the 80/20 rule holds in almost all walks of life. 80% of horse races are won by 20% of jockeys. 80% of all flight delays occur in 18% of major U.S. airports. A year after the state of Colorado legalized marijuana, 22% of the state's tokers accounted for 67% of the state's legal pot sales. 26% of the songs in my iTunes collection account for 80% of my listens.

The process of gathering that information and weaving it into a story that others will find interesting taught me a valuable lesson about research and writing. The tales of people who interest us and characters we care about will enliven any story – even one as arid as the tale of the 80-20 rule.

I enjoy presenting to business audiences, and of the different presentations in my arsenal, Pareto's story is the most fun to deliver.

Once I start reading a book, I almost always slog through it to the end. I "never" give up and stop reading partway through;

unless, that is, I'm reading a book in my chosen field - sales forecasting – a genre that produces some of the most dreadfully boring books ever written. In all likelihood, 80% of the books I've abandoned in my life are forecasting books.

A number of years ago, I was excited to find a remarkable exception. After reading a couple of glowing reviews and then finding a short excerpt, I picked up a copy of Nate Silver's *The Signal and The Noise: Why So Many Predictions Fail – But Some Don't*. I carried it with me on planes and trains, and I read it three times. It was – and is – the most interesting book about forecasting that I've ever read.

Signal ... has nothing to do with the type of forecasting that our software performs. There are no chapters about how to forecast ice cream or polo shirts or laboratory diagnostic kits. Instead, Silver devotes individual chapters to: how he applied his interest in baseball – "the world's richest data set" – to hone a unique agglomeration of statistics to project the success of his fantasy baseball selections, how weather forecasters apply satellite views of actual weather patterns to improve computer-generated weather forecasts, and how the lessons he learned from playing poker can be applied to forecasting – in particular that the best poker players understand that while they have no control over the cards they're dealt, they are in control over the decisions they make about those cards, as well as their reactions to the other players at the table. *Signal* ... certainly is not your father's – or your professor's – forecasting book, which is why it's so interesting and so practical.

Energized and inspired, I distilled Nat Silver's ideas into a paper titled "12 Supply Chain Forecasting Lessons from The Signal and the Noise," and wrote about how businesses can benefit by applying lessons that include:

#1. More information doesn't mean better information
#5. Your forecasts should tell the story of your business, not the story of your data. (My favorite)
#7. Data is useless without context
#8. Collective wisdom trumps individual brilliance

Although they shared a vaguely connected theme, each lesson was written as an individual one-page essay. The paper is intentionally snackable. Readers can pick it up on any page and digest it in small bites. Even though the original ideas were someone else's, the challenge of adapting and writing my "12 Lessons …" paper was grueling. I truly wanted it to be great. The finished product was a big step up in quality from my "Manage What Matters" paper. It's my best long piece of business writing, and still receives friendly feedback.

LinkedIn is a valuable business tool. Before I contact a prospective customer, I look her up on LinkedIn to get a sense of her work experience, educational background, and to see if we have any common connections. My LinkedIn profile outlines my work experience and my education, and it includes links to much of what I've written. I hope – indeed I expect – that anyone I'm about to engage with will check me out as well.

LinkedIn also provides a publishing platform. Any LinkedIn member can write and publish an article on any topic. One of the best things about posting on LinkedIn is the real-time feedback you receive from readers. You can see how many people have read your post, how many appreciated it enough to click the "Like" icon, and you can also read – and respond to - their comments. Unless you're a horrible writer or have picked an awful subject, it's a great source of instant gratification.

LinkedIn enabled me to fly under the radar when I began to write in earnest.

While LinkedIn is principally a business site, its members post on every topic imaginable. I usually stick to business subjects, with a goal of establishing an impression that my company and I are worthy of additional interest, and with the hope that a reader will be interested enough to visit our website to learn more about our software. As you might expect, my articles on LinkedIn include several about Vilfredo Pareto and a few about forecasting. But I've also stretched a bit and have written about such off-business topics as the original and very moving home-spun Flight 93 Memorial in Shanksville, Pennsylvania, and a perfectly true inspirational story that weaves together my encounter with Rollerblades, angels and cow-selfies.

My most widely read piece was one that I posted on a Thursday evening. I sat at my desk and watched in amazement as it exploded in readership (relative to my typical experience).

The day before, while waiting for a flight out of Baltimore/Washington International Airport (BWI), I noticed that a gauntlet had formed from the jetway at my gate. A number of people stood in the two parallel lines wearing a common tee-shirt, something about an Honor Flight.

Here's what I saw and here's what I wrote:

We can't all be heroes. A moving airport experience

I hereby resign my self-assigned "Road Warrior" commission. I totally denounce any reference I've ever made to "running the gauntlet" of business travel. Instead, I will simply clap as true heroes and warriors make their way by.

Yesterday started out as a typical day of business travel. Snarled traffic on the way to an early morning flight. Even worse congestion in TSA's security line. Terribly clumped groups on both sides of the carry-on scanner. Slow moving lines for overpriced coffee, and - to top it off - my chocolate glazed donut could have used more chocolate. Feeling sorry for me yet?

I actually enjoy the routine of frequent travel. Maybe I'm just numb from experience, but nothing mentioned above is more than a very minor inconvenience. It's rare, though, to enjoy a truly moving experience in an airport.

Because of their no-assigned-seats and group-boarding practices, some consider travel on Southwest Airlines to be an inconvenience. I've learned to embrace Southwest for their flexibility, their value and their service. (Please note: aside from my hard-won - argghhh, another cliché to banish - A-List status, I have absolutely no connection to Southwest).

Frequent Southwest fliers are well acquainted with the practice of lining up early. Sure enough, as I approached Gate B14 at BWI, I could see a large group of people already lined up. But it seemed too early - about 45 minutes before our scheduled departure time. And they weren't lined up in positions 1-5, 6-10, etc. No, instead they were lined up at the end of the jetway, forming a special aisle for exiting passengers to walk through.

Several held small flags. A good number wore vivid lime t-shirts printed with "Honor Flight Ground Crew" logos. A handful wore military uniforms. A sailor held the hands of his two young daughters. A quick scan suggested that every military service was represented.

Most of the observers were much like me - in a fog about what was going on, but joining the line to see what was coming. And then the clapping began. An enthusiastic gentleman standing by the jetway's door confidently proclaimed: "Here he comes!" An elderly man - a veteran of World War II - walked slowly up the jetway. As he passed through the doorway, the clapping grew louder. The men and women in uniform leaned forward to shake his hand. More tentatively, so did the sailor's two daughters.

Then another "Here he comes." And so came another vet. Like most who followed, he sat in a wheelchair. Then another, and another ... perhaps two dozen in all, in a slow parade of reverence and spontaneous joy. Some were pushed by Ground Crew volunteers. Some were pushed by family members. Most beamed with pride and happiness. A few fought back tears, not always with success. Many in the terminal fought back tears as well, even less commonly with success.

And then it got even better.

Sounding at first like an echo, but streaming in a slow wave, the clapping flowed to the far end of the terminal. Travelers set down their iPads, their coffee and their magazines as they drifted into spontaneous lines that spanned the entire length of the terminal. The clapping continued until the final hero made his way to the end.

I learned that the travel and the seed of the greeting were the work of The Honor Flight Network. I later read this on their www.honorflight.org website:

"Honor Flight Network is a non-profit organization created solely to honor America's veterans for all their sacrifices. We transport our heroes to Washington D.C. to visit and reflect at THEIR memorials. Top priority is given to the senior veterans - World War II survivors, along with those other veterans who may be terminally ill."

These visits to our Capital typically span 3 days, and include tours of such exceptionally meaningful sites as the Iwo Jima Memorial, the World War II Memorial and Arlington Cemetery. The Honor Flight Network covers all expenses for travel and accommodations for the genuine road warriors who served our country before many of us were born. The group that we saluted had flown in from St. Louis.

I mentioned that a number of people in the gauntlet by the jetway wore t-shirts with Honor Flight Ground Crew logos. The shirts also carried this quote from Will Rogers:

"We can't all be heroes. Some of us have to stand on the curb and clap as they go by."

Practice was having an effect. My writing was becoming tighter, more interesting and more clear. I'm my own toughest critic, and I could tell I was raising my skill level by doing more.

One writing project confounded me – not so much because the story was a challenge to write, but because I could not find its ending.

Early in World War II, a short time before the serious fighting began, France and Britain made a solemn pact that neither would seek an armistice with Germany without their ally's assent. Three months later, when it was clear that France would soon bow out of the war, Winston Churchill agreed to allow France to query Germany for their possible armistice terms. But Churchill insisted on two conditions:

France would have to sail its largest warships to British or American ports to ensure that its navy would not be absorbed into Germany's Kriegsmarine. And since France held roughly 400 German pilots in captivity, and since most of those pilots had been shot down by Britain's Royal Air Force, Churchill insisted that those Luftwaffe airmen be transferred to British custody to prevent them from re-entering the battle.

The story of the French fleet is, of course, worthy of a book.

As for the captured pilots, it is not likely that France would have turned them over to Britain under any circumstances. At a time when France was desperate for any glimmer of German mercy, the transfer of 400 members of the Luftwaffe to Britain would surely have driven Adolf Hitler to a vengeful rage.

As it turned out, Paul Reynaud, France's Premier, resigned three days after he promised Churchill that he would transfer the pilots. Reynaud never followed through on his promise. The new French government was likely not aware of Reynaud's commitment. They ignored Churchill's subsequent pleas for the pilots' transfer.

As Churchill noted in *Their Finest Hour*: "These German pilots all became available for the Battle of Britain, and we had to shoot them down a second time."

I wondered if Britain ever did shoot down any of those German pilots a second time. The Royal Air Force estimates that 2,692 German planes were shot down during the Battle of Britain between July 10 and October 31, 1940, a rate of about 24 per day.

Many of these German airmen died, but some parachuted or crash-landed their way into British captivity. I thought it would be an interesting and valuable exercise - a challenging project and an especially helpful writing practice exercise - to write a piece about a German pilot who was shot down over France and then again in the Battle of Britain ... if only I could find him.

I can be downright arrogant about my ability to find *anything* on the Internet. On the topic of downed German pilots in the summer and fall of 1940 however, my options were somewhat constrained since I do not read or write German. Despite hours of online, library, and used bookstore searches, I came up empty. I found interesting stories about several pilots who were shot down over France. One of the more fascinating stories was about Werner Molders, one of the first Luftwaffe aces in World War II. He was shot down in the waning days of the Battle for France and was held prisoner for just two weeks before the French handed him back to Germany. Molders died during the war, but ... I will hold those details for another time.

I was never able to find a pilot who was shot down over both France and Britain and captured twice. For me at least, that will be a never-finished story. Perhaps another writer with better resources or more highly developed research and language skills will find this story worthy of taking up and completing.

CHAPTER 14

Keeping Track
& Keeping Score

So, how's the book going?"
"Oh, you know ... it's going."
or
"It's a great mental health outlet, my one break from reality."
or
"Man, there are a *lot* of different ways to tell a story."
When family members, friends, and the small number of co-workers who I'd whispered to about my project would ask how my book was coming along, my replies were every bit as imprecise and uncharted as my actual progress.

The truth was, I really didn't know.

My work was all over the place. *I* was all over the place. I wasn't sure how far along I was with my project, or what I needed to do to pull my research into an outline, and an outline into a draft. I did know that I was precisely nowhere in terms of actually writing the story.

I had finished reading through most of my source materials, but the task of transcribing those documents into a collection of useful notes was still massive.

There was no doubt that I was busy. I worked on the book in some fashion almost literally (if not literary-ily) every day, typically early in the morning or in the late-night hours. If I missed three days in a month, that was a lot. What I did not really know, and certainly was not able to quantify, was whether or not I was making meaningful progress. My project had so many pieces and provided so many different ways to spend my time.

The funny thing is that in my real job, I preach and write about the benefits of managing what matters and the tangible impact of simply keeping score. I realized that I needed to apply Atul Gawande's Rule #3; I needed to count something.

I had to start keeping score – not just to track and measure my output, but also as an ongoing incentive to regularly advance my quantified progress. I've found that the simple act of tracking my activity helps make me more productive in every part of my life. The story of my life – the current version of it in particular – just might be that counting and writing go hand in hand.

Before I could quantify my progress on the book, I first had to document all of the many different fragments of the process – from reading books and transcribing notes to pulling together an outline and then writing an initial draft. I needed to make sure I was doing the right things. There were additional archives to visit, and old magazines and newspapers to track down. I needed to figure out how to read French. I had 700 pictures from the Churchill Archives that I needed to transform into words. There was a lot more to this than just reading, distilling, and writing.

When I begin work on a major new presentation or a webinar to promote our software, one of my first steps is to literally lay out my rough ideas, sometimes using Post-it Notes, sometimes rearranging index cards on our kitchen table, and often using Microsoft PowerPoint – which lets me reposition slides as well as reposition text boxes within slides by dragging them around on my computer screen.

The book that you are reading was a simpler challenge. It began as a stack of index cards – each with a two-to-five-word idea for a chapter – that I moved around on our kitchen table to form a crude initial outline.

I put together the PowerPoint slide that's shown below to get a better sense of the individual tasks that I would need to organize in order to keep my other, bigger book moving along. I needed to visualize the individual pieces of the project, and I needed a way to organize those pieces in some coherent form. With PowerPoint I could easily reposition my various tasks into logical, orderly relationships. This finally provided clarity on the many different pieces of the project that I had to address.

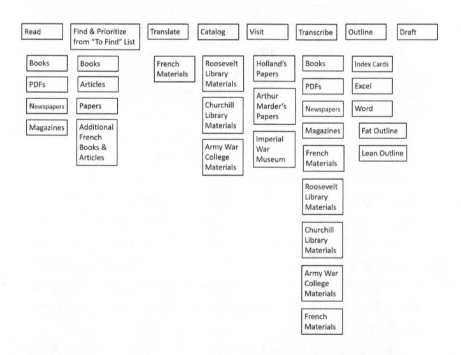

I know there are other tools – perhaps even better tools - for managing a writer's work. On one of my birthdays, my daughter Brittany - in "what does dad don't have" mode - gave me a copy of Scrivener, a thoughtfully integrated outlining, writing, and source-management software package developed specifically for authors. I was already so comfortable with the tools in Microsoft Office that I abandoned Scrivener after trying it for several weeks. The combination of PowerPoint for organizing and visualizing, Word for outlining and writing – and of course, Excel for keeping score and organizing my initial outline - provides me with just the right amount of free-form flexibility that I need to be productive.

The map of my work in PowerPoint finally provided some reassurance that I was not missing anything important. It also served as a handy reference for those times when I wondered: What do I do next? Or what should I be doing more of?

But it was no help whatsoever in measuring my progress.

In work and in life, I frequently look for ways to track my progress and to keep score. I bike, rollerblade or use our basement treadmill for exercise – and I routinely track the miles, elapsed time, and average speed for each workout. Multiple columns in multiple spreadsheets tell the story of individual workouts and cumulative performance. Graphs … well yes, of course graphs … help me visualize my progress. At the beginning of each year, I set monthly and annual mileage goals. This simple habit of keeping score even helps motivate me. I often skated or biked a few miles farther than I otherwise would have to ensure that I would make progress towards a monthly goal. I know I would not exercise as frequently or ride as many miles if I did not keep score.

Perhaps the goofiest story about my mania for tracking my progress is that I once found a way to quantify how hard and how subjectively smart I worked, and then crudely correlated that data to my commission-based income.

In the early days of running my own business, I tracked the number of letters I sent, calls I made, and presentations I delivered each day. (That was long enough ago that email was not yet a thing, so yes, letters). I assigned points to each type of effort; meetings were valued higher than calls, and calls were valued higher than letters. I tracked my daily, weekly, and monthly points. The urge to add a few more points often led me to crank out a handful of extra letters or make a couple of extra calls at the end of some days and weeks. When I graphed my monthly point totals against my monthly commission income, I noticed an uncanny relationship: with about a three-month lag, the harder and smarter I worked and the more points I racked up, the more money I made. As a result, I started working smarter, focusing more time on the high value efforts, and I started making more money.

Late one winter night, I collided with another player during what was supposed to be a no-check ice hockey game and broke my right collarbone. Since the Acura I was driving at the time had a stick shift, I didn't drive for thirty days. As a result, a month passed with no face-to-face meetings. Even with more time to make calls and write letters, my points for that period dropped off ... and sure enough, three months later, so did my income. I'm more of a fanatic than anyone I know when it comes to the value of keeping track and keeping score. But I know it works for me

But how do you quantify progress on a book? Obviously, when the serious writing started, I knew I could – and definitely would - count and chart words and pages.

At the time I first thought about this in earnest, I was deep into my research phase. Much of my time was spent transcribing excerpts from books that I had marked as interesting and potentially helpful. Since I was typing my notes into Microsoft Word, and since Word provides dynamic word counts and page counts, I tracked how many pages of notes I had typed each day. Of course, that led to a graph that showed my daily output, and then a similar graph that showed the total number of pages typed each week. And then, hey, why not add a seven-day-moving-average line to my daily bar graph for an additional dimension of progress? When I started work on my outline, I added a couple of new graphs – daily and weekly progress reports to myself on the number of pages in the outline.

Even though I work from home and have a flexible schedule, I run a small business which entails daily responsibilities to my customers, to the team I work with, and to the company whose software we sell and support. I have to make a conscious effort to carve out blocks of time for work on my book. My spreadsheets and graphs help ensure that I consistently make that time. As much as I want to show steady progress, I also really want to not show a lack of progress. Business travel sometimes prevented me from working on my notes or my outline or my initial draft for a few days. The holes and declining moving averages that sporadically appear in my spreadsheets and charts provide bothersome negative reinforcement. I want those gaps to be few and, literally, not-so-far between.

My spreadsheets and graphs reinforced my good behavior and encouraged my persistence. They enabled me to compete with myself to continually do more and to surpass my previous performance. It worked – at least in terms of the *quantity* of my output. My process continually encouraged me to write something every day.

This book is a smaller undertaking. I did only a small bit of separate research and, aside from rearranging index cards to re-order the sequence of the chapters in this book, I worked without an outline. In keeping with my typical experience, my first stab at each chapter was just brutal, painful to write, and even more painful to read. As I polished each chapter, and every paragraph within each chapter, I decided to try – very subjectively - to quantify the *quality* of my output. I assigned a score to each chapter, ranging from 5 (absolute slop), to 1 (I can't wait for someone else to read this).

I hold myself to high standards and grade myself on a tough curve, requiring significant improvement before changing a chapter's score from a 5 to a 4, from a 4 to a 3, etc. I demanded dramatic improvement – and significant re-writing - for a chapter to progress to a 2 and then a 1. I only used one graph for my work on this book, a daily chart that showed the average score across all 32 chapters. This was the one graph where a steady downward trend towards a perfectly adequate average score of 1.000 was the goal.

And yes, of course I calculate the quality of my work to three decimal places.

CHAPTER 15

Tout Le Monde Sait ... (*Everybody Knows ...*)

I f I write another book, the subject will be one that does not require a second language.

My book tells a story about the French fleet at the beginning of World War II. Much of the action takes place on French soil or in French colonial waters. I began my research with the assumption that the most likely villain in the dispute between France and Britain would be France's most senior Naval officer, Admiral of the Fleet Francois Darlan.

A bit off to the side, one small but intriguing player was Helene de Portes, mistress of France's premier, Paul Reynaud. Regrettably, but understandably, Reynaud neglected to mention Mme de Portes in his autobiography, but her meddlesome role in his government is whimsically noted in a number of other accounts.

Reynaud's biography, along with other major works from and about that period can be found in English translations, but there was no way to find and know and tell the full story without being able to read French. Without the ability to access and understand books, journals, newspapers, letters, and other documents that are available only in their original French, I would have just one side of the story.

I had taken French in high school and college, lightly studying my way through two years of introductory classes in both places. I retained slight familiarity with *bonsoir, s'il vous plait*, etc., and as I looked over several French-language resources - including websites and a few books in Notre Dame's library - I recognized occasional words and a few simple phrases. I was in better shape than if my antagonist had been German or Russian, but in reality, only the slightest degree of fluency remained from my eight semesters of study more than forty years before.

I realized that I was not sufficiently prepared to absorb the volume of information that my research required. I knew I would have to re-learn French - another task for my project and another box for the PowerPoint slide on which I mapped out this project. In my typically stubborn way, I set about re-learning the language on my own.

I had traveled down that road once before, when I tried to learn Spanish on the go after contracting to provide several days of software training for a customer with an office in Cali, Colombia. Since I regularly drive long distances for work, I bought a Berlitz "Think & Talk Spanish" cassette collection to make productive use of my car time in the weeks leading up to that trip. The first 15 minutes of the first cassette went extremely well. I learned a handful of words and basic sentences and was able to count to ten. I thought: "this might work," until the instructor commanded "Now open your workbook." Since my commitment to learning Spanish extended only to the limits of my idle mind on the highway, that venture ended quickly.

For this project, I have a one-way, single-lane objective. I just want to re-learn how to read French well enough to understand it. I have no desire to speak French or to write French. Once I made up my mind to re-learn how to read French books and other documents, I looked into different options for learning the language.

My first thought was to try Google Translate, which provides dynamic translations to and from more than 100 languages ranging from Afrikaans to Zulu. It's a free smartphone app, and it's also freely available at translate.google.com, which is where I took my first stab at binge-learning my chosen language.

One of the books I had partially scanned at Notre Dame's Hesburgh Library was *L'Amiral Darlan Parle*, by Alain Darlan, the Admiral's polio-stricken son. "Admiral Darlan Speaks" was written in French, and I assumed it would be an essential source ... if only I was able to read it. To test Google Translate, I started by typing in snippets of French from *L'Amiral Darlan Parle* – first a word, then a sentence at a time.

The individual translated words seemed plausibly correct, and although some of the translated sentences seemed a little bit stilted, I had a good sense of what the author was trying to say. As translated by Google, Alain Darlan's book begins:

> Two main reasons have led me to write this book, in which is finally hear, ten years after his tragic death, the voice of Francois Darlan, Admiral of the Fleet and Vice-President of the Council ... my father.

I gave up on Google Translate after a several weeks though, not because its translations weren't helpful, but because the process I created for myself was so tedious. I manually typed each sentence from Alain Darlan's book into the "translate from" box on the screen, read the real-time English translation, and then reviewed the original French entry. Then, since I wanted to keep a record of the translated text for future study, I pasted both the original French sentence and the English translation into a Word document. My comprehension was improving, but my progress was depressingly slow. I wasn't convinced that I had found an effective way to re-learn French, and I decided to check out other options on the web.

Not surprisingly, there are a number of helpful and even cheerful Internet sites that promise to help you learn the language of your choice. Two of the most popular are Duolingo and Babbel, and I gave them both a try. Both sites are free, and they take similar approaches, starting at an elementary "See Spot run" level of engagement, and gradually advancing you towards conversational fluency. Both sites use multi-sensory reminders and reinforcement: pictures, multiple-choice selections, spoken words and repetition. They begin with cheerfully simple multiple-choice options with suggestive clues that all but whisper the correct answers in your ear as you are guided through increasing levels of complexity.

For example, one of the early challenges presented by Duolingo was to select the French translation of "the apple." In addition to providing these 3 options – "*la pomme*," "*la chatte*" and "*la femme*" – a picture of an apple, a cat or a girl appeared above each word. I got that one right. On a whim, I tried the introductory questions for Turkish – a language I had never before seen or heard – and aced that one as well. Maybe the questions are too simple. Or maybe the application is so effective that even I could learn Turkish while also re-learning French. No doubt, their goal is to draw you in with a "seems simple" initial experience.

If you're looking for a path to polite conversation, these language sites are ideal. But my reading material pulsed with edgy confrontations and deadly skirmishes. I wasn't looking for help in placing a restaurant order, picking up dry-cleaning, itemizing my medical symptoms, or chatting about the weather. I had no desire to read breakfast French or grocery store French; I needed to read naval base French, contentious cabinet ministers' French, and I must with profound regret require you to sink your ships within six hours French. *(Je dois, avec un profond regret, vous obliger à couler vos navires dans les six heures).*

So I returned to Google Translate, this time with a simpler plan. I no longer wasted time pasting French sentences and English translations into a Word document. It seems like a little thing, but in addition to saving time, this added a helpful degree of continuity as I plowed through Alain Darlan's memoir, followed by *De Mers-el-Kébir a Londres*, in which Jean Boutron describes his experiences under fire on a French ship on July 3, 1940.

My previous attempts at learning French had lacked commitment and a consistent effort. My "learning time" was too sporadic and unfocused. I needed to learn how to read French and I needed to retain more of what I learned. Since I was doing this on my own, I needed to make a deeper commitment than if I was using a structured program like Duolingo.

I committed myself to spending 15-30 minutes with Google Translate every possible day, a more consistent commitment than my previous attempt. Work, travel, and family commitments sometimes made it impossible to find the time, but the more time I spent with Translate, the less of a drudge it seemed. I spent more time reviewing sections that I had previously translated, and that cycle of repetition and review helped quite a bit.

I learned to appreciate the value of reading and translating entire paragraphs at a time. The benefit of context would often help me translate individual words and sentences that I might otherwise have struggled to comprehend.

Google Translate, of course, does not provide reliably precise translations of phrases, sentences, or paragraphs. Words in combination have nuances that defy any translation app. For me to rely on Google Translate would be to risk my authenticity and credibility on quotes like "this book, in which is finally hear, ten years after his tragic death…" I used Google Translate to help identify passages worth digging into in more detail and worthy of a precise translation. For those translations, I relied on fluent friends and colleagues.

I maintained and regularly updated a spreadsheet with the French words that I most commonly stumbled over, and I periodically reviewed that ever-growing list of French words and English translations. For travel study, I even printed little flash cards with those words, their translations, and an example of each word in a short phrase. Pro tip: Use PowerPoint and use one slide per word. Print the slides six to a page and cut out the individual slides. Yes, you will feel like an absolute loon, and you will not mention this to a soul until you write a book about your project.

I actually began to enjoy my French studies. Of course, I considered keeping track of my progress. But tracking minutes is messier than counting pages. It would have taken too much time to track my time. So I simply focused on my work. I was that committed.

I would never claim that my approach is a best practice that I would recommend to anyone else with an interest in learning French, Turkish, Afrikaans or Zulu, but this focused, incremental approach to learning how to read selective bits of French worked well enough for me as it significantly extended my comprehension of written French.

One nice advantage of teaching myself French by translating topically relevant sources collected during my research was that my effort was now directly focused on the words and phrases common to my area of interest: the idioms of French ships, sailors, soldiers, and politicians.

Instead of the French version of "What is for breakfast?" or "That color looks great on you," I learned to read: *"le gout d'agir manqué"* (the taste for action is lacking), *"sa prétendue haine contre les Anglais"* (his alleged hatred of the English), and *"Les Britanniques ouvrent le feu sur les Francais."* (The British opened fire on the French).

I included one other small learning aid in my regimen. When Barbara and I visited Paris for a week, I made a one-day solo side trip to the site where Germany surrendered to France at the end of World War I, and France signed its armistice with Germany at the beginning of World War II. The small museum store there sells a 32-page booklet titled: "1918 and 1940: The signing of the Armistice in the forest glade of Compiegne." The booklet is available in both English and French, so I also bought: *"1918 et 1940: La signature des Amistices en foret de Compiegne."* I studied them side-by-side as another small step to extend my comprehension of written French.

One of the books I read in the course of my research was *The Path to Victory: The Mediterranean Theater in World War II*, by Douglas Porch. One of the sources cited by the author was an article titled "Could Admiral Gensoul Have Averted the Tragedy of Mers-el-Kébir?" I tried to find a copy online but found that it had been published in *The Journal of Military History*, which is not accessible to civilians or non-academics.

So, I took a short trip to a rich source of military research. I spent a day in the library of the Army War College in Carlisle, Pennsylvania, which is just about an hour from where we live. I had hoped to access military publications that are otherwise inaccessible to non-students and non-military personnel. I had a short list of publications in mind (*The Journal of Military History*, *English Historical Review*, *The Field Artillery Journal* ... you know, all the popular periodicals), and when I was not able to find them in the library's stacks, I asked a librarian for some direction. He was anxious to help, and was very generous with his time, as he used his privileged credentials to expand my on-line search capabilities for the day.

He quickly found - and very kindly printed - a copy of the Gensoul paper that I was seeking. I then asked if he would mind searching for additional articles about Mers-el-Kébir in military journals. He was happy to oblige and typed "Mers-el-Kébir" into the search box on his screen. As a long list of articles filled his display in a slow scroll, his face and his voice dissolved into disappointment. He quickly scrolled back toward the top of the list and said: "These all look pretty old, plus they all seem to be in French"

"Hey, wait!" I stopped him.

To my slight surprise, even though all the titles were in French, I understood every word.

CHAPTER 16

Three Loathsome Figures

M y research helped fill in the stories of dozens of people whose lives I thought I understood. The despicable characters were the most interesting to learn about and the most fun to write about. When I decided to profile a few of the most loathsome figures that I encountered, Adolf Hitler was, of course, just so off-the-charts obvious (not to mention off-the-charts evil) that he was never a candidate for this chapter.

Two of the three people I've written about here are peripheral scoundrels in my other book. That book is further enriched by a roster of additional villains, and I prefer to save their stories for those pages.

As I dug into the exploits of the men and women who created history in 1939 and 1940, Joachim von Ribbentrop of Germany got under my skin like no other person I encountered. I was tempted at one point to simply list his name three times in this chapter. So, let's start with him.

Joachim von Ribbentrop

Although there is a very long list of Nazis who were more vile and criminally wretched, Hitler's Foreign Minister Joachim von Ribbentrop merits the universal disdain that he received as much for his utterly contemptible temperament and personality as for his decisive influence on Adolf Hitler's decision to go to war with France and Great Britain.

Every book and every article that includes any mention of Ribbentrop includes at least one story of his boundless ignorance. He was an equal-opportunity ignoramus, every bit as uncouth to royalty as he was to commoners. He was knighted "von Brickendrop" by a British journalist after he demolished court etiquette during his ritual introduction to King George VI as Germany's new ambassador in 1937. Disdaining the customary modest bow to Britain's sovereign, Ribbentrop sharply clicked his heels, locked his right arm in an upward angle, and barked "Heil Hitler" ... and then repeated the Nazi drill two more times. The shy king smiled wanly and bowed slightly.

A schoolmate remembered Ribbentrop as "the most brainless boy in his class," a kid who was remarkable for his "pushiness and vanity." Andre Francois-Poncet, France's ambassador to Germany recalled: "One could not talk to Ribbentrop; he only listened to himself." His biographer called him "a shrill bully." Nevile Henderson, Britain's Ambassador to Germany and frequent target of Ribbentrop's rage and distorted reality described Ribbentrop as "a combination of vanity, stupidity and superficiality," and wrote: "there is no hell in Dante's inferno bad enough for Ribbentrop."

His German colleagues were equally unsparing in their disdain. Ernst von Weizsacker: "I honestly hated him." Hermann Goering: "Germany's No. 1 parrot." Count Otto von Bismarck: "He is such an imbecile that he is a freak of nature." Interpreter Paul Schmitt, who frequently assisted in Ribbentrop's negotiating sessions called him: "a dangerous fool" and noted "If Hitler was displeased with him, Ribbentrop went sick and took to his bed like a hysterical woman."

Born a Ribbentrop, he assumed an air of faux nobility as a *von* Ribbentrop after Gertrude von Ribbentrop, a titled aunt and widow of a Prussian officer, adopted him in 1925 when he was 32. In addition to his strategic adoption, Ribbentrop married well. Annelies Henkell was heiress to a wine and champagne fortune. Her father sent him to Paris to help expand the family business. Ribbentrop's mother-in-law would lament "Of all my sons-in-law, the most foolish became the most prominent." Joachim and Annelies had two daughters and three sons, one of whom they named Adolf.

While in his twenties and early thirties, Ribbentrop worked a series of jobs in Canada, the U.S. and France. Sir Eric Phipps, who represented Britain to both Germany and France as Ambassador noted: "Ribbentrop is the only member of the Nazi party who goes abroad and has foreign friends." The span of his travels and his fluency in English and French were unique in the German High Command, which emboldened him to flaunt a cosmopolitan aura that contributed to his influence with Hitler on foreign policy. American journalist William L. Shirer noted however that while Ribbentrop spoke French and English, his linguistic competence "was not accompanied by the slightest comprehension of France and the French," nor of Britons or Americans.

Ribbentrop made his mark on history with a trio of significant pacts that would ultimately empower Hitler to wage war with assumed impunity. He burst into international diplomacy in 1935 with his belligerent negotiation of the Anglo-German Naval Agreement, which boosted the German navy's tonnage in relation to Britain's. This agreement not only removed the last remaining naval restrictions from the Versailles Treaty, it also drove a temporary wedge between Britain and France, since Britain's ostensible ally had been excluded from the negotiations. The Pact of Steel, which Ribbentrop signed with Italy's Foreign Minister Galeazzo Ciano (Mussolini's flamboyant son-in-law) in May 1939, formalized the Rome-Berlin Axis which welded the warring alliance of Hitler and Mussolini. Finally, the Molotov-Ribbentrop Pact (a.k.a. the German-Soviet Pact) signed in August 1939, aligned Germany with Russia just as Germany was about to invade Poland, eliminating (temporarily, as history would prove) any threat from Germany's potential enemy on its eastern border as World War II dawned.

Ribbentrop's singular talent was his ignorant and offensive persistence. Paul Schmidt noted "I often saw him keep at it so long without the least regard for tact or politeness, that the other side gave in through sheer exhaustion." Although he was fluent in English, Ribbentrop often reverted to German and insisted on Schmidt's participation as a translator in many of his meetings with British envoys.

Joachim von Ribbentrop, with his dull eyes, pursed lips, and overall sullen visage, carried a passionate contempt for Britain. Herr Brickendrop had been mocked by British society, and his son Rudolph had been rejected for admission to Eton. Britain and France's refusal to interfere with Germany's incursions into Austria and Czechoslovakia had convinced the German Foreign Minister that the Allies lacked the will to support Poland if Germany attacked. Ribbentrop's confidence helped sway Hitler, and on September 1, 1939, Germany launched a vicious *blitzkrieg* attack on the Poles. Two days later, when Nevile Henderson delivered Britain's final ultimatum, which promised a declaration of war, Ribbentrop refused to meet with the British Ambassador, leaving the task to a most unlikely envoy - interpreter Paul Schmidt. After Schmidt rushed to Hitler's office and translated the British ultimatum to a small audience that included Hitler, Ribbentrop, Hermann Goering, and Joseph

Goebbels, Hitler turned to Ribbentrop and snapped: "Now what?" Ribbentrop quietly replied: "I assume that the French will hand a similar ultimatum within the hour." Schmidt heard Goering mutter: "If we lose this war, then God have mercy on us."

Winston Churchill had multiple cordial encounters with Ribbentrop during the German Foreign Minister's time in London in the late 1930s. Their final meeting was at a luncheon on March 12, 1938, the day German troops marched into Austria. Churchill later recalled: "That was the last time I saw Herr von Ribbentrop before he was hanged."

Ribbentrop was one of ten German leaders who were hanged at Nuremberg on October 16, 1946. With its subjective entries and edits, no one considers the Wikipedia website an attributable source of written history. However, if you scroll to the bottom of the Wikipedia entry for Joachim von Ribbentrop – or any of the other nine German war criminals who hanged that day - you will find undisputable gruesome truth: a photograph of his corpse, eyes closed, freshly cut from the gallows.

Countess Helene De Portes

Countess Helene de Portes was the very public mistress of French Prime Minister Paul Reynaud, the direct counterpart of Winston Churchill during the war's critical early months. Madame de Portes was much more than the affectionate focus of Reynaud's private life. She was also a frequent and detrimental influence on his public responsibilities.

The French and British prime ministers reached their countries' highest seats of government precisely 50 days apart, Reynaud on March 21, 1940, Churchill on May 10. During that spring and the early days of summer, as German forces smashed Holland and Belgium, as Germans swarmed France and occupied Paris, as British and French soldiers were swept off the beaches of Dunkirk, and as Reynaud desperately pleaded for aid from Britain and America to help keep France in the war, the heaviest burden he carried was Helene de Portes' unrelenting pressure to surrender - to abandon the commitment he had made to England that France would not seek an independent peace with Germany. The countess aspired for France to assume a role as Germany's most favored conquered state.

His agreement to the pact that neither side would seek a separate peace without the other's approval was one of Reynaud's first acts as Prime Minister. American emissary Sumner Welles later noted that Mme de Portes and the "termites" in the French cabinet "sought tirelessly day and night" to breach that agreement.

As France's fortunes crumbled after four weeks of German onslaught, Countess de Portes' appeals for a betrayal of England grew increasingly desperate. As Churchill and Reynaud headed into a meeting on June 13, she implored a minister: "Tell Paul that we must give up. We must make an end of it. There must be an armistice!" As it would turn out, France independently signed an armistice with Germany just nine days later, and Churchill and Reynaud would not meet again until after the war. Reynaud was confined in German prisons for most of the next five years.

Reynaud and Mme de Portes shared a small apartment at the Place de Palais Bourbon in Paris. Details of their official-if-less-significant others are sketchy. Reynaud appears to have been separated from his wife, and *Time Magazine* reported that the countess had been widowed two years before the war. *Time* also crammed their short piece with an anonymous reporter's un-chivalrous and un-Timely depiction of Mme de Portes as: "short, homely, plain, dark, nervous, jealous and not very bright."

From most accounts, the countess was not a joy to be around. The American journalist Vincent Sheean wrote that she "chat-tered like a magpie and lost her temper with ease. She was not chic, she was not charming and she was not intelligent." To Brit-ain's General Edward Louis Spears, she was "untidy" and "de-void of charm." Sheean added that the countess "behaved at times like a sovereign, at times like a fishwife."

After a late-April trip to London, Reynaud was bedridden for several days with the flu. Pierre Lazareff, editor of *Paris Soir*, called on the prime minister to discuss an urgent matter and was taken by surprise when he arrived to find Mme de Portes seated at Reynaud's desk, meeting with "generals, high officers, mem-bers of the Parliament, and officials. She was ... giving advice and orders right and left."

Possibly her most egregious encroachment was an instance when Reynaud's aides were not able to locate an important and highly confidential cable that was to be discussed in a meeting with British Ambassador Sir Ronald Campbell and Churchill's liaison, General Edward Louis Spears. After searching for some time, Reynaud's *chef de Cabinet* Roland de Margerie suggested to Spears: "Wait a moment. I think I know where it might be."

Moments later he returned with the crumpled communique. He replied in exasperation to Spears' question about where he had found it: 'Chut. It was in Madame de Portes' bed.'

She exerted strong influence on Reynaud's cabinet selec-tions. When the author Andre Maurois criticized one pick, Rey-naud responded: 'Ah, you don't know what a man who has been hard at work all day will put up with to make sure of an evening's peace.'

After reporting the details of his June 13 meeting with Reynaud to his cabinet, Churchill added with characteristic twinkle: 'Paul Reynaud returned to Tours with the Countess de Portes. She had a comfort to give him that was not mine to offer.'

Reynaud, who had worked so hard to marshal opposition to Germany before and during the war, bitterly opposed the colleagues who favored an indirect contact with Germany to learn potential armistice terms. With his stance in the minority, and in the face of unrelenting momentum of the German forces, Reynaud resigned his post on June 16, 1940. Countess de Portes was jubilant. Not only did France's new government seek an armistice, they also provisionally selected Reynaud as their Ambassador to the United States.

To assist with the transition of the new ambassador and his mistress, two aides quickly set off for Madrid, with plans to sail to America. To their surprise, and despite their claims of diplomatic immunity, Spanish authorities insisted on searching their baggage. In addition to Mme de Portes' personal wealth – currency, bonds and jewels – they also discovered two million dollars in gold. The well- connected aides insisted that the gold was from a secret fund which the French government had earmarked for propaganda use in America in support of their cause. The valuables were returned to France and Reynaud's assignment was quashed.

Reynaud, who claimed not to know about the gold, surmised that his aides had been overzealously proactive in planning for his new role as the face and voice of France in America. He later told U.S. Ambassador William Bullitt: "It's going to be most difficult to prove that I had nothing to do with it. But I gave Leca (his aide) no orders to do what he did. As for the gold and jewels, they belong to the countess." De Portes sheepishly claimed that the money was intended for her two children who had recently departed for the U.S.

Earlier that spring, Bullitt, a Francophile, the most ebullient of men, and outwardly a friend to de Portes, noted in a typically chatty cable to President Roosevelt: "The people of France ... deserve better ... than to be ruled by a Prime Minister's mistress.... In the end she will be shot. Meanwhile, she will rule the roost."

On June 28, 1940, Reynaud and de Portes enjoyed lunch at a café near the port city of Sete. After their meal they went on their way down a winding road in the former prime minister's Renault Juvaquatre. Several miles into the drive, Reynaud lost control and swerved from the road. As the car hit a tree, the load of baggage that was piled in the back seat surged and toppled forward into the front seat. Reynaud was seriously injured and would be hospitalized for days. The countess was killed instantly. Some versions of the story say she was nearly decapitated by the tumbling, heavily laden bags.

Marshal Philippe Pétain

Try this: call to mind any iconic American general – Ulysses Grant, John Pershing, Dwight Eisenhower, George Patton – any iconic American general, that is, whose triumphs in war earned him perpetual reverence.

Now stretch your imagination to picture the passage of 20 years, and the esteemed general's recall to duty in advanced age to lead America in a fresh war against our country's previously beaten foe. Imagine that as we all looked to him for leadership and inspiration that he cowed and caved and meekly surrendered to the invader. Then imagine surrender slipping into collusion, and collusion corroding into betrayal. Imagine the general's silent assent at the persecution, imprisonment, deportation, and selective execution of the people he had pledged to defend. If you can imagine that horror, you might then understand the story of Marshal Philippe Pétain of France.

Pétain was an authentic hero of World War I. It is conceivable that France and its allies could have lost that war had it not been for Pétain's leadership - on the battlefield for certain, but also for his sure-handed resolution of the fragile and volatile French Army's internal conflicts near the end of the war – enabling France to endure as a viable fighting force until American troops joined the Allied cause.

In battle, he led French Armies to victory at Verdun in 1916 - the war's longest and deadliest battle. Pétain was remarkable for his compassionate leadership during the 299 days of brutal fighting in which each side suffered more than 100,000 fatalities. Pétain was reluctant "to throw warm bodies at barbed wire and machine-guns." He scorned reckless all-out assaults in favor of targeted attacks by rested troops backed by overwhelming artillery support.

Even more important, the Victor of Verdun's firm but humane leadership helped subdue the little-known but widespread mutinies in the French armies in 1917. War-weary and dissolute, thousands of *poilus* (the common term for French infantry men) openly rebelled against their officers. Some refused orders to attack, some deserted, some took to the battlefield drunk and without weapons. Just under half of France's artillery divisions in 1917 were infected with mutinous soldiers. The author

Richard M. Watt wrote that the mutinies had "reduced the French Army to impotence for almost a year."

Pétain, who once said "They call me only in catastrophes" was called on to suppress the mutinies. By that point some men had been fighting for as long as 18 months without relief from front-line hostilities despite a promise of seven days leave every four months. Pétain ordered the reinstatement of the 7-day leave policy, and also pledged to halt major offensives until American forces arrived to join the French and British in the conduct of those offensives.

Amid the turbulence, Pétain drove each morning to the encampment of a different infantry division. He mounted the hood of his car or stepped atop a tree stump to rally his men and share his thoughts on the war, his strategies for battle, and his plans for winning back the allegiance of the men who were fighting for France. He reinforced why Frenchmen were fighting this war with a simple and convincing message:

We fight because we have been attacked by Germany
We fight to drive the enemy from our soil

Empathy and compassion alone would not end the epidemic of mutiny that had infected the French Army. Pétain understood the need to severely punish the most malignant mutineers. Thousands of men were imprisoned, with many shipped to overseas prison colonies. 554 men were condemned to death by firing squads. Only 49 of those sentences were carried out; enough to send the desired message. To this day, many details of the mutinies of the French armies in World War I remain shrouded in secrecy. What is clear is that the mutinies subsided under Pétain's leadership, and in the war's final months the French Army was once again a cohesive fighting unit.

One month after the fighting ended in 1918, sixty-two-year-old Philippe Pétain was declared a Marshal of France by President Raymond Poincaré, a distinction he shared at the time with just two living military icons – Marshals Joffre and Foch.

In the twenty-two years between the World Wars, Pétain enjoyed the laurels of a distinguished commander of the winning side. After service on the Supreme War Council through the nineteen-twenties, Pétain had a brief turn as Minister of War in 1934. He helped shape French strategy for future wars, and naturally embraced tactics that helped him win a Great War in 1918: massive forces embedded in static defensive positions supported by relentless artillery bombardments. In his lectures and writing Pétain scorned tanks, "aeroplanes" and mobile attack forces - the new, risky and unproven tools and tactics that went against his experience-borne principles.

Pétain was in Madrid at the start of the Second World War, posted to Spain as France's ambassador. In the face of catastrophe, and in desperate need of personal, military and public inspiration, Prime Minister Paul Reynaud called Pétain home just eight days after Germany's invasion.

Reynaud counted on Pétain to invigorate and inspire the French military and the French populace. He believed that the Marshal would somehow stem the Germans' advance. In a radio address on the evening of May 18, Reynaud joyfully announced that Pétain had joined his government as deputy prime minister. "The Victor of Verdun, Marshal Pétain, returned this morning from Madrid. He will now be at my side ... putting all his wisdom and all his force in the service of the country. He will remain there until victory is won."

In his 85th year Pétain was still the embodiment of a leader. His remaining grey hair was close cropped on the sides and back, and his balding pate was often covered by his gold-braided kepi. Beneath the narrow brim of Pétain's flat-tipped circular cap, the wrinkles that framed the octogenarian's piercing, gray-blue eyes did nothing to diminish their brilliance. His mustache, once a bushy flag of flamboyance was now a tight, grave accent. Although he stood just 5 feet, 7 inches tall, his trim figure and erect bearing helped project an imposing command presence. He had the haughty countenance of a man who expected others to take him as seriously as he took himself.

As Reynaud would quickly grasp however, Pétain was no longer the inspiring leader of the First World War. At a time when all of France looked to the Marshal for bold and confident leadership, Pétain's gloomy defeatism was a final blow to French hopes. As early as May 26, Reynaud conveyed his impression to Britain's Secretary of State for War Anthony Eden that if a large part of France was occupied by the Germans, Pétain would speak in favor of an armistice. France had been attacked by Germany once again. But now, Pétain lacked the will to drive the enemy from French soil.

General Spears described Pétain's countenance in a May 31 meeting as "glacial and morose." Churchill lamented: "...his serene acceptance of the march of adverse events." As Reynaud, Churchill and Anthony Eden were about to enter a meeting on June 12, Reynaud remarked as Pétain approached: "He looks buoyant this morning. There must be some bad news."

Paul Reynaud resigned as Prime Minister four days later - on the evening of June 16. To no one's surprise, he was immediately replaced by Marshal Pétain. Shortly after midnight the French Government sent a note to Germany asking if they would be willing to propose peace terms.

A short time after noon the next day, Pétain broadcast a radio address to all of France from a makeshift studio in a classroom at the Lycee Longchamps. Pétain, described by American journalist Eric Sevareid as "a vain, doddering old man," announced that France would cease fighting – despite the fact that an armistice had not yet been negotiated. In the preamble to his announcement, Pétain memorably huffed: "I give to France the gift of my person to lessen her misfortune."

After two days of anxious silence, the German government conveyed their conditional assent to talks – which began the path that led to the signing of the armistice on June 22 at Compiegne, and then to the breakup of France's alliance with Britain, and the suppression of all that France stood for and fought for.

By the terms of the armistice, France was broken in two. Germany now occupied three-fifths of the country. The gerrymandered German-controlled territory included Paris and the coastlines of the Atlantic Ocean and the English Channel. The remainder was ostensibly under French control, with Pétain as Prime Minister.

Pétain quickly assumed a dictatorial role. At one of the most vulnerable times in his country's modern history, Marshal Philippe Pétain betrayed the hope and the trust of the people he had been asked to lead. He acquiesced to German demands for food and materials that were pillaged to supply Germany and Italy. He accepted the existence of the Milice, a paramilitary organization that ruthlessly harassed, tortured, and murdered members of the French resistance. Pétain bears responsibility for the enactment of anti-Jewish legislation that stained France, and he acquiesced to the arrest and deportation of French Jews by the Milice and German authorities.

In the years just after the First World War, Pétain had been a mentor at the *Ecole de Guerre* to a young officer, Charles de Gaulle, who was thirty-four years his junior. De Gaulle would become an early and eloquent proponent of mobile tank warfare. Unfortunately, his tactics were embraced more avidly by Germany's self-proclaimed "Panzer Leader" General Heinz Guderian than anyone in France. As de Gaulle's and Pétain's views on how to fight the next war diverged, their relationship grew cold. By 1940 they barely spoke. De Gaulle had been promoted to general shortly before one of their final meetings in June of that year. The Marshal remarked: "You're a general! I don't congratulate you. What good are ranks in defeat?"

De Gaulle flew away to Britain in the company of General Edward Louis Spears the day after Pétain became Prime Minister. The new general was horrified by the defeatist posture of the Marshal and his cabinet. He also knew that he would have no role in France's government or military. When he landed in Britain, he was literally a man without a country. With help from Spears, Churchill, and others in Britain, de Gaulle launched his lonely campaign for the liberation of France. The new French government in Vichy, with Pétain at its head, sentenced General de Gaulle to death for desertion and treason.

After the Allies won the war in 1945, Charles de Gaulle was appointed Chairman of the Provisional Government of the French Republic. His government tried Pétain and sentenced him to death for treason. Offers of asylum for the Marshal from Britain, Switzerland, Brazil, America and other countries were rejected.

De Gaulle commuted the Marshal's sentence to life in prison, and he remained captive on the tiny Ile d'Yeu off the western coast of France for the remainder of his life. Philippe Pétain, Victor of Verdun, Marshal of France, and Hitler's willing partner in the oppression of French people, the disgraced hero who had been muddled with severe dementia in his final years, died a prisoner in 1951 at the age of 95.

CHAPTER 17

Journey to the Edge of Word

"Of all the practical skills a student develops while at LaSalle, typing is the one skill which will become more and more invaluable as the student pursues his educational and vocational goals."

La Salle College High School, 1970 Blue and Gold Yearbook

I've had my wireless keyboard for so long that the A, S, D, L and C keys are blank, the letters completely worn away from years of typing. I rarely look down at my keyboard, so that's OK. Those blank keys and their insignificance are a nice testament to the touch-typing skills that I learned from Brother Edmund Miller during my freshman year at La Salle College High School in the Philadelphia suburbs, and to the frequency with which I still put Brother Edmund's lessons to work.

I have surely done more typing than necessary during this project. Early on, when I realized I needed to impose some semblance of organization on the bundles of research that I had gathered, I began to collate my notes into about two-dozen high-level categories. They included: The Buildup to War, The Fall of France, Negotiations at Mers-el-Kébir, The Battle, etc. I created a file for each topic in Microsoft Word, and I've been manually typing my notes ever since.

As tedious and inefficient as this might be, the process of typing my notes provided one additional pass at the information I had harvested, hopefully helping me absorb the most meaningful bits. More important, with my notes now typed into Word I'm able to quickly search my files for names, locations, dates, ships, and authors.

Over time, as I typed note after note after note after note, some chapters spanned hundreds of pages, several have passed the thousand-page mark. One – "The Fall of France" – contains more than 2,900 single-spaced pages of notes

Well before I crossed the thousand-page threshold, I wondered if there was a finite limit to a Microsoft Word file, a maximum number of pages that you could type or paste into a single document, and then go no further.

I had once "blown up" an old contact management program, pointlessly adding notes about potential customers after I had passed the word limit that the software provider had neglected to document. I work with numbers in my real job, and before Excel expanded its capacity sixteen-fold to just over a million rows, I would occasionally max out spreadsheets with more data than a single worksheet could handle.

As I work on my book, I would hate to belatedly learn that an evening's worth of typing about the brotherhood of seafaring men had been for naught. Until this project, I never had to think about filling up a Word file.

As it turns out, the maximum size of a Word file is not defined in pages; instead, it's defined in Megabytes. A Word file is fully saturated when it's filled with 32 MB worth of text.

It takes quite a bit of typing to create a file of that size. My "Fall of France" file, with a bit more than 2,900 pages (and about

920,000 words) is just under 9.5 MB in size. I would have to reach about 10,000 pages (and over 3 million words) in a single document before I bumped into the outer edge of Word. The letters Q, Z and X would probably be the only remaining readable keys on my keyboard if I ever got that far. (And I will never get that far).

In case you're curious, there are 783,137 words in the King James version of the Bible and a mere 587,387 words in Tolstoy's *War and Peace*. "The Fall of France" is just one chapter's worth of research notes. I have a lot of notes. This book, by the way, has about 65,000 words.

Megabytes were not a thing when I sat in Brother Edmund's class in the late 1960s. He graded our typing on accuracy and on words-per-minute. If he knew I would one day do the math for how many minutes it would take me to type 750,000 words, Brother Edmund would have thrown a chalkboard eraser at my head. (Teachers could do those things back in the days of Remington typewriters ... and to this day, my classmates and I cherish those memories).

I learned all kinds of things from the Christian Brothers at my Catholic high school in the Philadelphia suburbs: how to speak halting French, why to question conventional wisdom, how to pray, how to write with imagination, and how to type with precision and speed. All of those lessons – not just what I learned in typing class - truly have become more and more invaluable over time.

CHAPTER 18

Rick Atkinson – Outlines and Fine Brushstrokes

All of those photos and scans and typed up bits of research that I had accumulated had come together – not into anything resembling a coherent story – but as 13,000 pages of notes, loosely organized within several dozen binders, labeled according to their content.

By then I had a fairly decent process for collating my findings, although at the time it was more in the form of rough thematic groupings than a tight chronology of events.

When I first thought about how I might like to organize my information, I broke it down into about three-dozen different topical segments. Those topics included: The Buildup to War, British Concerns About the French Fleet, The Fall of France, Churchill as Military Planner & Tactician, etc.

I created a separate Word file for each topic, and methodically typed my notes into the appropriate document. I curated a stock of blue binders, initially one binder per theme, although some themes eventually spanned four or five fat binders. In addition to the previously listed subjects, there was also a binder filled with biographical bits about the principal characters in the book, and another with notes about civilian life in England,

France, and Germany. In hindsight, I wish I had taken a more chronological approach, but this still worked pretty well for me.

Any book that I read could potentially be a source for stories that fit into a handful of different topics. I might find a chapter on the buildup to World War II, maybe an anecdote about Churchill's clumsy attempts to speak French, and perhaps a few pages touching on the close and comfortable working relationship between the French and British navies in the initial stage of the war.

I kept a steadily growing stack of my recently printed pages on a shelf in the wall unit behind my desk. On any given day, the pile would include thin clusters of pages destined for seven or eight different binders. I used yellow Post-it notes to separate and label the first page in each topical section. Every few days, as the pile of printed notes grew, I would hole-punch and load the pages into their respective binders.

I still think of my research as my big historical stew.

Since I've always spent more time than most people with my nose buried in books, I cannot say I stepped up my reading as I researched admirals, diplomats, journalists, and politicians in pursuit of details for my story. Instead, my pleasure reading evolved from a couple of weeks spent immersed in the latest mind stretcher from Michael Lewis or a new John Irving novel to a 45-minute skim through a 75-year-old diary from a starchy old member of Britain's House of Commons.

On top of all the reading I did for research, I also maintained a parallel track, reading the works of a select group of narrative non-fiction authors – an attempt to go to school on their research, organization, storytelling, and writing talents. Six authors whose work I especially appreciated, and whose books I was alternately inspired and intimidated by, were Erik Larson, Laura Hillenbrand, Tracy Kidder, Michael Lewis, Lynne Olson, and Rick Atkinson.

Of that group, Rick Atkinson is the one author who focuses on military history. He won a Pulitzer Prize for his book *An Army at Dawn*, which told the story of the Allies' battles against German forces in North Africa in 1942 and 1943. That was the time when the American and British armies learned to fight together, and the place where they first learned to despise and kill their common enemy. The book describes their challenges and triumphs, their narrow brushes with defeat, and ultimately, how the British and American forces routed the Germans from Africa.

An Army at Dawn was the first installment in Atkinson's *Liberation Trilogy*. I had also read *The Day of Battle*, its follow-up. The first book had closed with "... just over the horizon, another continent waited." *The Day of Battle* picked up with the Allies' invasion of Sicily and continued with their ferocious struggle up through the boot of Italy.

I devoured both books (1,129 total pages of narrative and 226 pages of end notes and acknowledgements), and also listened to their unabridged audio versions, which spanned thirty-two 80-minute CDs. I spend quite a bit of time in my car, and the *Liberation Trilogy* was with me on many long drives.

I will never write remotely as well as Rick Atkinson, but I look to him every day as an inspirational model. In addition to studying his written work – re-reading several pages at the start of each day - I also tried to learn everything I could about his approach to researching and writing.

I found the transcript of a televised interview that he had done on C-SPAN's *Booknotes* program in 2002. The program's host, Brian Lamb, asked Atkinson about how he kept such a large quantity of information - "battles and people and all that stuff" - organized.

Atkinson mentioned that he first completes his research, and then outlines his book in great detail. "I'm an inveterate out-liner." He then reviews the material that he's collected during his research phase, "and I go through and I decide that this is a fact that goes in the trash.... This looks interesting. This goes in Chapter 3."

That general approach – starting with some form of an out-line, and then fleshing it out with interesting and relevant bits of information was what I had in mind for my historical stew (or, perhaps, for stirring a theme into my pudding), and it was how I would eventually approach my writing. Finding that little bit of guidance and reinforcement was one of the most encour-aging moments in this solitary project.

I certainly needed help. My initial challenge was how to or-ganize my research into at least a shell of a book. There were so many events, people, conflicts, details, dates, implications, and lessons that I did not know where to start. I actually made sev-eral starts, but quickly got lost along the way, unsure and not at all confident how best to proceed.

I thought a spreadsheet might help, and began typing brief notes, sequenced by date. My spreadsheet eventually grew to 11,286 rows. It helped to frame my thinking, and the ability to sort by date or to search by word in Excel helped me begin to transform my binders of information into the skeleton of an ac-tual story.

But Excel is more appropriate for numeric data than it is for sentences, or even the cryptic phrases in my outline. Although my spreadsheet helped me accumulate and organize dates and facts, I still struggled to manage all of the many pieces of information that I would have to tie together in my book. I knew I needed a better way to harness the details of the conflict between Britain and France in the early days of their mutual clash with Germany.

Fourteen years after Rick Atkinson started researching and writing *The Liberation Trilogy*, his concluding volume - *The Guns at Last Light* - was published in 2013. I saw that his book tour included an appearance at Politics and Prose Bookstore in Washington, DC in mid-May of that year, and made it a point to be there on the evening of his talk.

I arrived early, as bookshelves on wheels were being rolled aside to transform a section of the store into an open space, and watched erstwhile booksellers unfold portable metal chairs to fill that space with tight rows. P&P's coffee bar was doing a thriving business. Wine and beer could be purchased at an ad hoc serving table. Great stacks of *The Guns at Last Light* awaited purchase through the evening. I bought a copy.

The event was not a "reading." Rather, Atkinson shared stories about "the greatest catastrophe in human history." He described many of the fascinating little details that his research had uncovered, frequently signaling a shift to a new topic with "I tell the story of ..." As he does in his book, he shined a light on the fascinating personalities and horrific events of the war. He outlined the arc of his trilogy, starting in Tunisia, moving through Italy, capped by the invasion of France on D-Day, and ultimately, Germany's surrender.

I roughly counted 400 people in the tightly packed room when his talk began. I arrived early enough to claim a seat, but

I'm fidgety in any situation, and was grateful to join those who stood along the shelves at the edge of the room.

The audience was well dressed, absolutely engrossed and completely quiet, with the hush broken only by occasional waves of laughter. (Toward the end of the war, desperate to replenish its ranks of riflemen "the army didn't really examine eyes, it just counted them"). Atkinson, in his early sixties, with sandy brown hair, rimless glasses and a military bearing, is an engaging speaker. A video of his talk can be viewed on Politics and Prose's YouTube channel, and you will notice the rapt attention of the audience, heads tilted, gazes sharply focused. He sprinkled his talk with compelling statistics (one person died every three seconds) and somber tales (the foreign grave of each fallen American soldier was re-dug by hand after the war, and families were given the option of having their son or father sailed back home or interred for all time where he fell).

He spoke of the challenge in writing about World War II in a fresh way when Amazon.com already stocked 60,000 hardcover books about the War. He mentioned the importance of differentiating via voice, narrative, and archival spadework. A former newspaperman, he becomes visibly excited when talking about his research. He refers to himself as an "archive rat" who treasures the surprises and discoveries he finds in boxes and folders.

He has affinity and affection for many of his subjects, a number of them lesser-known officers. He mentioned Ted Roosevelt, Jr. and Lucian Truscotte, Jr. - who have been "with me through all three volumes." He has his guys.

After speaking for just under 30 minutes – followed by a round of solid applause - he invited questions. Lines were beginning to form at standing microphones on both sides of the room. I jumped in quickly and was the third person in line on

the left side of the store, holding my newly purchased copy of
The Guns at Last Light.

The questions before mine were asked by people who were
interested in the deep details and lessons from World War II.
One asked his opinion on how the War was fought. Another
asked about the long-secret Operation Tiger, a badly botched
rehearsal for the D-Day invasion in which 700 to 800 soldiers
and sailors died, and which still has a shroud of some secrecy.

My question was probably the longest and certainly the
strangest of the night:

> Rick, I hope you won't mind a question about how you
> research and write. In reading the first two books of the
> trilogy, I was just dazzled over and over by how you bring
> the story to life by bringing us to people's neighborhoods
> and into their lives. And I've seen you talk before about
> your passion for outlining. You spend months on an out-
> line and then you start to fill in the facts. I have this image
> of a wall filled with Post-it notes, and I sense that's not
> how you do it. I'm just curious about the tools you use and
> then as you start to weave in the facts of your research,
> how do you keep track of it all.

He took a deep breath and faced me with a wry smile.

"Well, this crowd really wants to hear about my outlining
techniques."

There was laughter. I replied with a feeble "Sorry." And then
he told me everything I needed to know.

"Well, you know, the heart of your question is really: how do
you distinguish between this that you use and this that you don't
use. And I'm always looking for fine brushstrokes that bring
something or someone to life."

He mentioned a quote from Keats that was often used by Civil War historian Shelby Foote: "A fact is not a truth until you love it."

"And so, somebody like me, and narrative writers, we're looking for facts to love that tease coherence and intimacy from the past. And that is part of what the researching art is about. And it is an art form."

He briefly discussed the appreciation for timetables and deadlines that he gained during his days in the newspaper business.

"And the outlining process – you know, I use the outlining software in Word. I think it is the greatest invention since the plow! It's fantastic.... And for me, it works not only as a road map, to show me where I'm going to go in this big book, but it also tells me where everything is in my notes. "

He added that he had spent seven or eight months outlining *The Guns at Last Light* and that "the outline was three times longer than the book."

He stressed the importance – and noted the incredible tedium – of the outlining process.

"But once I'm done, I do have a map, I know where I'm going. I've got a sense – I know where things are – which is pretty critical. And I have a sense of how this is going to play out."

I use Word every day, but I had never noticed its Outline functionality. Of course, I jumped in as soon as I got home, and immediately saw just how helpful the Outline feature could be.

After the questions, I joined the long line for personal book signings. As I handed him my copy of *The Guns at Last Light*, I said: "Thanks for humoring my question about your research. I'm just a software salesman who writes for my mental health." Rick Atkinson smiled and replied: "That's fine. When I start talking about research I can go on for a long time." And he signed my book.

I rode the Metro back to Union Station, then an Amtrak train to Baltimore, and drove the rest of the way home to Lancaster, knowing, for the first time, with confidence ... I can do this.

CHAPTER 19

I Went to School on Laura Hillenbrand Too

Laura Hillenbrand's *Seabiscuit* captivated and inspired me more than any book I've ever read. (I know; bear with me. This is about one of the best writers on the planet, not about Churchill and the war; although, come to think of it, one significant thread in her book was Seabiscuit's rivalry with a horse named War Admiral).

If you've read her book or watched the perfectly-cast movie (let's begin with Jeff Bridges and Tobey Maguire, and then you have narration by David McCullough and music by Randy Newman ... I mean, come on!), you know the inspiring tale of this gutsy racehorse and his troubled and fragile jockey Red Pollard.

You might remember "Silent Tom" Smith, who nurtured and trained his horse through onerous weight handicaps and crippling injuries. And of course you have Charles Howard, who owned Seabiscuit and was the passionate ringleader of a thoroughbred racing and public relations machine. As they individually and collectively overcame a continual torrent of life-wrenching obstacles, their passage mirrored and inspired multitudes of Americans who still struggled to find their way through the final years of the Depression in the late 1930s.

In the opening chapters of *Seabiscuit*, as you begin to care about her characters, Laura Hillenbrand immerses you into an era when horse races were routinely broadcast to living room radios across America. You become feverishly embroiled in rivalries with owners of other horses. And she walks you down to the rail as she describes nine major races in riveting detail, with each race brought to life in a unique, breathtaking account, with vivid descriptions that bring you to your feet in anticipation and excitement, even after multiple readings.

Laura Hillenbrand's legion of fans also includes Daniel James Brown, best known for his best-selling book *The Boys in the Boat*. Before I read *The Boys in the Boat*, I found an article that mentioned how Daniel James Brown had meticulously studied *Seabiscuit* before he wrote his narrative nonfiction account of the 1936 U.S. Men's Olympic Rowing Team and their quest for a gold medal at the Berlin Olympics.

Brown proudly admits to having "dissected" his paperback copy of *Seabiscuit* during a family vacation, blurring it with notes on every page, "… just studying all the writerly decisions she made; why she started this scene this way and that scene that way, and the language choices in how she developed the setting." He added: "I went into the whole research project with a list of guidelines, which were drawn from this close study of 'Seabiscuit.'"

In a *New York Times Magazine* interview, Brown mentioned that although he admires other nonfiction writers – particularly Tim Egan, Jon Krakauer, Nathaniel Philbrick and Erik Larson - he considers Hillenbrand "a model to aspire to." Also, simply: "I think she is the best."

After reading *Seabiscuit* many years before, after watching the movie (which doesn't really count) and after listening to the unabridged audiobook, I brought my paperback copy with me on a family vacation to Montana.

Using my own primitive hand-scrawled version of Microsoft Word's outlining technique on a stack of 8" x 5" index cards, I outlined the entire book. That process was incredibly enlightening; I saw what Daniel James Brown had seen. That outlining process was especially helpful in understanding how Laura Hillenbrand's characters were introduced, developed and seamlessly mingled with the other jockeys, owners, sportswriters and family members who had enjoyed their own orderly introductions into the flow of the story.

My outlining work produced one funny side effect. Our family was on a vacation trip to Yellowstone National Park, and Barbara had found a grand house for us to rent on a bluff in Emigrant, Montana. One evening I mentioned to our son Billy that I was diagramming *Seabiscuit* in an attempt to at least partially decipher Laura Hillenbrand's writing style. He gave me a quizzical look and asked, "so now you're writing about Seabiscuit instead of Churchill?"

I explained more clearly what I was trying to do and confirmed that "my Churchill book" was still a thing. I also mentioned that Laura Hillenbrand set such a lofty standard that there's no reason and no room for *anyone* to ever write another book about Seabiscuit ever again.

I never expected to apply the specific outline that I created from *Seabiscuit*. And, as it turned out, my story about prime ministers, admirals, and massacred sailors has progressed down a different path. However, the process of deconstructing Laura Hillenbrand's masterpiece taught me the value of a solid structure, and it provided incredibly helpful insights into how to outline, construct, and enliven the story I was trying to tell.

CHAPTER 20

Every Side of the Story

To this day, the tale of Dunkirk – the bombing and strafing of long lines of haggard soldiers waiting on beaches with superhuman discipline, the improvised armada of small civilian boats that joined in their rescue, and the sheer number of men who were saved - is venerated as a tale of deliverance and renewal. The rescue of the British Expeditionary Force from the beaches in France saved close to a quarter of a million British soldiers from captivity or slaughter. The many tales of heroism from the beaches and the small ships inspired Winston Churchill's island nation at a time when almost all of the war news that preceded it had been grim.

The French, however, tell a different story.

The French version of Dunkirk is a tale of abandonment and betrayal. In the eyes of the French, not only had British forces contributed little on the ground or in the air in their joint combat against the German invaders, the British retreat across the English Channel left France to face the full onslaught of Germany's tanks, infantry and dive bombers virtually on their own.

And then there's the German version.

The scope and pace of their advance through France astonished the German High Command every bit as much as it shocked the English and the French. The temporary halt at the fringe of Dunkirk called by Adolf Hitler is one of the mysteries of the war. German officers were frustrated and enraged at this lost opportunity to quickly crush the Allies at their most vulnerable juncture. Germany's failure to land a knockout punch in 1940 was a contributing factor to Britain's survival during the perilous nineteen months that followed (when she and her Dominion nations fought alone), and to the Allies' ultimate victory in 1945.

The example of Dunkirk, with the different sides so clearly drawn, perfectly demonstrates the challenge of how to tell a story from multiple perspectives. In researching and writing about the clash between the French and British navies, I've worked to capture and understand the actions, motivations, decisions, and personalities from all sides. Gathering facts was the easy, if time-consuming, part. The facts are straightforward. The interpretation and weighing of those facts from each perspective was a bigger, more subjective challenge. My goal has always been to distill the details and shape the information into a convincing three-dimensional tale.

Tracy Kidder, who collaborated with his editor Richard Todd on a book called *Good Prose: The Art of Nonfiction*, notes: "The fundamental elements of a story's structure are proportion and order." The order of the events in my story took care of itself, but finding the right proportion was a persistent challenge.

My writing was also guided by Rick Atkinson's answer to my question at Politics and Prose … that when it comes to organizing a story, the heart of the challenge is: "how do you distinguish between this that you use and this that you don't use." I've learned that just because a bit of treasure from my research is interesting to me, it does not necessarily add value to my narrative of Winston Churchill and Britain's clash with the French Fleet. (Hey, did you know the Swedish Army has no generals – except during world wars)?

In contrast with the cleanly drawn stories from Dunkirk, the different perspectives of the French, British and Germans on the optimal disposition of the French Fleet in 1940 are less clear and more of a challenge to present in the appropriate proportions.

Britain and France shared a common goal: to prevent the French ships from falling into German hands. But their plans for how to achieve that goal could not have been more different.

On the surface, and in the way the story is commonly told, the conflict over the French fleet was very straightforward. France was about to be vanquished. Its fleet was a valuable asset, one that could significantly tilt the balance of naval power in favor of Germany and Italy if they obtained control of France's ships. All that the leader of the French navy - Admiral Francois Darlan - had to do to prevent the loss of his fleet was to order his unequivocally loyal officers to sail their ships to British, American or neutral harbors. How could he possibly decide otherwise? Only a traitor would align himself with Hitler and Nazi Germany.

That's the conventional wisdom. The British and Americans pressed France for possession of the ships based on understandable self-interest and their perception of allegiance and loyalty. To the French though, the decision was a matter of honor and assets. Admiral Darlan had given his word multiple times – to Winston Churchill and to Darlan's counterparts in the British Admiralty - that no French ship would fall under foreign command – which, although the British did not know it at the time, included British command.

By that time, French mistrust of Britain was almost on par with their concerns about Hitler. In the eyes of many in France, Britain had dragged them into an unnecessary war, then fought poorly, and, when France desperately needed additional air support, Britain held dozens of Royal Air Force squadrons back for the defense of Britain against the inevitable invasion by Germany. Britain's retreat across the English Channel was a decisive death knell for the Franco-British alliance.

Perhaps more important, Darlan and many others in France expected Germany to defeat Britain shortly after France's fall. Although the nation of France had been vanquished, her navy had not been defeated. Until an armistice was signed, her navy was her best bargaining chip in the inevitable negotiations with Germany.

And then there was this significant blind-spot: no one in Britain or France knew how Hitler intended to use his Navy. The Allies had little sense of his outlook on naval warfare in general and were naturally inclined to assign malicious motives to his plans for the French fleet. Germany had aggressively built up its navy in the years leading up to the war, and most of the battles in the first eight months of World War II had been fought at sea. The *Kriegsmarine's* most glaring weakness was in surface ships, a gap that Admiral Darlan's fleet could instantly fill. It seemed logical that Hitler was every bit as interested in conquering the seas as he was intent on dominating the air and the ground. If the political and military leaders of Britain and France knew what we know today about Hitler's posture on naval warfare and his ambitions for the German Navy, would either country have acted differently?

The answer to that question might surprise you. I've already given enough away, so I will save the rest for my other book. Thanks to gradually opened archives and the passage of time, and thanks to the advantage of hindsight and history, we now have all three sides of the story.

My job is now to tell the entire story in a compelling, meaningful, and appropriately proportioned way.

CHAPTER 21

Oh No!
I Already Read This

O n the night it started raining in my office, my books were not my first concern. As a slowly increasing flow of water dripped through a light fixture above my desk, I moved my laptop and monitor to a safe spot, switched off the light, and then did what I always do when there's a household emergency – called out to my wife Barbara.

Barbara quickly reasoned that the light fixture was just the most convenient drain for the invading precipitation, and that we had better punch a hole in the ceiling closer to the source before a buildup of water poured through and did serious damage to my room. Since my office extends from the rest of our home, and since there's a junction of gutters where the office meets the front of the house, that front corner seemed to be the most likely source of the weather system that hovered above my desk.

Barbara divined the most likely spot in the ceiling and punched a hole that let a steady trickle of water drip down to the bucket that I held in perfect fulfillment of my level of expertise in every home emergency. (To borrow a quote from Tracy Kidder's longtime editor Richard Todd: "I am incapable of fixing anything that isn't made of words").

The forecast called for outside-rain through the night, and the impromptu drain was perilously close to a wall unit that held about a hundred books, so the two of us carted books by the armful to the dry safety of our dining room. With each short trip, we each picked up as many books as we could carry, paying no attention to titles or to the erratic system in which my shelves had been organized.

As the stacks slowly rose on our dining room floor, just one book caught my attention. It was the top book on one of one of the last piles that I rescued from a "Read & Transcribed" shelf - Alistair Horne's *Seven Ages of Paris*, a biography of France's capital city from its earliest recorded history in the twelfth century.

By then I had skimmed at least 400 volumes, and most of the books on my "Read & Transcribed" list were whipped into what was now, at best, a general blur of recognition. *Seven Ages of Paris* was one of those rare books that I specifically remembered reading - but I knew I had not read this physical copy.

About a year earlier, Barbara repeatedly told me how much I would like *Seven Ages of Paris* - a book she had read and absolutely loved. She had devoured a paperback copy shortly before we visited France's capital, and after exploring the city for a week, she wanted to read it again. She knew how much Paris had also charmed me, and suggested time and time again how much I would enjoy Alistair Horne's tales of the city's intoxicating and tangled past.

At that time, I was exclusively focused on books related to my research into military and personal hostilities in 1939 and 1940. The history of Paris from centuries before Columbus set foot in America had no practical value to me, but Barbara's persistence won me over. (Barbara has that knack). I finally gave *Seven Ages* a shot, and by the time I was about a dozen pages in, I was so completely engrossed - drawn into Alistair Horne's tales of kings, torture, priests, cemeteries, food, clothing, emperors, mischief and malice, disease, and debauchery - that I enjoyably persisted through all nine centuries' worth of history.

The only drawback was the tiny 9-point font in our paperback copy. (This book is printed in an 11-point font. The notes in the back are in a 9-point font). That small type was a challenge for my moderately failing eyesight, even with reading glasses. Still, I read the stories from all seven ages, all the way through the epilogue, and I loved the book every bit as much as Barbara knew I would.

So, when I saw that I owned another copy of *Seven Ages* – this one a hardcover volume, with every word printed twenty-two percent larger than in our paperback copy, I was surprised – but nicely so.

What surprised me even more was the discovery of one of my 5-by-8-inch index cards lurking in the book's back pages. When I'm reading for research and I come upon a note-worthy event or the story of a fascinating character, I write the page number on an index card. Rather than continually interrupt the flow of my reading to capture notes, I then scribbled the first few words of the section that interested me, gradually filling each card with page numbers and sketchy notes. At some later point – while in "transcribe-mode" - I return to the book and type the relevant information into one of my Word files. This enabled me to read without continual interruptions to record my findings.

This particular card had lines drawn through my sketchy notes, which signified that I had not only read this copy of *Seven Ages of Paris* but had also transcribed the relevant information into one or more of my Word files. Alistair Horne's book was one that I read for the first time with a very precise focus. Of the 422 pages in *Seven Ages of Paris*, I only read the forty or so pages that covered the two World Wars.

As a result of my narrow concentration on that sliver of history, I initially missed out on a rich biography of a place that fascinates me. I'm glad I eventually treated myself to the rest of the book. No doubt I have dozens of other books that I should probably revisit – and almost certainly never will. My commitment to the book I'm writing is more important.

After the ceiling was patched, I began the slow process of returning the books to their logical clusters. The most basic sense of order was to separate the books I had already read from the books I had yet to read. In addition to updating my color-coded spreadsheet, whenever I finished reading a book, I tagged it with a Post-it Note. My process was a bit haphazard, and there's a limit to the stickiness of Post-its, so my system was not perfect.

A couple of months after the cloudburst in my office, during the search for a new book to dissect, I glanced at my shelf of ostensibly unread books and picked up the slim, 214-page *Britain Alone, June 1940-June 1941* by mid-century American journalist Herbert Agar. As always, as I read *Britain Alone*, I kept track of each interesting, research-worthy section on the index card that served double-duty as a bookmark.

With his journalist's eye, Herbert Agar provided a number of interesting insights and anecdotes, but this was also one of those books that I did not have to read all the way through. Since my area of interest extended only to July, 1940, I only read the first third of the book.

Before transferring *Britain Alone* to a "Read but Not Transcribed" shelf, I flipped through a few pages in the back of the book for a quick look at Agar's notes and other sources. Here again, I was surprised to find a marked-up index card, smoking-gun-level evidence that I had previously skimmed *Britain Alone* some months before.

I've read so many books on similar topics, it did not really shock me that I had inadvertently read at least a couple of books a second time. What really surprised me though was what I found when I compared my two sets of notes from my two readings of *Britain Alone*. Almost every section I had highlighted during my first reading was not highlighted during my second pass, and almost every section that I highlighted during my second time through *Britain Alone* was new.

On the index card that used to track my first passage through the book, I had marked 30 sections to include in my notes. On my just-completed second pass, I had marked 21 sections. 17 of those sections were new, only four were repeated from my first reading. There was even one page on which I had highlighted one paragraph during my first pass, and a completely different paragraph on my second pass.

It makes sense that my perspective and interests had evolved over time. When I first started my research, just about every fact, every story, and every personality was new to me, and just about everything I read seemed important enough to capture.

As my research evolved, I gradually compiled a more robust outline of the facts – in my mind and in my notes. What I was looking for now was perspective and color. In the words of Rick Atkinson, I was searching for "facts to love [in order] to tease coherence and intimacy from the past." My second reading revealed finer details that had not seemed as relevant during my first pass.

For all of my attempts to keep track of my sources and keep score of my progress, these accidental re-readings provided some reassurance that my book was no longer just an accumulation of words or a linear collection of facts. It was rounding into a continually more interesting story.

CHAPTER 22

Compiegne

Although it had no direct connection to either the French or British Navy, the town of Compiegne, 45 miles northeast of Paris, provides an important thread to my story. I visited Compiegne more to gain a sense of the place than to pick up additional details to add to my research. I came away with a deeper appreciation of the contrast between its quiet and majestic solitude and the monuments to conquest and vengeance that were installed, demolished and reinstalled there. To my surprise, I also encountered an unexpected reminder of the unfathomable evil of Adolf Hitler and his Nazi devils.

World War I's fighting ended in 1918 when Germany and the Allies signed an armistice at Compiegne. In 1940, Adolf Hitler avenged that perceived stain on German pride by summoning French negotiators to Compiegne to sign the armistice that affirmed Germany's subjugation of France at the beginning of World War II. Both pacts were signed in the same quiet clearing in a French forest, and, more remarkably, in the same French rail car parked in that clearing. Let's start with that rail car.

American Journalist William L. Shirer was at Compiegne in 1940, sitting unobtrusively at the edge of the woods as Hitler and his entourage paraded in and briefly participated in the opening of the armistice talks that halted France's participation in World War II. Shirer made a number of casual references to a "wagon-lit" in his radio broadcasts and in his books. He was clearly referring to a rail car - specifically the private rail car in which both armistice agreements were signed.

While "wagon-lit" might have been a common reference in 1940, it was a fresh addition to my vocabulary. A wagon-lit is a sleeping car on a European railway. The *Compagnie Internationale des Wagons-Lits*, which was founded in 1872, provided sleeping cars and dining cars to the state railways of countries throughout Europe. Even if you've never heard of the *Compagnie*, you probably know of its fabled Orient Express.

Rail cars were routinely confiscated for military use as the First World War expanded across Europe after 1914. Wagon-lit #2419D was commandeered in October 1918 and remodeled by the *Compagnie* into a rolling office for Marshal Ferdinand Foch of France, Supreme Commander of the Allied Forces. By then, the war was tilting in the Allies' favor, but few realized just how close it was to its end.

Just one month after Foch acquired his wagon-lit, the Allies selected Compiegne as the site for armistice talks with Germany, due largely to its quiet seclusion. In 1918 the site was little more than a path to battle. A pair of rail lines – built to carry heavy artillery – stitched their way through a dense forest of oak trees and beech trees. There would be no distractions in the forest as the two warring parties met to end the killing.

A train that carried a team of negotiators from Germany pulled into Compiegne at 7:00 on the morning of November 8, 1918. The German party had been escorted to the site in secrecy, in a rail car with drawn shades. When their train rolled to a stop and the shades were opened, all they could see were the dense surrounding trees, a few slices of grey sky through the branches as a gloomy day loomed, and, on an adjoining track, another sitting rail car.

The German delegates were told that Marshal Foch wished to see them in his private car at 9:00 that morning. Foch's rail carriage sat just a few yards away. A duckboard walkway – planks of wood laid flat – was improvised between the two trains to spare the participants from having to slosh through the marshy ground.

At the appointed hour, the adversaries took their places on opposite sides of a long rectangular table set in the middle of Foch's wagon-lit, with four chairs on either side. All of the men stood as the glass door to Foch's private compartment opened. The Marshal entered and crisply saluted the visitors. They shared no pleasantries and engaged in minor formalities. After introductions, the German delegates presented their credentials. The talks began with an abrupt question from Marshal Foch.

"What do you want, gentlemen?"

Matthias Erzberger, Germany's recently appointed Secretary of State replied: "We have come to receive the proposal of the Allied Powers for an armistice"

Foch snapped: "I have no proposal whatsoever to make."

Plenipotentiary Minister Count Alfred von Oberndorff responded: "Tell us, *Herr Feldmarshall*, how do you wish us to express ourselves. Our delegation is prepared to ask you the conditions of an armistice."

Foch: "Do you formally ask for an armistice?"

After Erzberger and von Oberndorff responded "*Ja*" in unison, Foch replied "Then please sit down and I will read the conditions of the Allies to you." Foch's Chief of Staff General Maxime Weygand then read the Allies' terms for the cessation of battle and the capitulation of Germany.

Notwithstanding Marshal Foch's strident opening, the two sides negotiated over the next three days. The armistice was finally signed at 5:15 on the morning of November 11, 1918. At 11 o'clock that same morning, soldiers at the front heard the order to cease fire and laid down their guns. The fighting was over but the complex challenge of settling accounts remained. Seven months later, on June 28, 1919, the treaty that finished the war, punished Germany, and re-drew the map of Europe was signed at Versailles.

After the armistice was signed and the guns were silenced, Wagon-lit #2419D was returned to *Compagnie Internationale des Wagons-Lits*. In September 1919, after a final tour of duty as a dining car, France's most prominent rail car was donated to France's *Musee de l'Armee,* and was displayed in a courtyard at *Les Invalides*, the vast shrine to France's military history, surrounded by a tight array of decommissioned cannons and mortars.

To commemorate the armistice and the neutralization of its despised foe, France opened the carefully groomed "Glade of the Armistice" at Compiegne on November 11, 1922. Trees had been cleared and an oval space - a carefully tended lawn - was sculpted out of the forest. A broad 250-yard stone and dirt avenue was laid to provide a dramatic entrance into the glade. Flat granite monuments, each the footprint of a rail car, marked the placement of the two historic rail cars that had served France and Germany respectively during the armistice discussions in 1918.

Additional monuments were added to the Glade in the years between the wars. Arthur Henry Fleming, an American lumber magnate, underwrote the construction of a small museum at the edge of the park, and then financed the restoration of the museum's primary attraction – Marshal Foch's wagon-lit, which was restored to its November 11, 1918 condition, including the table where the armistice had been signed. Place cards showed where Foch, Weygand, Erzberger and the other participants sat. Marshal Foch and General Weygand were among the dignitaries who participated in the museum's opening on November 11, 1927.

A towering statue of Marshal Foch was unveiled at the site ten years later - in September 1937. Set just a bit off to the left of the oval as you walk into the glade, Foch, standing with a walking stick in his right hand and a packet of papers – maps? the armistice agreement? – in his left, looks down upon the clearing, across to the museum, and down on the monuments to where the two rail cars stood in 1918. Participants in the ceremonial unveiling of the Foch statue included General Weygand and the widow of Marshal Foch, who had passed way in 1929 at the age of 77.

France's simmering ire was most evident in a monument to the liberation of the long-disputed regions of Alsace and Lorraine from German rule. This monument stands outside the park, just across the curve in the road where the park's boulevard entrance begins. Its focal point is a large dead eagle – the German Imperial Eagle - gruesomely sprawled across its base, impaled by a large bronze sword, in grim celebration of Germany's defeat in World War I.

In June 1919, with the ink from 67 signatures barely dry on the treaty of Versailles, Marshall Foch predicted the inevitable next war. Unhappy with the just-signed terms that he felt were too lenient toward Germany, Foch declared: "It is not a peace treaty. It is a twenty-year armistice."

He was deadly accurate. World War II began on September 1, 1939 when Germany attacked Poland. Two days later, Britain and France declared war on Germany. Although a number of deadly clashes at sea took place in the months that followed, the Battle for France did not erupt in earnest until Germany launched its *blitzkrieg* attack on Western Europe on May 10, 1940. The fall of France was swift and shocking. By June 14, German troops were casually breaking baguettes and brioches in Parisian cafes after France's capital was surrendered without a fight.

Two days after the surrender of Paris, the French government, on a brief layover in Bordeaux after fleeing their capital, asked the Spanish ambassador to approach Germany "to find out on what conditions Chancellor Hitler would be prepared to end operations and conclude an armistice." In response, and again through the Spanish ambassador, Germany directed France to appoint plenipotentiaries for the negotiation of an "agreement to end hostilities." Germany would reveal the meeting location upon receipt and approval of those names.

There were no immediate volunteers to negotiate with the Germans. There was, in fact, heated debate over the appropriate composition and leadership of the French negotiating party. General Maxime Weygand, who sat across from the Germans at Compiegne in 1918 and was now Supreme Allied Commander, refused to participate. Weygand argued that since the declaration of war was a political act, the politicians who started the war should be accountable for its termination. After some debate, the French delegation was led by a different officer - General Charles Huntziger – who was compelled into service as France's lead negotiator.

Early on the morning of June 20, the German government wired the French their approval of the French negotiating team.

Six hours later, a second message directed the French party to travel to the Loire bridge near Tours. The French team left at 2:30 P.M., and after a long, frustrating day spent weaving their way through crowds of civilian and military refugees in aimless drift away from perceived danger, the French negotiators arrived at the bridge at 10 P.M. A German convoy escorted them to Paris, where they were permitted a short overnight rest. They were driven to Compiegne at 1:30 the following afternoon.

It had been almost a full day since they left Bordeaux, and the French high command was panicked, blind to their whereabouts and to the status of negotiations. Also, Hitler and his generals had declined France's plea to cease hostilities until an armistice was signed. The carnage continued as France's leaders waited to learn Germany's terms for pausing the fight.

In 1918 there were no third-party witnesses to the armistice talks in the dense French Forest. On June 21, 1940, Compiegne's Glade of the Armistice was a movie set. A German film crew was on hand – as was American journalist William L. Shirer, who had been tipped off by a German officer - for the preliminary German pageantry leading up to the negotiations.

As German newsreel cameras captured the scene, the tall statue of Marshal Foch still looked on from the Eastern edge of the glade. At the far end of his gaze, the Armistice Museum building was newly scarred. A large hole had been carefully punched through its front wall with pneumatic drills, just barely wide enough and just barely tall enough to drag a wagon-lit through. Foch's rolling office was pulled out of the museum and rolled over rusty tracks to the center of the glade – to the precise spot where it rested in 1918.

The scene had been carefully staged to maximize its propaganda value and to ensure the humiliation of the French. At about quarter-past-three in the afternoon, a small caravan of gleaming black Mercedes, carrying Adolf Hitler and Germany's most senior military leaders drove up to the curve in the road where the wide path leading into the park began. Ahead of him, an honor guard of Wehrmacht forces lined the walkway, standing three-deep. At his back, the sword-impaled, fallen German Imperial Eagle was completely shrouded for the day by an immense swastika banner.

With the swastika-draped monument at their backs, the German high command paraded down the stone and dirt pathway toward the center of the glade: Hitler, Goering, Raeder, Keitel, Hess, von Ribbentrop, Brauchitsch, and Jodl. Eyes left, Hitler proffered the stiff-armed Nazi salute as he strode past the guard of honor that stood in rapt attention. Reporting from the site, William L. Shirer noted Hitler's solemn and grave countenance. Hitler's true emotions were conveyed by his "springy step," and a visage that expressed "a note of the triumphant conqueror, the defier of the world." Hitler also displayed "a sort of scornful inner joy at being present at the greatest reversal of fate – a reversal he himself had wrought."

When he reached the center of the glade, Hitler paused and absorbed the scene. For a moment he stood with his arms folded in front of a broad, flat granite block in the center of the clearing that rose to knee level. Hitler silently glared at the inscription: "Here on 11 November 1918 succumbed the criminal pride of the German empire vanquished by the free peoples which it tried to enslave."

William L. Shirer stood fifty yards away. Hitler's expression, viewed through Shirer's binoculars, made a deep and lasting impression on the American journalist. The Fuhrer was "afire with scorn, anger, hate, revenge, triumph." Shirer later wrote about Hitler's "burning contempt for this place now and all that it has stood for in the twenty-two years since it witnessed the humbling of the German Empire."

The German party walked a few steps over to Marshal Foch's wagon-lit. Hitler paused briefly, and after a courteous "enter please" gesture from an aide, was the first to climb the three steps into the rail car, with the rest of his party close behind. The name cards at each seat identified the places of each negotiator in 1918. Hitler took his place in Marshal Foch's chair at the center of the table.

After the Germans entered the wagon-lit, the French contingent of negotiators, with an escort of three German officers, briskly marched down the path into the glade in the direction of the carriage. General Charles Huntziger saluted stiffly as he passed in front of the German honor guard that still lined the path.

The French walked haltingly into the rail car, their faces a blend of strain and humility. The German party stood as the French entered, and each side saluted its counterparts in their own way, the Germans thrusting their right arms in their *Sieg Heil* salute, the French wearily touching their foreheads in the more traditional military manner.

On behalf of Adolf Hitler, General Wilhelm Keitel opened with a statement in which he recounted grievances that had simmered since the last war ended.

The 1914 armistice "ended a war which neither the German people nor its government had desired and, in which, despite their overwhelming superiority, our adversaries had succeeded in decisively beating neither the German navy nor air force."

Also: "Thus did November 11th, 1918, inaugurate, in this railway carriage, the sufferings of the German people." That suffering included: "dishonor, humiliation and moral and material suffering."

More recently, in September 1939, "France and Britain again, without the slightest cause, declared war on Germany."

And now, "France is beaten. The French government has requested the German government to announce terms for an armistice."

For perspective, "The fact that the forest of Compiegne has been chosen for the handing-over of those conditions is explained by the determination to efface once and for all, by an act of reparative justice, a memory that was a far from glorious page in the history of France and that was felt by the German people to be the greatest dishonor of all time."

Finally, for good measure, soldier to soldier: "France has collapsed after resisting heroically and being beaten in an uninterrupted series of bloody battles. That is why Germany has no intention of giving the armistice terms and negotiations a flavor that would humiliate a gallant adversary."

Twelve minutes after the French entered the car, and just after Keitel finished his preamble, Hitler, Goering, and all the Germans except Keitel left the rail car. Keitel, who would be hanged at Nuremberg five years later, then presented the 21 articles of the armistice agreement.

Finally, at 8:15 that night – five hours after the French negotiators entered the glade, and 30 hours after they left the temporary French capital of Bordeaux - General Huntziger was permitted to telephone his anxious military and government leaders, who were still completely in the dark as to the negotiators' whereabouts.

Huntziger told Weygand: "I'm in the wagon."

Weygand replied: "*Mon pauvre ami.*" He knew the location and immediately grasped its significance.

Huntziger informed him "The terms are harsh, but they contain nothing conflicting with honor."

Over the next hour, Huntziger then dictated the agreement to Weygand over the phone.

After a number of requests for clarification and minor revisions to several articles, the armistice was signed at 6:50 P.M. on the following day, June 22, 1940.

With its role as a prop complete, the railway carriage now became a trophy. Wagon-lit #2419D was wheeled onto an immense flatbed trailer and towed out of the forest behind a large truck. Marshal Foch's carriage was taken to Germany and prominently displayed on the *Lustgarten* in the heart of Berlin.

Back in Compiegne, a German work crew quickly razed the shrine to the events of 1918. With pickaxes and dynamite, the reminders of France's victory and vengeance were destroyed. Tracks were yanked from the ground; memorials were hacked to pieces. The large stone monument at the center of the park and the museum with the hole in the wall that had previously housed the wagon-lit were dynamited. The Alsatian monument with the sword-defiled German Imperial Eagle was dissembled into packing cases and shipped to Germany (and then returned to France after the war). The single vestige of 1918 that remained untouched was the looming statue of Marshal Foch. It was temporarily encased in wood for protection when the museum was blown up, and then left in place as a sign of Hitler's respect for a fellow soldier in the Great War.

There are conflicting stories about precisely how the Compiegne wagon-lit was destroyed at the end of the war. One story holds that it was blown apart during a massive American bombing run on Berlin. Another story claims that the rail car had been hidden but then purposefully destroyed to keep it from the Allies. What is not disputed is that the wagon-lit was burned almost completely to ashes.

From the earliest days of my project, I planned to visit Compiegne. The significance of the dual armistice signings and Hitler's diabolical use of the site had established it in my mind as a must-see historical destination.

During the course of a week-long trip to Paris, I travelled to Compiegne by myself on a day when Barbara visited Claude Monet's house and gardens at Giverny. Thanks, as always, to Barbara, by then I was comfortable with France's public transport system. I took the Metro to the massive Gare Nord train station, and from there booked a 47-minute mid-morning train to Compiegne.

I had read that the Glade of the Armistice was about 20 minutes from the station in Compiegne, on the road to Rethondes. You could get there by taxi, and a guidebook suggested that you arrange your return trip to the station in advance - since the site is not on a major thoroughfare, and the likelihood of idling taxis was slim. (This was a few years before Uber and Lyft became options). Also, since I would be away from a major metro area, I knew I could not necessarily count on finding an English-speaking driver.

A short line of taxis waited at the station at Compiegne. I jumped in the first car and asked the driver if he spoke English. "*Un peu*" [a little].

OK, I was prepared. I also spoke a little of his language, and asked, in Philadelphia-accented French "*Pouvez-vous me prendre a la clairiere?*" ["Can you take me to the clearing?"]

When he nodded and said *"Oui,"* I handed him my phone into which I had already typed into Google Translate the one question that I wanted to be sure I communicated with no risk of error or misunderstanding: *"Pouvez-vous revenir pour moi dans une heure?"* ["Can you come back for me in one hour?"] Once again, he nodded, and said "Oui."

Over the course of about twenty minutes, the car crossed through the small town, passed open fields, and then drove into a wooded area. There is a break in the woods off to the right, just as the road curves to the left. As the car slowed to a stop as the road curved – right at the spot where Hitler alighted from his car in 1940 - the driver interrupted our silence with: "One hour, yes?"

Hopefully I replied, *"Oui, une heure,"* but honestly, I forget. I jumped out right at the unpaved lane leading off to my right into the park. I remember a surge of excitement and relief – partly from a reasonable sense of assurance that I would not be stranded in the forest and would make it back to Paris that evening. To be extra-safe, when I paid the driver the 20-euro one-way fare, I added a 15-euro tip.

Before entering the park, I walked across the street to where the Alsace-Lorraine Monument stands once again, restored after World War II. The monument is striking not just for its size – including its massive rectangular stone frame and bronze sword – but especially for the unique hostility and bitter vengeance in its design, with the Imperial Eagle of Germany oddly splayed across the base of the monument, stabbed to death by the sword. There was no hint of celebration. It spoke purely of disdain and defiance.

I re-crossed the road from the monument and walked down the path leading into the glade. In 1940 a Wehrmacht honor guard, standing three-deep at attention, had lined this same path. It runs for about 250 yards and opens into a wide oval clearing that is defined by a dense ring of beech trees of varying heights.

As you make your way down the path, you see a low stone slab at the end of the clearing. As you walk into the clearing, the tall, imposing statue of Marshal Foch stands to the left.

Two sets of railroad tracks stitch the ground – one set on either side of the large granite block that sits at the centerpiece of the glade. Smaller, low-set stone monuments are set on the spots where the French and German rail cars had rested in 1918.

It's a very quiet place, even when visitors are present, as if solemnity is desired and quiet is expected. I'm not sure if my day was a typical day, but I counted no more than eight other people in the park during my one-hour early-afternoon weekday visit. The few voices that I heard were hushed.

I felt a deep sense of personal solemnity, sharply conscious of the activities surrounding the signing of the armistice in 1914, and – especially - the armistice of 1940. Hitler's presence at this site added an additional dimension, a disturbance of the force. I stood precisely where he stood, in front of the granite slab (which was restored after the war), marked: "Here on 11 November 1918 succumbed the criminal pride of the German empire." I imagined his fury as he read those words. I remembered William L. Shirer's description: "scorn, anger, hate, revenge, triumph." Seriously, I felt the aura of evil.

There is a new museum building at the site, off to the right, in Foch's direct gaze from the opposite side of the clearing. Once again, a wagon-lit is on display inside the museum. It's an exact replica of wagon-lit #2419D, and was donated by the *Compagnie Internationale des Wagons-Lits* in 1950. It was built in the same year as the original and outfitted as closely as possible to replicate the carriage used by Marshal Foch.

A few small remnants of the original wagon-lit survived the fire in Berlin – small shards of the chassis and pieces of bronze decorative elements. Like the relics you see under glass at Notre Dame, Sainte-Chapelle, Sacré-Cœur and other churches in Paris, the bones of the carriage are on display under glass in the museum.

Even in the solemn presence of history, I am at my very core a tourist, and of course I purchased a few souvenirs from the gift shop at the museum, including a key chain with a tiny metal representation of the *"wagon de l'Armistice de Compiegne"*, as well as two copies - one in English, one in French - of the booklets that describe the museum, the glade and – mostly - the historic events that took place there.

One hour at the site worked out perfectly for me. I was relieved, but not surprised, to find my driver waiting at the end of the path. We picked up where our silence had left off and drove quietly back to the train station in Compiegne. I saw everything there was to see, and experienced deeper extremes of emotion than I had expected.

I was absolutely buoyant when I exited the taxi in front of the train station in Compiegne. The logistics had worked out perfectly, and my visit was even more moving than I had anticipated.

With a bit more than an hour to kill before my return train would leave for Paris, I wandered into a boulangerie a block away from the station and purchased a baguette and a bottle of water for lunch. I walked around the small town-center, and made my way back to the station, still with plenty of time before my train would depart. I sat my backpack on a bench, and, as I typically do while waiting for a train, I paced the length of the platform.

Two wooden rail cars with rusted wheels sat on a siding at the far end of the station. With faded red paint, they looked like freight cars – actually more like cattle cars - but they had small, window-like openings a short way below the roof at each end. Where there might have been panes of glass, I saw strands of barbed wire. The sliding door on each car was secured with a padlock.

These cars were clearly not built for comfort. They were clearly not wagons-lits. These cars had been used to transport Jews and other unfortunate souls from Compiegne to German concentration camps.

I knew a bit of Compiegne's history before I travelled there on my comfortable train. I knew that Joan of Arc had been captured at Compiegne in 1430, and that rounds of golf had been played there during the 1900 Paris Olympics. However, I was blindingly and embarrassingly unaware of its role in the Holocaust. I read later that night that Compiegne had served as an internment and deportation camp - primarily for French political prisoners, captured resistance fighters, and Jews.

A sign in front of one of the worn wooden red rail cars listed the dates on which the German "destination convoys" departed, along with the number of passengers in each convoy. The destinations included Auschwitz, Buchenwald, and Dachau. According to a sign at the station, 39,564 victims were carried away from Compiegne.

Early in my research, I read about the British Naval Mission that was first established in Paris just before the war. That Mission - along with the French Ministry of Marine – was relocated to the small commune of Maintenon the day after war was declared. The new naval headquarters was established on the grounds of the Château de Maintenon, which was owned by the family of the Duc de Noailles. When I later dug through my research to fact-check myself, I noticed a story about the duke's son, Jean de Noailles, who joined the French resistance after France capitulated to Germany. After he was captured and tortured by the Gestapo early in January 1942, Jean de Noailles was briefly held in Compiegne before he was transported to Buchenwald. He was processed through a series of concentration camps during the war and died at Bergen-Belsen shortly before the war ended.

I traveled to Compiegne intrigued by Hitler's diabolical quest to avenge the 1918 armistice. I left even more thoroughly repulsed by his toxic heart. The stories that come together to form history weave their way along and together in so many surprising, interesting, and sometimes horrifying dimensions.

I haven't researched or written about the Holocaust. Although the legacies of Joachim von Ribbentrop, Marshal Philippe Pétain, and even Admiral Francois Darlan, are forever stained by the roles they played in this monstrous crime against humanity, the very worst of this systematic genocide fell outside the time span and the scope of my story, and I feel its horrors are well beyond my ability to do them justice as a writer.

The sight of those two rail cars provided the most jarring dose of reality on that day, and the most chilling manifestation of diabolical cruelty that I have ever encountered. Less significantly, I learned a priceless lesson about the striking contrast between reading about history, and walking the ground where history was made.

CHAPTER 23

Eleven Men with Whom It Would be Agreeable to Drink a Pint

I've studied and written about an intriguing variety of mostly British and French soldiers and sailors, diplomats, members of parliament, world leaders, and mothers and fathers who sent their sons off to war. All of them shaped history to varying degrees. Some of them wrote history and therein shaped their own stories. Of the hundreds of individuals I encountered and have written about, eleven stand apart as even more interesting than the rest.

In 1911 when Winston Churchill and his close friend F.E. Smith (later Lord Birkenhead) were denied membership in a dining club called The Club, they started a club of their own which they named The Other Club. The standards for selection to this invitation-only club included: "men with whom it was agreeable to dine." This, at least, is the commonly told tale.

Historian Andrew Roberts has written that Churchill and Smith had *not*, as legend claims, been blackballed by The Club. As my late friend and business mentor Steve Johnston would say with a hearty laugh, "never let the facts get in the way of a good story," so feel free to believe your favored version of the story of the origin of the dining club that Churchill and Smith indisputably inaugurated.

I've written here about men with whom it would be agreeable to drink a pint of beer or two. I did not set out to exclude women from my virtual club. Women just were not prominent among the key players in my story from the war zones of 1940.

Winston Churchill is not one of the eleven subjects in this chapter. It would be the thrill of a lifetime – hey, who would not want to sit down for drinks and a conversation with the greatest man of the 20th century? – but his story would have overwhelmed all of the others ... in word count and significance. I should note that while Churchill would have preferred to sit across from a whisky and soda, or a flute of Pol Roger champagne, he was alert to the mass appeal of lager and stout. Sir Martin Gilbert wrote that after Churchill received news of Germany's surrender in May 1945, the Prime Minister directed Scotland Yard and the Ministry of Food to ensure that the exuberant masses in London had an adequate supply of beer to help lubricate their celebrations.

Here, then, is my own personal Other Club of eleven men who helped shape and enrich my story in their own unique and fascinating ways.

Admiral Sir James Somerville
Commander of Britain's Force H, at Mers-el-Kébir

Admiral of the Fleet Sir James Fownes Somerville vocally opposed the use of force against Britain's recent allies. Somerville of course had no alternative but to carry out the Admiralty's orders despite his personal misgivings. When I worked with Admiral Somerville's papers in the Churchill Archives, I learned the many facets of this good man's personal anguish in the days leading up to the clash at Mers-el-Kébir.

Over time I also learned of Somerville's unbounded sense of curiosity and his active participation in the interests and responsibilities of the men under his command. He was fascinated with aviation and was the rare commander who took the opportunity to sit in the observer's seat in open-cockpit bi-planes that either flew from carrier decks or were launched by deck-mounted catapults from smaller ships.

At the same time, Somerville was a taskmaster who acknowledged his impatience with those who were indecisive or overly deliberate. He criticized men who "have to go down each stair carefully instead of sliding down the banisters when the house is on fire."

Somerville's men were accustomed to the sight of the admiral rowing his skiff around his flagship and rippling by other ships in the harbor most mornings before breakfast. They watched him walk the steep paths of the Rock of Gibraltar at a brisk pace. And so, it was a shock when Somerville was invalided out of the service due to a suspected case of tuberculosis the year before war broke out.

Somerville fought the navy's decision – which was the result of a series of concerning but inconclusive tests and x-rays - and "with only vague authority behind him," he began working with the Signals Division of the Admiralty on the development and the rollout of radar. To this day, he is considered by some to be "the foster-father of naval radar."

Another ad hoc assignment in the early months of the war was "Inspector of Anti-Aircraft Weapons and Devices." Unofficially called the "Department of Wheezers and Dodgers," this outfit developed and tested a variety of devices – ranging from kites to rockets - to defend against low-flying German aircraft attacks.

After Somerville played a significant, if under-appreciated, supporting role in the evacuation of British and French forces from the beaches of Dunkirk, he was summoned by the Admiralty just a few weeks later to lead Force H - the Royal Navy squadron that was assembled to confront the French ships at Mers-el-Kébir.

Somerville's experience at Mers-el-Kébir was not the final chapter in his career. Eleven months after the attack on the French ships, torpedo-bearing aircraft from the carrier under his command contributed to the tracking and the sinking of the German battleship *Bismarck*.

Somerville had been knighted a Companion of the Order of the Bath in June 1939. When he was knighted a second time – as a Knight Commander of the Order of the British Empire in October 1941 - his good friend, Admiral Andrew Bowne Cunningham quipped: "What, twice a knight at your age?" Somerville received a rare honor in May 1945 - promotion to Admiral of the Fleet, the ultimate rank in the Royal Navy.

In the aftermath of the events at Mers-el-Kébir, in the wake of "this filthy business," Somerville's conscience was wracked by a note from his former allies and friends. I roughly read (and then photographed for more precise translation at a later time) a hand-written note signed by more than a dozen officers of the French battleship *Dunkerque* in the days following the clash. In memory of the nine officers and 200 men of *Dunkerque* killed by the Royal Navy at Mers-el-Kébir, they wrote to convey their "bitter sadness and disgust." The French officers accused their former ally of soiling "the glorious flag of St. George with an indelible stain, that of assassination."

Not many things went according to plan during that long, hot day at Mers-el-Kébir. As we sipped away, I would ask Admiral Somerville to walk me through his decisions and emotions as events cascaded and his options for a peaceful outcome dwindled away.

Paul Schmidt
The Germans' favorite interpreter

There is a common thread to every story I read of the meetings of English and French diplomats with Hitler, Goering, Goebbels, or von Ribbentrop. Paul Schmidt, the Germans favorite interpreter, participated in almost every conversation and meeting. He would have so many great stories to tell.

Schmidt's post-war autobiography was a letdown, with sanitized impressions of many German leaders ... with one shining exception: he simply could not hold back his loathing of Joachim von Ribbentrop.

Even while the foam was still settling on our pints of lager, I would have to ask, "C'mon Paul, it's just us. What were they really like?" I would, of course, especially hope for more dirt on Ribbentrop.

John "Jock" Colville
Assistant Private Secretary to Neville Chamberlain and
Winston Churchill

Twenty-five-year-old John Rupert Colville was Assistant Private Secretary to Prime Minister Neville Chamberlain. On the afternoon of Friday, May 10th, 1940, when it was apparent that

Chamberlain would resign and Winston Churchill would almost certainly succeed him, Colville opened his diary, picked up his pen, and wrote in black ink: "Everybody here is in despair at the prospect."

Colville was retained by the new Prime Minister, and he quickly noted Churchill's lack of patience and unsettling abundance of energy. One of the delights of reading John Colville's diary is to observe the gradual transformation of his relationships with the entire Churchill family. After five months in Churchill's daily presence as the new P.M. inspired and galvanized Britain against daunting odds, Colville wrote: "What was constant was the respect, admiration and affection that almost all those with whom he was in touch felt for him despite his engaging but sometimes infuriating idiosyncrasies."

As he assisted Churchill with his schedule and correspondence, Colville's reliability and affability won the P.M.'s confidence and affection in return. When Colville spoke of his plan to volunteer for military service, Churchill responded with heartfelt objections and noted that he could block Colville's enlistment. The Prime Minister gradually acquiesced to Colville's dream of flying in the Royal Air Force, and even acknowledged, with a touch of envy, during one late-night conversation "that a fighter pilot had greater excitement than a polo-player, big game shot and hunting-man rolled into one."

With his immersion in Churchill's political, military and family routines, if you could wish for one person to write a diary of his experiences in London in 1940, it would be John Colville. At the time, officials and their aides were discouraged from keeping diaries lest they end up serving as encyclopedic guides for invading Germans. Thankfully, like dozens of others, Colville ignored that prohibition. When I worked in the Churchill

Archives, one of the most stirring moments was when I first turned the pages of Colville's hand-written diary.

John Colville's daily account of his interactions and conversations - further enriched with his anecdotal impressions of Churchill, his family, and contemporaries - survives as a contemporaneous and engaging journal of the early days of World War II (which was my focus; the diary continues for another 17 years). The published version is a cherished source of anecdotes about Churchill's character, quirks, resolve, and humor.

I would ask Colville to share at least three stories that he left out of the diary (in which, by the way, he casually mentions a fondness for lager).

Admiral Marcel-Bruno Gensoul
French Commander at Mers-el-Kébir

I probably would not have had a story, and 1,297 French sailors almost certainly would not have perished if Admiral Marcel-Bruno Gensoul had been willing to parley with the British at Mers-el-Kébir in the morning hours of July 3, 1940.

Admiral Gensoul commanded the French fleet at Mers-el-Kébir. As an officer, Gensoul was understandably insulted when the upperworks of a British destroyer, followed shortly by 16 additional warships – including 10 destroyers, 3 battleships and an aircraft carrier - silently filled the dawn horizon at the mouth of the harbor at Mers-el-Kébir - an unexpected show of belligerent force by France's former ally. On a personal level, he was offended that his direct counterpart, Admiral James Somerville, elected not to sail into port for face-to-face negotiations. Instead, Somerville sent the impeccably qualified Cedric Holland, who spoke French like a native and had previously worked closely with members of the French naval brass in Paris - including Gensoul. Holland's perceived flaw was that he was a mere captain.

Although I question a number of his decisions, I did not find Gensoul sufficiently loathsome to include him in the group of characters on whom I would be more inclined to spill a drink. Just as Somerville had orders to follow, Gensoul's actions were similarly constrained by his Admiralty, who were far removed from the scene, and operating in chaos with crippled communications under German control. I found no reason to like him, but my dislike was tempered with a degree of sympathy.

Honestly, from the accounts I've read and the pictures I've seen of the rigid, unsmiling Gensoul, he does not seem like he would be much fun to share a couple of beers with. I'm a salesman though, and I know I could get him to open up. I would love to hear his personal stories of the negotiations, his garbled communications with France's admiralty, the battle, and the aftermath at Mers-el-Kébir. He was literally right in the middle of it all.

Captain Cedric Holland
Somerville's Negotiator at Mers-el-Kébir

No Briton was more directly involved in the tense negotiations at Mers-el-Kébir than Captain Cedric Swinton "Hooky" Holland. The former British Naval Attaché to France, and the former Head of the Naval Mission to the French Admiralty, had the ideal experience, relationships, and language skills to negotiate Britain's terms for the fate of the French fleet. He was good friends with many French officers and had mutually respectful relationships with key members of the French Admiralty.

The French and British navies had worked in close collaboration in the years leading up to the war. In comparison with their armies and air forces which never meshed in harmony, the French and British navies smoothly executed joint operations in their pursuit of German and Italian warships. Holland had sailed the North Atlantic with France's Admiral Marcel-Bruno Gensoul, and he proudly wore the ribbon of France's *Legion d'Honneur* which Admiral Francois Darlan had presented to him in recognition of his liaison work with the French Navy.

This son of an admiral was an affable and charismatic leader who bore the nickname Hooky – which derived from his uncommonly sharp and prominent nose - with humor and grace. One month before the German attack on France in the spring of 1940, the Royal Navy ended Holland's formal liaison role with the French Navy and assigned him a plum seagoing command aboard the aircraft carrier *Ark Royal*.

Holland's crisp written account provides the most detailed version of the day's events in the harbor at Mers-el-Kébir. I would ask him for additional details of his frustrating discussions through the day with his designated counterpart *Lieutenant de Vaisseau* Bernard Dufay, and, ultimately, his fateful negotiations with Admiral Gensoul in the cabin of the French admiral's flagship. I would also want to hear how it felt to be fleeing the harbor in a small motorboat as shells began to fly overhead in both directions. If I could pick just one person to drink a pint of beer with, it would be Holland.

Lord Halifax
Almost a Prime Minister; Secretary of State for Foreign Affairs

Joseph Kennedy, the U.S. Ambassador to Great Britain, said of Halifax: "He is the noblest Englishman, almost a saint." He is, to me, the panoramic embodiment of the British Empire. A former Viceroy of India, a member of the House of Lords, Britain's Foreign Minister, and the eventual Ambassador to the United States, Edward Wood (as he was born), 1st Earl of Halifax spanned heaven and earth with his life and his interests. "Lord Holy Fox" devoutly embraced his father's Anglo-Catholic religious beliefs. His faith shaped his character and helped guide key decisions.

When Neville Chamberlain resigned as Prime Minister, both Chamberlain and King George VI preferred Halifax over Winston Churchill as his successor. After serious temptation, Halifax reasoned that as a member of the House of Lords it would not be feasible for him to lead the House of Commons and serve as Prime Minister. Instead, he served Britain as Churchill's Foreign Minister in the first year of the war, until his posting to Washington as Ambassador to the United States in December 1940.

Early in the war, when Halifax was Foreign Minister and Churchill was still First Lord of the Admiralty, Halifax stretched the bounds of international law when he approved Churchill's request to raid a German ship suspected of carrying 299 captive British merchant seamen as it sailed in Norwegian waters. The successful raid and the liberation of all 299 prisoners – with a cry "the Navy's here!" - boosted British morale at a time when positive news about the war was scarce. The daring rescue also boosted First Sea Lord Winston Churchill's standing in public, within Neville Chamberlain's Cabinet, and throughout the

Royal Navy. "That was big of Halifax," Churchill remarked at the time.

In his personal life Halifax handled great hardship with quiet dignity. Six foot, five inches tall and quite thin, he led an active life – even riding and shooting – despite being born with a withered left arm and no left hand. One of his sons was killed in the war, the other lost both his legs to a German bomb.

As a salesman, I've learned to toss out a topic and just let the other person speak. To be honest, I would not know where to begin with Lord Halifax, but I would lift a pint with confidence that he would have a fascinating tale that would enrich any subject I raised.

Since it was such an out-of-character observation for the aristocratic peer, I would also have to ask: "Did you really, as John Colville wrote in his diary, once refer to the German Foreign Minister as 'that swine Rib?'"

Admiral Francois Darlan
Admiral of the Fleet, French Navy

Admiral Francois Darlan is the villain in every English-language account of the clash of the British and French fleets. British and American authors typically assert that Darlan had a moral obligation to order key elements of the French fleet – battleships, destroyers, and cruisers in particular – to sail to British or American waters to prevent his ships from falling into German hands. Had he done so, some say he would have been the first major hero of World War II. In his biography of General Charles de Gaulle, Jean Lacouture writes that Churchill claimed: "If Darlan had chosen to fight in June 1940, he would have been a de Gaulle raised to the tenth power."

I started researching and writing my book pleased to have an indisputable villain to work with. But as I continued digging for additional perspectives, and when I eventually began to question the conventional wisdom, I recognized that Darlan's decision about the fate of the French fleet was not automatic or beyond dispute.

During the pre-war and early war periods when the French and British navies planned and sailed in close cooperation, Francois Darlan's lifelong contempt for Britain was one occasionally discordant exception. Darlan's antipathy toward Great Britain was a family tradition that traced back several generations to the Battle of Trafalgar in 1805, where Darlan's great-grandfather had fallen to the Royal Navy. He disparaged the civilian oversight of Britain's navy and questioned Britain's commitment to the Battle for France. After the evacuation of more than a quarter-million British soldiers from Dunkirk, Darlan remarked with his typical derision: "the British lion seems to grow wings when it's a matter of getting back to the sea."

The disdain was mutual. Churchill once referred to Darlan as "a bad man with a narrow outlook and a shifty eye." Churchill was resolute in his mistrust despite multiple solemn assurances from Darlan that he would never permit a single French ship to fall into German hands. Ultimately, Churchill determined that the risk of accepting Darlan's promises was too great and felt compelled to take matters into his own hands.

As France and Britain's mutual allegiance crumbled in the early summer of 1940, so did their ability to communicate with one another. France's armistice agreement with Germany specifically crippled the French Navy's communications capabilities. Darlan further complicated matters by relocating the Admiralty to his remote, inland hometown of Nerac in early July. On a day when Admirals Somerville and Gensoul pressed their respective admiralties for split-second decisions from the harbor at Mers-el-Kébir, the routing of two-way communications between French officers sometimes took hours to complete.

There is so much I would want to ask Darlan. In our conversation over a beer or two I would press him for his sense of how his life – and history - would have changed if he had sailed his ships to Britain or America, and also why he never pursued much more than symbolic revenge against Britain after the attack at Mers-el-Kébir.

Max Aiken, Lord Beaverbrook
Press Baron, Churchill Antagonist and Minister of Aircraft Production

Lord Beaverbrook, who owned Britain's most widely read newspaper, was the most unlikely and most breathtakingly effective member of Winston Churchill's first Cabinet. Before the War his *Daily Express* supported Neville Chamberlain's policy of appeasement and routinely criticized Churchill for his unrelenting warnings of a coming war.

Despite their antagonistic history, and without concern for a press lord's aptitude for running a critical wartime cabinet department, Churchill asked Beaverbrook to build and lead the Ministry of Aircraft Production, an organization that did not exist at the time. After reviewing the makeup of Churchill's proposed cabinet, King George VI sent his first letter to his new Prime Minister - an urgent, hand-written note asking Churchill to reconsider Beaverbrook's appointment.

Michael Korda, who knew Beaverbrook, and whose 21 books include *With Wings Like Eagles: A History of the Battle of Britain*, wrote that while "Beaverbrook knew little or nothing about manufacturing airplanes ...what Beaverbrook did know how to produce was results."

His turbulent management style was typified by a sign in his office: "Organisation is the enemy of improvisation." A shameless pilferer when it came to battling other ministries for materials and skilled workers, Beaverbrook was frequently – and fairly – described as a pirate.

As Minister of Aircraft Production, Beaverbrook quickly increased monthly production of new Spitfires and Hurricanes by more than 50%. He also returned almost as many damaged planes to the air as he had built from scratch. With the Battle of Britain fought in British airspace, and with most downed British planes crashing on British turf, Beaverbrook built an organization – largely staffed by civilians – to scrounge and recycle every salvageable part from damaged aircraft. His tireless, improvised methods helped Britain fend off the Luftwaffe during one of the most perilous periods of the war.

Churchill embraced Beaverbrook, once a harsh critic (the press baron had even cancelled Churchill's weekly newspaper column) as one of his most trusted advisors during the early months of battle. "The Beaver" bluntly counseled Churchill as he dealt with the mercurial emotions of the leaders of the French government and military forces. Beaverbrook's most relevant impact on the story I am writing occurred on a stroll with the Prime Minister through the garden at 10 Downing Street on the eve of the battle at Mers-el-Kébir. Beaverbrook firmly reinforced Churchill's commitment to mortal action.

The force of his personality would make Beaverbrook the most intimidating person in this chapter. As I raised a beer with a trembling hand, I would ask him to share the details of his conversation with Winston Churchill during that garden stroll.

William Bullitt
U.S. Ambassador to France

When the international diplomatic corps followed the French Government as they abandoned Paris to escape their capital's imminent occupation by the Germans, one ambassador stayed behind. Ignoring directions – but not firm orders - from President Franklin Roosevelt and Secretary of State Cordell Hull to follow France's leaders, U.S. Ambassador William Bullitt remained in Paris to help mitigate the impact of German occupation. By that time Bullitt was so completely absorbed into French society that he was asked to fill the governing void and serve as provisional mayor of Paris. Over the next two weeks, Bullitt helped coordinate the inevitable transfer of control of the city to German authorities as he arranged the safe passage of American and British citizens from France.

Bullitt was a free-wheeling diplomat. A garrulous friend of FDR, he typically bypassed the State Department with the steady stream of chatty calls and cables that he sent directly to the president. I would have loved to have shadowed him in the first six months of 1940.

Even his backstory is fascinating. When Philadelphia-born Bullitt graduated from Yale in 1912, he was voted the most brilliant student in his class. He was a sometimes-caustic member of Woodrow Wilson's negotiating team at the Paris Peace Conference in Versailles in 1919. After his first marriage ended in divorce, Bullitt wed Louise Bryant, the widow of American Communist revolutionary John Reed. (That marriage also ended in divorce. Warren Beatty played John Reed in the movie "Reds."). Bullitt wrote a psychological profile of President Wilson – with his co-author Sigmund Freud. In November 1933 he became the first American Ambassador to the Soviet Union. He was appointed U.S. Ambassador to France in 1936.

Bullitt developed an extraordinary affection for France and the French. He spoke the language fluently and spent weekends at a centuries-old chateau that he rented in Chantilly. He developed warm relationships with all the leaders in the continually rotating French Government – to the extent that one joked of his wish that Bullitt would one day become France's Ambassador to the U.S.

Bullitt knew everyone who mattered in France, including both Helene de Portes and Admiral Darlan. You know I would like to pick his brain about those two over our beers.

General Sir Edward Louis Spears
Author and Churchill's Liaison to French Leadership

After reflecting on his role in the suppression of mutinies in the French Armies in the First World War, Marshal Philippe Pétain remarked "they call me only in catastrophes." Major General Sir Edward Louis Spears, who Winston Churchill sent as his direct representative to Premier Paul Reynaud, wrote a two-volume book about his attempts to keep Pétain, Reynaud and France in the war. The two volumes – *Prelude to Dunkirk* and *The Fall of France* – were published under the umbrella title: *Assignment to Catastrophe*.

It's a perfect title for a fascinating account by the perfect man to represent Churchill to Britain's brittle ally. Spears served as a military liaison to France in World War I and continually nurtured his relationships with senior officers who were still in command at the beginning of World War II, and with Marshal Pétain in particular. Several colleagues in Britain's House of

Commons joked that Spears was the "Member for Paris." Spears spoke impeccable French with no accent. He knew his way around the tangles of the French government and military hierarchies every bit as well as he knew his way around the countryside.

He was also the perfect man to write about the events and intrigues in France in the spring and summer of 1940. He wrote with a sharp eye for detail and a flair for capturing the tension and emotions as the mutual resentment between the French and British sides grew more toxic by the day.

In addition to the marvelous details that Spears provides about Paul Reynaud, Helene de Portes, Marshal Philippe Pétain, and other key figures in his writing, it is a special joy to read Spears' impressions of his friends and foes. Every one of his character descriptions is a rollicking delight. Take, for example, the little-known Gaston Palewski, principal private secretary to Paul Reynaud:

> A man in his early forties, he was amiable but not prepossessing. Had anybody said his complexion was good, that person could hardly have escaped grave doubts being cast on his veracity. Very dark, rather short and square, a slight oiliness was common to hair, face and manner. His conversation too was well lubricated, as were his hands, which frequently shook each other in unexplained and inexplicable self-congratulation. Beady intelligent eyes peered through the wrinkles of a permanent but not unpleasant smile, over a wide, loose, full-lipped mouth. Funnily enough he fancied himself as a ladies man.

Spears not only wrote about his contemporaries and their impact on history, Spears made history ... of so he claimed. After

France yielded to Germany, Spears helped smuggle Charles de Gaulle from Paris to London – the first step in France's renewed participation in the struggle against Hitler's forces. (De Gaulle disputed Spears' account in his autobiography).

If the many reasons why I would so enjoy downing a pint in the company of General Sir Edward Louis Spears are not clear by now, perhaps you should stop reading and tuck this book away. (But please don't)!

If, by chance, you are inclined to stop here, I should let you know that you will miss out on a couple of stories about how my "relationship" with this multi-faceted British general became more interesting and complicated over time.

William L. Shirer
American Journalist and Historian

It wasn't just that he wrote about the German *Anschluss* in Austria, and that he wrote about Hitler's furious harangues to packed stadiums in Berlin and Nuremberg, and that he wrote about the betrayal of Czechoslovakia by Neville Chamberlain and Edouard Daladier at Munich, and that he wrote about Hitler's ritual staging of the armistice signing at Compiegne ... No, it wasn't just that William L. Shirer wrote those stories; he was there – in Vienna and Berlin and Nuremburg and Munich and Compiegne - to report all of those stories.

William L. Shirer, who will forever be known for his best-selling book *The Rise and Fall of the Third Reich*, was the preeminent correspondent and historian of the opening chapters of World War II. While he is most widely known for his books about the war, its buildup, and its aftermath, Shirer, along with Edward R. Murrow was also a pioneer on some of the first wartime radio broadcasts for the Columbia Broadcasting System. Shirer, who was fluent in German and French, had a remarkable knack for being on the scene at unique moments in history. He chronicled events and personalities across Europe – in Germany and France in particular – as the embers from World War I reignited.

On the morning of Friday, June 21, 1940, American radio listeners could hear over their crackling sets: "Hello America. ... This is William L. Shirer... We've got our microphone at the edge of a little clearing in the Forest of Compiegne." Compiegne will always have a special meaning to me. Shirer's first-hand account from the fringes of that forest as a vengeful Adolf Hitler and his German cohorts marched by and then climbed the steps to the restored rail car would of course be the one thing I would want to hear more about over a couple of beers.

One final note:

Of the six Britons profiled in this chapter, only one – Lord Beaverbrook – was invited by Winston Churchill to become a member of The Other Club. John Colville was the club's honorary secretary for several years.

CHAPTER 24

Just Who Do You Think You Are?

I mean, really, Whiteside, who do you think you are? What makes you think you can write a book that anyone would ever read?"

I am one of the most positive, carefree, and quietly confident people you could ever hope to meet. I'm a salesman after all. And yet there was no escaping these periodic moments of self-doubt, these temporary encounters with imposter syndrome.

There's a great book called *Good Prose*, in which Tracy Kidder - whose books include *The Soul of a New Machine* (for which he was awarded the Pulitzer Prize), *House*, and *A Truck Full of Money* - comments on the "distorted sense of reality" that helps sustain a writer's faith in his project. "It's as if you are required to think your work more important than it is in order to make it seem important at all."

There was never any doubt in my mind about the importance of the story I'm writing. (OK, maybe a small bit of doubt. I dealt with that back in Chapter 3).

But my lack of pedigree as a writer was another issue to overcome. Here, a willfully warped sense of reality helps drive my belief in my ability to successfully transform myself from a software salesman to a professional author.

I think I've pulled it off. I hope it's a good sign that you've read this far. Hopefully, you are also now intrigued by my book about Winston Churchill and the events at Mers-el-Kébir.

My credo has always been "just watch me." I believe firmly that actions count, and words are cheap. Here, though, words mean everything. Figuratively – and quite literally – my words will have to speak for themselves.

CHAPTER 25

My Almost First Book

Hi Bill,

My name is Zzzzz Zzzzzz, I am a business book editor at Zzzzzzzzz and I would love to speak to you about a possible book project....

This completely unexpected email popped into my inbox late one Friday morning. By that time, I had written several well-received and widely read papers to promote my work, and I had been absolutely promiscuous in building a list of email contacts to whom I promoted my writing. My email list included multiple people at multiple publishing houses. This intriguing email came from an editor at Zzzzzzzzz, one of the larger publishers of business books.

The message continued:

I receive your e-newsletter updates about the work that Demand Solutions does in the area of business strategy and planning, and I am very impressed. I was particularly intrigued by your most recent update about your upcoming "Manage what Matters /

Pareto Analysis?" - themed webinar. I would be thrilled to discuss and address any ideas or questions you may have for a possible book tied in with the work that Demand Solutions does around the world.

I was, if I may, completely chuffed, extremely flattered, and practically levitating with joy, pride, excitement, and hope.

OK, a business book had never actually been in my thoughts or plans, but one of the great unknowns for me was whether I would ever be able to break through to an agent or a publisher ... and now a major publisher had contacted me completely out of the blue.

After waiting two hours so as not to appear unduly eager, I replied that of course I would be interested. (Heck, I would have been happy to write another software manual, an Amish cookbook, a biography of Vilfredo Pareto ... just about anything he might have had in mind).

In a follow-up note, the editor mentioned the formality of a book proposal. When he sent the promised template – a simple Microsoft Word document - it took just a day for me to complete and return the proposal for my first book. (I've since learned to put significantly more time, thought, and creativity into my book proposals).

The template that he forwarded – basically just an outline – was remarkably simple. The information it directed me to provide included:

Brief Description of Your Content
What Makes Your Concept Unique?
Chapter Outline & Summaries
Your Biography
Sales & Marketing Hook

Who is Your Audience?
Existing Opportunities for Marketing & Sales
Competitive Books / How Does Your Book Compare?

During our next call - after he had an opportunity to review my proposal – the editor – *my* editor - had a couple of minor questions about my response, and he asked for a few more details about what I would do to help sell the book.

We had three follow-up conversations and exchanged several additional emails. During each exchange, he asked for increasingly sharper details about what – very specifically – I planned to do to ensure sales of my book. I felt that I had a well-stocked arsenal of sales ammunition.

"Well, I have more than 90,000 names on my marketing email list"

"When I send an email about a new paper or presentation, somewhere between 15,000 to 20,000 people read each message."

I mentioned a couple of speeches that I made to an international forecasting association, as well as presentations to our software company's bi-annual user group meeting. Audiences commonly numbered in the low hundreds at these events. I also routinely spoke to one or two regional trade group dinners per year, typically attended by 15-50 people.

He made it very clear that he was not very confident that my activities would help sell a sufficient quantity of books. My marketing efforts were way too passive for his tastes.

"Well, when I've spoken at national conferences for the American Production and Inventory Control Society (aka APICS, aka my people) in San Antonio, Denver and Las Vegas, the rooms were packed to capacity, with about 300 attendees, and I've always received exceptional feedback"

He could not have been less impressed.

What, he wanted to know, would I do to guarantee that my book would sell at least 10,000 copies at $40 per copy?

"Huh?"

He recalled that in one of our early conversations I mentioned that 2,000 companies had purchased our software, and that about 10,000 individual managers used the software on a daily basis.

Would the management of our company be interested in purchasing several thousand copies of my book to distribute ... even as goodwill paperweights ... to our customers?

What could I do to speak more frequently and to larger audiences, especially if those engagements led to sales of my book?

Would I be willing to purchase several thousand copies of my own book to either hand out or sell to my customers, prospects, and presentation audiences?

Although I still consider myself to be a marketer at heart, my primary role is to sell the software that our company represents. I'm a salesman.

When I started my business to sell Demand Solutions software on January 1, 1990, my background in sales consisted of the inconvenient truth that in addition to the fact that I had never sold a thing in my life, a respected colleague once reinforced my conviction that I was not cut out for a career in sales.

While in my first job at Mrs. Paul's (where I worked on marketing and advertising campaigns for fish sticks, onion rings, and candied sweet potatoes), I once had this conversation with "The Booner," one of our company's senior sales managers. Booner had just received an award for record sales in his region.

"Booner, you're amazing. I don't know how you do it. I know I'd never survive in sales."

"You're right, Billy. You'd be horrible. You'd never make it."

Booner was absolutely right at the time. Fortunately, I was in a different frame of mind by the time I started my business about ten years after that conversation. I was selling a product that I passionately believed in – one that I unreservedly knew would help make companies more profitable, and one that I had used to great effect in my job for three years. I knew more about the software than the people I was selling it to, and I was able to convey its features and benefits with contagious enthusiasm. In addition, by that time my personality had blossomed to the extent that I was more outgoing and confident, and I was comfortable speaking to groups after dozens of internal company presentations and several doses of kind encouragement bestowed by members of our senior management team.

I recognized that selling was a skill that could be learned and refined – and that I still needed to learn ... well ... just about everything. I subscribed to several sales magazines and newsletters. Since I spent so much time in my car, I became a devotee of audio cassette and CD collections of the books and seminars of such sales luminaries as Zig Ziglar, Brian Treacy and Harvey McKay. My brother-in-law and I once attended a memorable and inspirational presentation by Zig himself.

One of the best sources that I found in my pursuit of ideas and inspiration as a rookie salesman was a sales trainer named Art Sobczak. I paid for a subscription to Art's 8-page monthly newsletter of sales tips, and I bought his books and audiotapes. I got more out of Art Sobczak's material than any other sales resource I found. I still have every newsletter that I ever received from Art. Each monthly newsletter provides a solid handful of innovative ideas and practical tips that helped add polish and originality to my sales efforts.

I learned to handle price objections and overcome stalling tactics. I learned how to identify a potential customer's most significant interests and how to tailor follow-up activities to address those interests. I learned that this really was not about making a sale, it was about helping people buy. I certainly wasn't consistent in my application of Art's ideas, but there is no question that his coaching helped elevate my sales career.

Our software company has an annual sales meeting. Every couple of years we are "treated" to a day of sales training by an outside expert. In addition to his prolific writing, Art Sobczak conducts on-site sales seminars for individual companies. I really wanted to meet Art, so I put my sales education to work and sold our company's management on paying for a day of Art's time at one of our meetings.

I did not typically look forward to those 2 ½ day ordeals, always held in February in a frigid suburb of St. Louis, but I was incredibly excited about Art's session. And he delivered. At a time when many in his field continued to preach the benefits of robotic script-driven cold-calling, Art was a pioneer and outspoken evangelist for social selling, which advocates the use of information that's available on social media to support well-informed discussions that could organically evolve into personalized sales opportunities.

I made it a point to sit by Art during our lunch break, and in a brief conversation, he delivered the most valuable lesson that I've learned about the book business.

After I clumsily asked about how he launched the writing side of his career, and how he got his books published, Art kindly shared this: "Publishers are in the business of printing books. They aren't looking for great authors as much as they are people who can sell a lot of books."

In my final conversation with Zzzzz Zzzzzz of Zzzzzzzzz, I told him that our company would not be interested in purchasing thousands of copies of a book written by me. I also mentioned that my focus was on selling software, and that I would never have the time or the interest to devote myself to book sales in the extremes that he required. I certainly had no interest in buying thousands of copies of my own book. I did not think to add that I made a pretty good living selling software, and that a concentrated effort to sell my book would make me less successful.

Just 38 days after that unexpected *"I would love to speak to you about a possible book project"* valentine, we wished each other well and my first book reverted to "almost book" status.

I know that publishers count on well-written content. But I also understand that publishing is a business, and that I have a personal stake in marketing and selling my book. In the years since that busted dream of a published book, I haven't forgotten the lessons shared by my almost editor and by Art Sobczak. As I've worked to improve my writing, I have also worked to build the platform that I know I will need to help sell my eventual first book (i.e., this one).

Hardly a day goes by that I do not fine-tune my very targeted mailing list. I've upped my Twitter game with frequent Tweets to a steadily expanding universe of contacts. I've actively written articles on LinkedIn as I've steadily built my list of connections. I've added additional white papers –they're now called

White(side) papers - to my body of work. I've conducted additional on-line webinars and I've reached thousands of additional potential readers. I built – and regularly update - a custom website to help introduce and support my book.

As much as I want to write a book that people will want to read, I also intend to do everything I can to ensure that potential readers know the book is there and is worthy of their interest. After more than 40 years of marketing other people's products, I am truly excited about marketing a product of my own hard work and imagination.

CHAPTER 26

Platform

Windows down and music blaring, my spirits were high on the drive back to my hotel after a presentation to a small group of supply chain managers in a country club dining room on a spring night in Indianapolis several years ago. My talk had been well-received, with members of the audience nodding and laughing in all the right places.

About two weeks after the presentation, the meeting organizer sent a kind and gracious note, along with a tally from the feedback forms that the attendees had filled out at the end of the night. Of the 18 people who completed the forms, 17 had awarded me a score of 5 on a 5-point scale. The one outlier had given me a rating of 4.

With that ego boost, I jumped up and walked from my home office through our dining room and into the kitchen to share my excitement with my wife.

Her reaction: "There were only 18 people at your presentation?"

Barbara has a blunt knack for keeping me humble. She is my biggest supporter, as well as my greatest source of motivation to surpass her and other people's expectations.

When my book is available, you can be sure I will let those 17 people know about it, hoping they still retain at least a faintly favorable memory of me and what I have to say. Hell, I will be in touch with that 18th "hater" as well.

But of course, to have a successful book – not to mention to impress Barbara - I will need to reach quite a few more people.

One unexpected lesson from my "almost first book" experience was the significance of my personal stake in the selling and marketing of this actual first book.

I'm happy to have that responsibility. I want to promote and support my book with an exceptional marketing program. I would expect there to be no psychic reward in writing a book that no one knows about. Certainly, no one has more of a vested interest in my book's success, and no one else will care as much about its quality and its appeal as me.

After marketing other people's products that were either manufactured in food plants or coded by software engineers in far off places, it's uplifting to market a product that's the direct result and complete reflection of my work; a product that I am unconditionally passionate about.

And this works both ways. As much as I want to write a book that captures and rewards the attention of a multitude of readers, I could not put my heart into marketing a personal product that I did not feel was exceptional. Each part of this project – the writing and the marketing – helps drive the other.

One benefit of running a small business with a limited budget is that I learned to use social media and email marketing to help boost interest in our company's products, services, and events. I was also fortunate that the company whose software I sold gave me free rein to use their email marketing tools. I learned how to build lists, write effective email messages, manage email campaigns, and analyze my results. My guerilla marketing paid off. Over time, as they kindly let me know, an ever-widening group of contacts looked forward to my papers and posts. More important, some of those people bought our software.

I didn't realize it at the time, but I was gradually building a platform. The author Ryan Holiday underscores the importance of a platform to anyone – an author, a songwriter, a programmer - who seeks to build an audience for his creative content. In Ryan Holiday's definition,

> ... a platform is the combination of the tools, relationships, access, and audience that you have to bring to bear on spreading your creative work - not just once, but over the course of a career. So, a platform is your social media, and the stage you stand on, but it also includes your friends, your body of work, the community your work exists in, the media outlets and influencers who appreciate what you do, your email list, the trust you've built, your sources of income and countless other assets.

Ryan Holiday's book *Perennial Seller* sparked a remarkable surge of enthusiasm when I read and then listened to the audio version during the course of this project. As the book's subtitle – "The Art of Making and Marketing Work that Lasts" – affirms, it is as much about marketing as it is about the creation of content. One important recommendation in *Perennial Seller* is that an author, performer, or programmer should begin building his or her platform as early as possible - well before their book or album or program is ready to be introduced.

The process of building a targeted mailing list and establishing yourself on social media can take as long as the production of your content. If you wait until your project is finished, you will face a daunting uphill marketing struggle, and will miss the most timely opportunity to properly introduce your work.

Ryan Holiday considers an email list "the single most important and effective way to communicate with your potential audience and customers." In this one case I'm fortunate to be a compulsive multi-tasker, one who's not averse to the tedious work of gathering names and email addresses – often when my attention should be focused elsewhere. I sit in on hours of conference calls and web sessions each week. I regularly distract myself with never-ending updates to a spreadsheet packed with names and emails from customers, consultants, downloaders, former classmates and teammates … connections from every path in my life.

I was very fortunate that I had the inclination to start building a platform (the email part of it, at least) well before I knew I would need a platform.

This book had a different working title early in its gestation. Because I was so charmed by the email that I received from my archivist contact at the Churchill Archives, and because it felt like an appropriate expression of my personality, I planned to call this book *Perfectly Adequate*. I knew all along that my platform would include a website, and with that title in mind, the website would of course be perfectlyadequate.com.

I've licensed the rights to a handful of sites through the years, and I'm familiar with the drill: log into register.com, enter the name of your desired site, and seal the transaction with your credit card information. (A site can be licensed for a fee of roughly $38 per year. You can pay more if you include email and other options). Oh yeah, after entering the name of your site, there are those few seconds of uncertainty when you hold your breath, waiting to learn if someone else had previously grabbed that perfect website name.

As I was about to learn, my perfect name was already taken. When register.com delivered the grim news that perfectlyadequate.com was owned by someone else, the site's algorithms made an effort to ease the pain by cheerfully suggesting a handful of alternate names. Those suggestions included:

perfectlyadequate.org
myperfectlyadequate.com
perfectlysufficient.com
perfectlydecent.com

I was also informed that the name perfectlydrinkable.com could be instantly snapped up from its owner for a four-figure price.

I was not interested in anything but a dot-com address, and just could not get very excited about any of the suggested alternative website names. Since perfectlyadequate.com was not currently in use, I wondered if the owner might be interested in selling the rights to his inactive name. I set off to learn about the buying and selling of website names.

My brother-in-law's brother, who designs websites for a living, pointed me towards Network Solutions, a company that serves as a middleman between owners of websites and interested buyers, facilitating private anonymous bids and negotiations. For a fee of $39, they will contact the site's owner with an offer on your behalf. The owner is given 10 days to reply with an acceptance, a rejection, or – very likely – a counteroffer. Network Solutions even suggests a price for you to bid, based on their many haggles over similar sites. For perfectlyadequate.com, which was not a single, identifiable word and was not actively in use, they suggested a plausible bidding range of $230 to $460. I offered $375, and awaited the inevitable counteroffer – most likely a couple of hundred dollars higher.

Eight days later, the owner of perfectlyadequate.com came back with his counteroffer. It was not a couple of hundred dollars higher. It was $9,625 higher than my offer. In all likelihood he or she expected me to re-counter, but I decided not to bother. The gap between $375 and $10,000 was too vast to expect a mutually acceptable compromise.

Fortunately, a very satisfactory Plan B popped into my mind in the course of the bidding process for perfectlyadequate.com. Perfectly Adequate was going to have a subtitle, one that would work with just about any other title that I selected (even though I finally decided not to use that subtitle). I held my breath once again as I waited to learn if this name was available. It was.

I consider this a perfectly lucky turn of events. In sharing the tale of how a full-time salesman and business owner fell in love with a story, and then learned to research and write the details of that story, I could not do much better than to support my platform with a website named www.perfectlytruestory.com.

"Perfectly Adequate," by the way, lives on. When I created a company to self-publish this book, I named it Perfectly Adequate Press.

CHAPTER 27

I'm Now That Guy

In his Wall Street Journal review of Michael Kinch's book *Between Hope and Fear*, William F. Bynum praised the author's inspired incorporation of figures as diverse as Napoleon Bonaparte, Alexander the Great, and Adolf Hitler into a book written primarily about vaccines. We also learn that *Between Hope and Fear* is "far better documented than many popular-science volumes." It is "especially clear" and is a "masterly exposition."

The review ends, though, with some minor quibbles. "This is a fine book, marred only by a few factual slips. For example, Karl Marx was German, not Russian; Paul Ehrlich used Salvarsan for syphilis, not gonorrhea."

While I'm a stickler – actually I am a fanatic – about the accuracy of my writing, I have never been one to comment in those rare instances when I have the knowledge or the luck to recognize mistakes in the writing of others.

I've noticed recently however that after reading close to a thousand books, papers and other documents on a fairly narrow subject, I'm now that guy.

One example: I devour everything that the journalist James Fallows writes in *The Atlantic*. When I first signed onto Twitter, he was one of the first people I followed. As I was scrolling through my customary dose of music, sports, and political tweets one evening, I noticed a response from Mr. Fallows to a pundit who had tweeted about a cluster of politicians who: "… were given the choice between war and dishonor. They chose dishonor and they now have war." Fallows remarked that this was an "apt revival of Churchill's speech on succeeding Neville Chamberlain."

Within the span of several heartbeats, I tweeted an impulsive correction: "No! Churchill said this in reaction to Chamberlain's signing of the Munich Agreement."

I did not expect that he would notice my reply, but James Fallows kindly rewarded me with a "Yes correct" tweet a few moments later.

I loved that I got his attention – and, more importantly, that I did not misstate the context of Churchill's scorching quote. At the same time, I felt like such a scold. But that's the price you pay, I suppose, when you become that guy.

CHAPTER 28

Too Damn Interesting

My book covers the chaotic weave of expectations, ultimatums, and perceived violations of honor leading up to the violent confrontation between the British and French navies on July 3, 1940. There were, of course, reactions and repercussions in the aftermath, but the core of the story was essentially complete by the end of that July.

By then the bodies of the fallen French sailors had been buried. The initial praise for Churchill's difficult decision had begun to fade in some capitals, as did the bitter clamor against the British attack in others. The Battle for France was over for now, and British eyes turned from the Royal Navy to the Royal Air Force as the four-month Battle of Britain was being fought in the skies above England. The R.A.F., which Churchill had refused to fully commit to the defense of France, was now fully engaged in daily combat with Germany's Luftwaffe.

July 31, 1940 was a mile-marker for me and a clearly defined boundary. With the exception of a few small longer-term repercussions, the events that I was researching and writing about were - in a word - history. This meant that most books had a natural stopping point for me. When a story ticked over to August 1, 1940, I could stop reading, which freed me to re-shelve these partially read books to continue my research with the next book in my stack.

I consumed hundreds of books during the course my research. There was no sense in reading beyond my milestone; it was a waste of valuable time. For the most part, I complied. But there is a limit to my self-control, and some books were just too damn interesting to stop reading.

My hands-down favorite book about Winston Churchill was written by John Colville, his Assistant Private Secretary. *The Fringes of Power*, the published version of Colville's personal diary, flows more or less continuously from September 10, 1939 to May 31, 1945, with several additional chapters and addendums that extend Colville's account to the mid-nineteen-sixties.

In an earlier book of recollections, titled *Footprints in Time*, Colville confessed: "I kept a diary during the war years. I shall not publish it because it contains opinions of people and views of events which in the light of subsequent knowledge, I believe to be unjust." Much to our good fortune Colville changed his mind and eventually published his diary.

The Fringes of Power is dedicated to Mary Soames, the youngest of Churchill's five children, "... with affection and penitence for some of the less complimentary references to her in the early part of this diary." In one hardly scathing observation after sitting next to Mary at a dinner on the eve of her father's appointment as Prime Minister, Colville noted that "I thought the Churchill girl rather supercilious; She has Sarah's emphatic way of talking, and is better looking, but she seemed to me to have a much less sympathetic personality."

More harshly, Colville wrote about a drive with Clementine Churchill, Sir Winston's wife. After a clash over their respective opinions on whether the last nine months of Neville Chamberlain's government had been effective, Colville wrote: "her views are as ill-judged as they are decisive." The charm in these pages emerges gradually as Colville blossoms from a twenty-five-year-old Foreign Office underling whose reverence for his first boss - Prime Minister Neville Chamberlain - accompanied his initial misgivings and concerns about Chamberlain's successor, Winston Churchill.

It took just a few months for Colville to become a trusted confidant of the entire Churchill family and earn the P.M.'s fatherly affection. Two years into the war, eager to join the fight against Germany, Colville pursued a commission in the Royal Air Force. Churchill admitted: "You know I can stop you. I can't make you stay with me against your will but I can put you somewhere else." However, energized as always by the prospective thrill of combat, Churchill came around with his characteristic exuberance. One Colville entry notes that Churchill guided him away from bombers, with typically enthusiastic assurance that "the short, sharp battle of the fighter pilot was far better than the long wait of a bomber crew before they reached their destination."

This diary of a rather privileged young Londoner in the perilous years under German bombardment is packed with candid opinions and intimate sketches of the daily lives of the Prime Minister, his family, and his eminent contemporaries. It is a treasured window into every significant decision, event, and personality during the years that Winston Churchill earned the accolades that define him in most people's eyes.

In the published version of Colville's diary, his entry for Tuesday, July 30, 194`0 ends on page 206. (There was no entry for July 31 – my historical boundary). I should have stopped there. But I kept reading to the book's end on page 774 and relished every word.

The Ciano Diaries: 1939-1943 provided another engrossing set of personal recollections that I read well beyond my natural stopping point. Galeazzo Ciano, who was married to Benito Mussolini's daughter Edda, was the fascist dictator's Minister of Foreign Affairs as well as his son-in-law. His diaries offer a frank and irreverent view of the pre-war years and the war's proceedings from the truly dark side. Once I started reading the one-volume published version of Ciano's diaries, I sped right past my calendar demarcation and consumed 300 additional pages - through to the final entry in December 1943, written from Ciano's cell three weeks before he was executed.

With a puffed-up sense of his own importance, and with his peaked cap worn at an absurdly rakish angle (he was a captain in the air force), Galeazzo Ciano was a flamboyant character in public, and an unfiltered diarist with a candid appreciation of reality in private. In the summer of 1939, in a note about Italy's Axis partner just before war was declared, he acknowledged: "I am becoming aware of how little we are worth in the opinion of the Germans"

Ciano showed no fawning loyalty (in his writing, at least) to the malevolent personalities in his sphere - not to Hitler ("Either he is under hallucinations, or he really is a genius."), not to the German High Command ("that pack of presumptuous vulgarians"), not to his father-in-law (whom he accused of "base cowardice" in the shadow of Hitler), and especially not to Joachim von Ribbentrop, his loathsome German Foreign Minister counterpart. ("He is the exaggerated echo of Hitler").

Ciano and his wife fled to Germany in 1943 after Mussolini was overthrown for the first time. When the Germans arrested Ciano and returned him to Italy for trial, Edda unsuccessfully attempted to barter her husband's diaries, which she had smuggled out of Italy, for Ciano's freedom. The lure of half a decade's candid and embarrassing revelations about Italian and German leaders was not enough to save her husband. Benito Mussolini was temporarily back in power, and Ciano, who had earlier advocated Mussolini's overthrow, was convicted of treason and sentenced to death. He was executed on January 11, 1944. As a pronounced statement of disdain and humiliation, his killers tied the seated Ciano to a chair and shot him in the back.

I resisted for many months, but finally gave into the inevitable obligation to read *The Rise and Fall of the Third Reich*. Long books do not deter me, but I hesitated to pick up William L. Shirer's canonical 1,280-page chronicle of evil; dreading a murky web of loathsome creeps and unthinkable horrors that I did not expect to have much direct relevance to the clash between the French and British navies. Also, I carry books when I travel, and while most fellow passengers would understand the historical import of this widely recognized book, I did not like what a peripheral glimpse of the swastika on its cover might suggest about me.

There is no escaping the Germans' role in disrupting Europe and sparking World War II. When I finally dug into Shirer's masterpiece, I became completely absorbed in this essential foundation of knowledge about the architects of world disorder in the second quarter of the twentieth century. I carried a paperback copy of *The Rise and Fall of the Third Reich* through more than a few airports and train terminals, with the swastika covered by a mailing label. Shirer's stories enhanced my understanding of the backgrounds and motivation of the men who were most responsible for the war.

Originally a foreign correspondent for William Randolph Hearst's wire services, Shirer was recruited and posted to Vienna for CBS Radio by Edward R. Murrow. Fluent in German and French, Shirer had an uncanny, Zelig-like knack for being on the spot as the biggest stories in the world exploded. He was in Vienna on the day Germany annexed Austria under its Anschluss in 1938. Shirer was in Germany for much of Hitler's rise, where he discretely observed and chronicled the ever more inflammatory annual Nazi rallies in Nuremberg. Shirer, along with other accredited journalists, was allowed to accompany German forces into France in 1940.

Acting on a tip from a German officer, Shirer made his way to the forest of Compiegne, 45 miles outside of Paris on June 22 of that year. France was about to sign its armistice with Germany in a historic rail car that sat in a quiet glade. Germany had surrendered to France in this same clearing in that same car in 1918. Adolf Hitler had personally set this scene. Shirer estimated that he stood with his microphone just 50 yards from Hitler, just before he climbed the steps to the carriage, close enough to the Fuhrer that "I saw his face light up, successively, with hate, scorn, revenge, triumph..."

Although I admit to closing *The Rise and Fall of the Third Reich* with some relief with more than 500 pages left unread, Shirer's work had an extended impact on my reading and my understanding of the forces that brought Europe to a boil in the late 1930s. In keeping with my habit of searching out other books by favored authors, I ended up reading four additional books written by Shirer: *The Nightmare Years: 1930-1940*, *Berlin Diary*, *The Collapse of the Third Republic* [i.e., France] and *"This is Berlin": Radio Broadcasts from Nazi Germany* - which averaged more than 600 pages per title.

The Collapse of the Third Republic, with its sharply drawn portraits of the men who led the downfall of France and attempted to direct the allegiance of the French Navy was an especially valuable resource for my book. Shirer's instinctive blend of first-person journalism and reflective narration kept me company on quite a few plane rides and train rides.

I sat on *In Command of History: Churchill Fighting and Writing the Second World War* by David Reynolds for the longest time. I thought it would be more about Churchill the writer than Churchill the statesman and war leader. And it was. I thought it might not be relevant to my work. And, for the most part, it was not. But once I finally started reading *In Command of History* I simply could not stop.

As an aspiring author with deep admiration for Churchill and an interest in every aspect of his life, I was especially fascinated by these tales of Churchill the writer. When Churchill was pushed from office after World War II, he dedicated himself to the writing of his multi-volume history - *The Second World War* - which spanned six volumes. Those volumes had singularly majestic titles: *The Gathering Storm*, *Their Finest Hour*, *The Grand Alliance*, *The Hinge of Fate*, *Closing the Ring*, and *Triumph and Tragedy*. Churchill commanded a small army of researchers and writers, dealt with government secrecy laws, and the onerous British tax code that threatened to take 97.5 per cent of his royalties. As he wrote his version of the war, Churchill was also acutely sensitive to the feelings and reputations of important contemporaries like Dwight Eisenhower and Charles de Gaulle. When you read as much about a subject as I've read about Churchill, you encounter quite a bit of repetition. *In Command of History* turned out to be one of the most fascinating, refreshing, unique, and enlightening books about the man I so admire.

There is one book that I read from cover to cover, and almost wish I had not read at all.

After reading General Edward Louis Spears' account of the first year of the Second World War, I felt that I had gotten to "know" this British General through his own words. My admiration for Spears – and for his writing in particular - is clear in these pages, and I was interested in learning more about his life in the decades before and after the War. And so, I was thrilled to find a biography - *Under Two Flags: The Life of General Sir Edward Spears*, written by Max Egremont.

Even before picking up Max Egremont's biography, I had detected hints of Spears' emotional fragility. At times he seemed overly eager to receive affirmation of his significance, particularly in the eyes of Winston Churchill. *Under Two Flags* confirmed my perception. Egremont wrote about the "insecurity of unreturned affection … that often clouded his life."

Spears was married for 50 years to Mary Borden, an American-born author. Mary Borden brought inherited wealth into the marriage, and also earned a good living from her books, primarily novels. Ms. Borden founded and helped run a field hospital in France during the First World War, and a roving ambulance corps during the Second. Spears conducted an indiscreet affair with his secretary for decades, and married her in 1969, one year after his wife's death. Spears was a cad.

He was also a faithless friend. Spears had his hand in several business ventures after the war. He was loath to depend on his wife's income, and endured periods when he was barely able to maintain his lifestyle. An elder acquaintance who served on the boards of two companies hinted that he would eventually propose Spears as his replacement. The two men happened to be patients of the same doctor. Spears asked the doctor to recommend to the friend that he withdraw from the boards for health reasons. The doctor was offended by the suggestion and, of course, refused. John Colville wrote that Spears "had a streak of metallic ruthlessness."

One of the most brutal denunciations of another man that I have ever read was a broadside against Spears from Duff Cooper. A well-rounded diplomat and author, Cooper had served as Secretary of State for War under Prime Minister Stanley Baldwin, and as First Lord of the Admiralty under Neville Chamberlain. He was Churchill's first Minister of Information and, after the liberation of France, was posted to Paris as Britain's first post-war Ambassador. Spears and Cooper served together in Parliament as members of the Conservative Party and knew each other well.

In 1932, Cooper's nephew Rupert Hart-Davis was about to propose marriage to Catherine Comfort Borden-Turner, Mary's daughter from her first marriage. When Hart-Davis asked his uncle for his opinion of Spears, Cooper erupted: "If he had the word SHIT written on his forehead in letters of fire it wouldn't be more apparent than it is now. He's the most unpopular man in the House." Comfort Borden and Rupert Hart-Davis had a daughter and two sons before divorcing after thirty years of marriage.

I became a dog person late in life, and so I was initially delighted to read of Spears' devotion to his two dogs, a poodle and an Alsatian. However, I was horrified to read an account of how Spears "insecurity of unreturned affection" also applied to his dogs. On an occasion, when one of the dogs demonstrated more affection for the Spears' family housekeeper than for Spears, and refused to run to his side, Spears ordered the housekeeper to fetch his whip so he could teach the dog a lesson. She refused. That incident defines Spears' character in a manner that I just cannot get past.

I still consider Spears a generally reliable source of information, and I still admire his writing ability. After some deliberation, I decided not to rewrite two relevant earlier chapters in this book. However, as I learned these mortifying details of Spears' life relatively late in my project, I will admit to an inclination to cancel my wished-for pint of beer across a table from Spears, and an urge to write about him as my fourth loathsome character. (I guess I just did that). I also now realize that I would have thoroughly enjoyed sharing a pint or two with the remarkable Mary Borden.

And finally, there is *The Kings Depart*, by Richard M. Watt, a book about the Treaty of Versailles, which Germany was forced to sign at the end of World War I. My experience with Richard M. Watt was so unexpected and incredible in so many different ways that I just had to give that story a chapter of its own.

Everybody Knows a Salesman Can't Write a Book

Another book that I read from cover to cover was *The Kings Depart* by Richard M. Watt. While his book fascinated me and held my attention much longer than I had expected, the author's personal story – which I pieced together over time - absolutely astonished me in more ways than I could possibly have imagined.

Richard M. Watt's book tells the story of the contentious negotiations in the months leading up to the signing of the Treaty of Versailles in 1919. I initially skimmed *The Kings Depart* simply to verify a few details from the events that colored the signing of the armistice between Germany and the Allies. I found several fine brushstrokes of history in Mr. Watt's account of that meeting in the rail car in a small clearing in the Forest of Compiegne that I so revere. This was more of a routine fact-checking expedition than a quest to glean new information, but once I opened *The Kings Depart*, I found it so interesting that I ended up reading it all the way through to the end.

The shooting stopped on November 11, 1918, the day the Armistice was signed to end the fighting. That was seven months before the final treaty would be signed in Versailles to settle the terms that officially ended the First World War. Marshal Ferdinand Foch, the Supreme Allied Commander who signed the armistice for France, delivered that armistice document to Prime Minister Georges Clemenceau with the declaration: "My work is finished. Your work begins." What also then began was a sharp clash between the Allies' political leaders – who focused on their constituents' lucrative expectations for crushing financial reparations from Germany – and the senior military officers who sought to ensure that Germany's ability to wage war was crippled for all time.

I learned that as Germany's team of negotiators crossed France by rail on their way to Versailles for the presentation of the hastily stitched-together final version of the treaty in May 1919, their train was slowed to a crawl whenever they passed scarred battlefields or rolled through devastated towns. The French wished to leave no doubt as to why the Germans were so despised and why they would face such harsh penalties in the final treaty.

Germany's objections to the Allies' severe financial terms and crippling military sanctions were understandable. It was more of a surprise to learn of their leaders' fierce reluctance to accept the treaty's *schmachparagraphen* [shame paragraphs] in which Germany was forced to acknowledge guilt for starting the First World War. Watt's account of how that reluctance almost caused the war to reignite was a complete revelation to me.

If I had been efficient, I would have simply skimmed through the book's index and read just a handful of pages. However, captivation trumped efficiency, and I ended up reading all 530 pages of *The Kings Depart*.

I followed my usual practice after reading an especially interesting story. Curious about the author, and interested in other books he might have written, I Googled Richard M. Watt. I learned that he had published three favorably reviewed books, and ended up ordering his earlier book *Dare Call It Treason* from an on-line seller of used books. That account of the mutinous French Army near the end of World War I provided telling insights into the early career of Marshal Philippe Pétain and several other officers who would later play essential roles in command of French forces at the beginning of World War II.

I learned that Richard M. Watt was a Dartmouth grad, he served in the Navy, and he passed away in 2015. What really captured my attention and triggered my "oh man; are you kidding me?" reaction was that Watt was not a full-time writer. In fact, he worked for 45 years as a salesman and then a senior executive at a company called Crossfield Products Corporation in New Jersey. They sell flooring products and are the type of company I sell my software to.

His author's page on Amazon.com mentions: 'While he would say he was lucky to have never experienced the "starving author desperate to be published" [syndrome] he did feel the work of writing, while something he loved and found immensely satisfying, was hard work.'

In other words, he was just like me ... only more successful in both facets of his life. I was curious to learn more about his life and, especially, about how he fit his research and writing into his life.

His author's page on Amazon.com also provides a contact for information about his books: Linda W. Doyle, one of his daughters. Her address was listed, and I wrote her a letter.

It was a pure fan letter, written in spontaneous enthusiasm after reading *The Kings Depart* and learning about her father's dual career. I included my contact information, but - no surprise – did not hear back.

So, five months later, I mailed a second letter. In this note, I mentioned my attempt to replicate her father's parallel track of working and writing, and I asked if it might be possible to arrange a call to discuss her father's life as an author. I included this awkwardly worded request: "The favor I'm asking is to wonder if you wouldn't mind sharing some insights into how your father managed to write while also working fulltime." Her mailing address was in a town just north of Boston, and I travel that way about once a month for business. Once again there was no reply.

I travel quite a bit for work. At the end of one especially hectic week of meetings, flights, hotels, and rental cars, I had to connect through Atlanta's bustling airport on my way back home from a presentation to a shoe company in St. Louis. I was tired, I was rushed, and I just wanted to settle in with a book for my last flight of the week. As the plane began to taxi toward home, I took one last look at my phone before shutting it down. An email message had just arrived in my in-box, with a name I did not recognize, and with the Subject: "You Made my Day." I was not wearing my glasses and could not decipher the body of the message. A flight attendant was hovering over me, so I shut off my phone for the duration of the flight. It was not worth incurring her wrath for what was surely a note from a spammer, or, heaven forbid, another software salesman.

As I always do, I powered my phone back up as just as the plane's wheels hit the runway in Baltimore. Now there were three additional messages from that name I did not recognize. The first one began:

Hey Bill -

Lin Doyle (a/k/a Linda Watt Doyle) here.

Last night, I opened your letter to me about my father's book, The King's Depart. I so appreciate you taking the time to write.

It was a short note, actually an unfinished draft. She mentioned a Nantucket vacation with her husband and son, and the note then ended abruptly.

The second email, with the subject line "My last email," sent 20 minutes after her first email and two months after my second letter, began:

The email I just sent you (in error) has been sitting in my draft folder since last summer and your second letter to me in a pile of unopened mail.

Lin got me caught up in that surge of four emails. She mentioned that her father had written a number of short stories and something like 200 book reviews in addition to his books. She attached a photo-image of a story of his that appeared in a 1971 issue of Sports Illustrated – a surprisingly engaging tale of a boar hunting escapade in Turkey while his destroyer was moored there one Christmas season.

She also mentioned that a collection of her father's papers had been donated to the Howard Gotlieb Archival Research Center at Boston University, and that she had additional materials that she planned to send to the archives once she finished sorting through them.

The website for the Howard Gotlieb Archival Research Center provides a high-level outline of the materials in the Richard M. Watt collection. One selection in particular caught my eye. The archived correspondence includes letters to and from General Sir Edward Louis Spears. (I learned much later that the Howard Gotlieb Center also houses the donated papers of Spears' first wife, Mary Borden)!

As I've now learned, every archive center has its own minor quirks. Unlike Hyde Park and Cambridge, where cameras and smart phones are encouraged, visitors to the Gotlieb Center are forbidden from taking photographs of documents. This meant I had to take notes in my God-awful handwriting. The last time I focused so diligently on the slants and shapes of my cursive letters, a frowning nun from the Sisters of the Immaculate Heart of Mary was watching over my shoulder in third grade.

Another unique protocol is that each visitor must wear white cotton gloves when handling the Center's documents. The Gotlieb Center provides a pair to each visitor, gratis. I completely understand the rationale, but as I learned during my first day of work with Richard M. Watt's papers, it's a bit of a chore to sift through stacks of letters – many of which were thin carbon copies - and other documents while wearing loose cotton gloves. Try turning the pages of a newspaper while wearing gloves. It was that much of a challenge.

The Richard M. Watt collection at the Gottlieb Center spans 24 archive boxes. The archives include research materials, original manuscripts and quite a bit of correspondence. The archivist who was personally assigned to me on the day of my first visit (I went back a second time to confirm a few facts) supplied a typed list of the contents of each box. After reviewing that list, I requested five of the boxes for examination, including, of course, most of Richard M. Watt's correspondence.

The first page in the first folder in the first box that I opened was a letter – it was actually the beginning of a five-page typed letter – and it started me down another incredibly interesting path.

Dated August 18, 1959, the letter was written by Richard M. Watt to a man he had met while waiting to board the ferry from Greenport, NY to the more remote Shelter Island (both on the far tip of Long Island). After spotting a stack of books in the back of a car with New Hampshire plates, and thinking the driver might be a Dartmouth professor, Watt struck up a conversation.

As it turned out, Evan Hill was not a professor; he was a writer. Watt had a story he was eager to tell, and he shared it with Hill, hoping that Hill might be willing to write it. Richard M. Watt had been intrigued by the mutinies in the French Army toward the end of the First World War ever since he first read an account of that little-known bit of history in a *Reader's Digest* anthology as a 10-year-old. Hill joked later that in order to escape the conversation, he suggested that Watt send him an outline of his story. So, Watt sent him that five-page letter which began:

Dear Mr. Hill

I am in hopes that you will recall our conversation on the Greenport-Shelter Island ferry several weeks ago. We spoke of the French Army mutinies of 1917, and you suggested that I write you in the event that I ever decided to do something with it. Accordingly, I am setting my ideas down with the thought that you might find them interesting.

The next four single-spaced pages included a tight and very detailed summary of the events leading up to the mutinies, their suppression, and how they were largely covered up in history. Watt thought the story was worthy of a magazine article, and he wondered:

> Since you are a professional author, I believe that you can assess whether or not an article on these mutinies would be of interest to a magazine. If so, would you be interested in our getting together in some manner to write such an article?

Evan Hill replied nine days later. As would happen multiple times in Watt's sudden new sideline, his enthusiasm for his story was positively infectious. The seasoned writer wrote to the flooring salesman: "It is even more exciting than your explanation when we met on the Shelter Island Ferry." Hill saw even bigger potential than Watt. Perhaps the story could be told in a single magazine article, but he also raised the possibilities of an extended multi-part article or even a book.

Hill was not interested in writing the story himself or in collaborating with Watt, but he did a kind and very generous thing. He provided the addresses and phone numbers of his agent and another freelance writer, Don Murray, who was frequently published in *Reader's Digest*, the *Saturday Evening Post* and other magazines of the day. He also forwarded copies of Watt's letter to them.

Don Murray, who won a Pulitzer Prize for Editorial Writing in 1954, and who was a venerated author and writing teacher, quickly took up Watt's cause. A number of years later, he turned the story of Watt's unlikely side-career as a writer into an article titled: "The Secret Life of Richard Watt" in the *Dartmouth Alumni Magazine*. I failed to notice a copy of that article in the Gotlieb Archives during my first visit, but it was mentioned in a letter in one of the folders, and I later found it online. "The Secret Life of Richard Watt" was the single most helpful and inspirational source of information about Richard M. Watt's writing career.

After reading the outline of the story that Watt wanted to tell, Murray encouraged him to write the story himself. When the Watts and Murrays eventually met for drinks, Murray's wife Minnie May suggested: "Write a book. There's no future in writing magazine articles."

"So I wrote a book."

Dick Watt – as he was generally called - was every bit as ill-prepared for the challenge of writing a book as I am for my adventure. He had majored in English at Dartmouth "but took not a single course in writing and his only study of history was a one-semester freshman course in Modern European History."

After the stories of the mutinies of the French Army captured the attention of 10-year-old Dick Watt, he casually pursued additional details by reading books about World War I through his adolescence, teens, and twenties. Now, at the age of 30, with a book of his own in mind, he began to research his story with a passion. He haunted his local library in the small town of Glen Ridge, NJ as well as the vast New York Public Library. He visited the library at West Point and borrowed books by mail from the Hoover Institute Library at Stanford University in California.

As one might expect, the best published sources about the mutinies of the French Army were written in French, a language that Watt had never studied. So, he taught himself to read French. "Dick bought a paperback French grammar at a bookstore in the Buffalo Airport, cut out the lessons and pasted them on index cards. He proceeded to teach himself to read French ... in spare moments waiting for planes or customers."

He faced the additional hurdle of source materials in a second foreign language – German - and he outsourced that challenge. His papers include a receipt for $67.50 for the translation of 45 pages of German text.

He had a prior body of written work that was inspired by his impatient reaction to an encounter with poorly written instructional materials when he served in the Navy. Shortly after his induction, Watt endured a barely comprehensible lecture on the operation of the Navy's Mark 63 gunfire control system. When he found the available written documentation to be no more coherent, he wrote his own manual ... and it became the Navy's standard documentation in the years that followed.

When he outlined his first book – *Dare Call It Treason*, the story of the French Army mutinies - he used a spreadsheet – the original, circa 1960, paper version of a spreadsheet - a series of 18-column bookkeeping sheets on which he mapped the initial outline of his story. Those folded sheets of accounting paper are in the Gotlieb Archives today.

He found an agent, and his agent found him a publisher. At various points in his career his agent Herb Jaffe also represented Joseph Heller, Philip Roth, Paddy Chayefsky, and other elite authors. Jaffe's many letters to Watt reflect his breezy personality and the warmth of their relationship. One of the first, early in his quest to find Watt a publisher, written on February 27, 1961, began:

Dear Dick,

You are now a professional writer; we've had our first
rejection.

Doubleday was not interested in publishing Watt's book. But
Jaffe carried on and sold the book to Simon and Schuster. There,
Michael Korda became Watt's editor, and so began another fortunate relationship. Like Jaffe, Korda was a world-class talent
and world-class character, only more so. A British native who
had served in the Royal Air Force after the war, Korda would
have a distinguished career as Simon & Schuster's Editor-in-
Chief. He published the works of a sheaf of prominent authors
and personalities, including William L. Shirer, Richard Nixon,
and Ronald Reagan. He would also write more than twenty
books of his own. Watt was very fortunate in his mentors and
partners during every phase of his writing career, and, in return,
they were inspired by his enthusiasm.

After completing his spreadsheet-based outline, Watt continually honed his book in small bites. His initial rough draft "revealed the holes in his knowledge." Unlike authors who employ
strict and separate research and writing phases, Watt would periodically shift the focus of his research to fill in missing details
in his latest draft. "I could never do all my research first, before
writing a word, as I understand some authors do. As I write, I
understand how much I don't know, go after it, then fill in more
later."

Watt wrote everything in longhand; his wife Sandy typed
and re-typed every draft of his manuscript. After reading each
draft, "he'd mark that up and rewrite it, and rewrite that and

then rewrite it again." Dick Watt was transforming himself into a polished writer.

To help fill the holes in his knowledge, Watt combed the world for source materials. He contacted authors and officers. He wrote to the Library of Congress and the Department of the Army. He mailed questions to the U.S. Embassies of France, Germany, and Russia.

He was humble but not shy when it came to contacting other authors and historians for bits of information to fill in his knowledge. The letters in which he requested guidance or assistance typically ended: "I cannot think of any particular reason why you should help me by answering the above questions, except that my interest is sincere and I believe that the story of the French Mutinies is too important to remain a secret."

One of the experts he contacted to help fill the gaps in his knowledge was General Sir Edward Louis Spears. Spears was intimately familiar with the French military in general and had a close personal relationship with Marshal Philippe Pétain in particular.

Pétain, who was the most controversial figure in twentieth century French history, played the lead role in quelling the French mutinies and restoring the French army to an effective fighting force in World War I. In the next war, the heroic – but now defeatist – octogenarian Marshal of France was ushered into power just in time to surrender France to Germany, and he led the Vichy government which collaborated with Nazi Germany and willingly oppressed its own citizens. After the war, a French tribunal condemned him to death as a traitor. Charles de Gaulle commuted the 89-year-old Pétain's sentence to life in prison, where he died at the age of 95 after several years in the fog of severe dementia.

Watt characteristically introduced himself to Spears with a letter in which he asked seven questions about minute details related to the mutinies. For example, "What was Colonel de Grandmaison's first name and in what battle did he die?" and "What was the strength of a French infantry division at the time of the Nivelle Offensive?"

Spears replied three weeks later, first with a begrudging reminder of the imposition on his time, and then with answers that were quite helpful to Watt. Watt sent him a warm letter in return, noting his admiration and indebtedness to Spears' multivolume accounts of his experiences in both World Wars.

As *Dare Call It Treason* evolved, and as its publication approached, Watt endured a series of letters from editors at Simon and Schuster containing brutally frank critiques and recommendations for major edits. He accepted those suggestions in good humor, he revised his book accordingly, and his work continued to improve.

Watt, a salesman to his core, was very eager to assist with the marketing of his book, and even employed the 1960's version of his social network. He suggested to Michael Korda that they contact about 500 of his business contacts by postcard when the book was published. He did not believe – or even necessarily care – that those contacts would read his book, but he assumed that most would feel obligated to buy a copy. Korda eagerly agreed that Simon and Schuster would pay the cost of the postcards and the mailing if Watt supplied the addresses.

Since Watt was an unknown quantity in the realm of professional historians, he felt that a forward written by an actual historian would boost the credibility of his offering. Michael Korda agreed that such a forward would also "provide a protective cover against any possible attacks from professional historians, who are a pretty clannish bunch." Colonel John Elting, an author, historian, and educator at the U.S. Military Academy at West Point, who was also a personal friend of Dick Watt's, was recruited to write the forward.

With the research completed and countless edits honed to a final polished draft, *Dare Call it Treason* was published in the spring of 1963. Watt's book was widely reviewed, and the reviews – many written by esteemed members of that clan of professional historians - were sensational.

The *New York Times* enlisted author and historian Alistair Horne to review *Dare Call It Treason*. In his laudatory review, Horne – the future author of *Seven Ages of Paris* - noted "Watt has done superbly well" and "He writes engagingly well, yet never too well." Incredibly, Horne followed up with a personal letter to Watt in which he apologized for not being more effusive and for appearing to quibble over Watt's emphasis on the impact of political corruption on the mutinies.

Time Magazine noted that "Watt skillfully evokes the eerie, secret struggle of a nation to reform its will and its army in mid-war." Time also called *Dare Call It Treason* "all the more remarkable because its author is a complete amateur, a flooring-materials salesman who wrote the book (his first) in the children's playroom of his home."

William L. Shirer – William L. Shirer! - responded to an advance copy sent by Michael Korda with sincere admiration. "I found it fascinating. Once you get into it you cannot put it down." And: "Few persons perhaps realize how difficult it has been to get to the bottom of the story of the mutinies. As a young correspondent in Paris in the Twenties I once tried --- and failed. Understandably the French Army has no wish to publicize this painful chapter. The author is to be congratulated for digging out so much of the truth as he has. I think he has made a fine book."

When the venerable historian Barbara Tuchman responded to a request for a blurb by calling *Dare Call It Treason* "an original and valuable work of history," Michael Korda gushed to Dick Watt: "... Just think. If you do well enough people will be asking you for quotes for their books on the First World War!"

One of the best indirect compliments came from an editor at a different publishing house – Prentice-Hall - who mentioned in a letter he was aware that Watt was "well into a second book on Austria and Eastern Europe in the years following World War I." If Watt wasn't "contracted with S&S for it," he would be interested in publishing it. "Or if you want to talk about a third book, I'd also appreciate hearing from you."

With a well-regarded book to his name, Dick Watt continued to write. In addition to dozens of magazine articles and book reviews, he would go on to write two more books of history, both published by Simon and Schuster. Following *Dare Call It Treason* and *The Kings Depart*, he wrote *Bitter Glory: Poland and Its Fate, 1918-1939.*

While working full time, Dick Watt managed to forge a path to success as an author.

As he researched, wrote, revised, published, and then basked in the reviews of *Dare Call It Treason*, Dick Watt's relationship with General Sir Edward Louis Spears bloomed in a remarkable way.

Their correspondence retained an air of formality - Watt started each letter: "Dear Sir Edward," while Spears signed his "E.L. Spears." Once again, however, Watt's enthusiasm for the story that was "too important to remain a secret" helped create a warm and enthusiastic bond between the two men.

Michael Korda mailed a copy of the final proofs of *Dare Call it Treason* to Spears, hoping simply for a quotable reaction. Instead, Spears warmed to the task with twenty pages of notes and corrections, with microscopically precise insights and details that only this impeccably attentive British liaison to France's military and political leaders could have provided. They included:

"Clemenceau's gloves were not white but light grey."

[Writing about French Prime Minister Georges Clemenceau again] "I do not think it is quite correct to say that he enjoyed perfect health. He often suffered extremely badly from insomnia and when this happened he was even more difficult to deal with than usual."

And, "On page 204, Paragraph 1, line 5 ... I would suggest omitting the words "and dirty". If included this will be taken as an insult to the Foreign Legion and quite unjustified."

After reading the final published version of *Dare Call It Treason*, Spears saluted Watt: "You have in your first venture into authorship produced a really valuable contribution to history and one that is far more absorbing than most works of fiction. I congratulate you warmly."

Impressed with the details of Watt's research into the events of 1917, Spears – who had been in France at that time - noted that for one critical two-month period leading up to the mutinies "You know far more about the events ... than I did."

Incredibly, Spears' ambition was stirred by his long-distance encounter with Dick Watt. Their loose collaboration had inspired Sir Edward to dig into his long-neglected body of "very full information" about the events surrounding the mutinies and their suppression.

Spears had struggled with a dilemma for almost half a century, and he now revealed that predicament to Watt - that Marshal Pétain had entrusted him with his notes about the events in 1917, with the understanding that Spears was "the best person to write the story." But Spears had – to this point – demurred.

In his book *The Fall of France*, Spears touched on a conversation with Pétain in June 1940. Relations between Britain and France were approaching the peak of contention. These two old soldiers found time to reminisce on their mutual respect and one of the Marshal's crowning achievements. Pétain noted: "I was right to ask you to write the story of that period." Spears reflected in his book: "I had wondered if he remembered doing so, and rather expected him to ask for the return of his papers."

The outbreak of World War II had disrupted Spears' plans to write his account of the mutinies. After the war, with Pétain held in almost universal disdain, Spears confessed to Watt: "I did not feel that I could write a story of which Pétain would be the hero."

Now, with the passage of more than 15 years since the end of the Second World War, and inspired by Watt's depiction of Pétain's leadership, Spears decided to dust off the Marshal's notes, and tell a different version of the story he had originally intended to write two decades earlier. "I have come to the conclusion that the time is ripe to publish Marshal Pétain's account of the Mutinies."

Sir Edward Louis Spears' next to last book was published in 1966. Titled *Two Men Who Saved France: Pétain and de Gaulle*, it linked the stories of France's most prominent heroes in World Wars I and II respectively. By combining the stories of Pétain and De Gaulle, Spears partially overcame the prohibitive taint of Pétain's traitorous role in World War II, while writing his long-planned laudatory account of Pétain's subjugation of the mutinies in the French Army during World War I.

Although he was indisputably inspired by Dick Watt, Spears did not acknowledge him in *Two Men Who Saved France*. I was initially disappointed when I learned this, but ultimately was not surprised by Spears lack of gratitude and grace.

I never found Dick Watt's secret path to productivity and success. Of course, there was no secret path. It simply came down to the doing of it. As he worked long days and full weeks, he made time for his research and his writing. My reward in learning about Dick Watt was the confirmation that I was on my own good path, one that had a number of striking similarities with the trail forged by someone who found success as a writer while also working full time. That reassurance was immensely helpful.

Watt acknowledged that the work on his book was an obsession, one that filled his imagination and consumed most free hours. Like most obsessions, this one also had a downside – the time it took away from his wife and kids. As I know – and as my wife Barbara knows better – an obsession like his and mine will take over your life and steal time from your family.

As happened with most people in Dick Watt's universe, his editor Michael Korda also became a friend. A letter that Korda wrote in the spring of 1962 ended: "Best to Sandy. There are golf-widows, and fishing-widows and poker-widows. There aren't all that many historian-widows, and at least you can do a lot of it at home"

Dick Watt kept his side career as a writer relatively quiet until his first book was published. He once joked to Don Murray: "Everybody knows a salesman can't write a book, and I wasn't going to tell anyone about it and look ridiculous."

Same.

Epilogue

I met Michael Korda.

    He spoke in New York City in October 2017. The distinguished editor is also an accomplished author, and at the age of eighty-four, he had recently published his 20th book: *Alone: Britain, Churchill, and Dunkirk: Defeat into Victory.*

    Chartwell Booksellers – a bookshop that specializes in all things Churchill – hosted a late-afternoon reading and discussion with the author. The event was attended by a rather senior and decidedly reverent crowd of about 75 people. Many were in town for the annual gathering of the International Churchill Society, and the reading served as an unofficial kickoff for the society's three-day conference. My work colleague Noah Sferra, a like-minded history and music buff, joined me in the audience.

    Rather than read from his book, Michael Korda shared some of his raw content - stories about Dunkirk and the early days of World War II in his native Britain. He comes from a family of filmmakers and actresses; uncles of his were friends of Winston Churchill, Lord Beaverbrook, and other members of the wartime British Government. He spliced his family's engaging stories into his casually prepared discussion as well as into his answers to the audience questions at the end of the session. As the Q&A ended, we were told that Mr. Korda would sign copies of his new book inside Chartwell Booksellers, whose door opened directly into the atrium where we had settled in temporary chairs for a fast-paced hour.

I literally ran from the atrium and into the bookstore, purchased a copy of *Alone*, and was the third person in line for a signature.

As he signed my book, I asked Mr. Korda: "Is it OK if I ask you a question that's also a very unfair test of your memory." He looked up, smiled, and said he would be happy to give it a try.

I asked if he remembered an author whom he edited in the sixties named Dick Watt. He paused thoughtfully for a second, and then his already twinkling eyes further brightened.

The name clearly rang a distant bell. His recollection geared up haltingly, and then fell into place. "Didn't he write about the Polish Army?" I said that he had and reminded him that he also wrote about the French mutiny and about Versailles.

"I do remember. It was a very enjoyable experience working with him." He said "very enjoyable experience" with warm emphasis.

I know he was not patronizing me with a faux recollection. Michael Korda remembered Dick Watt's book about the Polish Army - the third book that he had written - without a prompt from me. His remembrance of Richard M Watt and the time in which they worked together clearly was the enjoyable and memorable experience that I hoped and expected it would have been, even after the passage of fifty years.

Author's Note & Acknowledgements

When my sister Mary learned that I intended to write a book, she gave me a thoughtful gift: a book about how to write a book. That was a number of years ago. So many years ago, in fact, that when I recently mentioned to Mary how her gift helped inspire me, she had absolutely no recollection of ever giving me that book. You might now understand how long it has taken me to finish writing *this* book.

Like the runner who staggers to the end of a marathon many hours after the winner rips through the tape, I have been blessed by family and friends who patiently lined the route and cheered me all the way to the finish line.

The longest and most loyal, of course is my wife, Barbara. It is only because I am not a historian that Michael Korda's "historian widow" honorific does not perfectly apply to Barbara. Instead, you should know how thankful and blessed I am that she endured the deficit of time and attention that I imposed as I worked on my book while she managed our home, our family – generally everything in our life - and enabled me to focus on my often-selfish avocation. The absolute luckiest strike in my life was meeting, loving, and marrying Barbara.

Our two kids, Billy and Brittany encourage and reward me with the loudest and most consistent cheers. Billy and Britt are my greatest source of joy and pride. A parent could not be any more blessed than I am.

My late mother, Eileen Ferrick Whiteside, the daughter of two Irish immigrants, encouraged everything I love about words, about reading, and about writing. More than anyone in the world, she would love that I have written a book. I am very fortunate that mom's brother, Uncle Dick Ferrick, exposed me to the *New Yorker*, to the author John McPhee, and to the craft of writing. Miraculously, those passions took hold, but UD's love for the Dukes of Dixieland and Richard Nixon did not.

I do not wear this on my sleeve - and only rarely on t-shirts or hats - but my time in South Bend, Indiana at the University of Notre Dame, significantly shaped the rest of my life. I owe that to my dad, the real Bill Whiteside, who graduated from ND 25 years before me and who provided my brothers and sisters and me with a lifetime of incredible family adventures and indelible memories. The fact that my research visits rekindled the indescribable (and I'm supposed to be a writer) feelings of comfort when I'm on campus, added to the wonder of this adventure.

This book tells of how I learned to research and write a book while selling software and running a business. I was a very contented one-man business during my first few years. I needed quite a bit of unsubtle coaxing from Steve Johnston (he of the "… but you're a complete idiot if you try" inspirational sendoff when I headed off to sell his software) to add a second person to my company. But once I did - and my little enterprise grew over time into a team (in every sense of the word) - my business thrived, and my life was enriched. I honestly still shake my head at my good fortune in getting to work with Dan Doran, Kristi

Gieseke, Matt Hoffman, John Koroluk, Dan Kroft, Mark Lania, Joe Cunningham, Keith McAlpine, Nancy Pastore, John Richard, Rhonda Roos, Paul Secraw (my longtime business partner), Noah Sferra, Katie Ward, and Peter Day.

This book draws on the experience, talent, and writing of others. I am grateful to those mentioned below for their kind permission to quote from their work.

Art Sobczak for permission to quote from our conversation about publishers and what they seek from writers.

Christopher Somerville for permission to quote from his email message in which he granted me privileged access to his grandfather's restricted papers in the Churchill Archives Centre.

Lin Doyle for her permission to quote from the papers of her father, Richard M. Watt, at the Howard Gotlieb Archival Research Center, Boston University.

Paul Reid for his permission to share the story he told about how William Manchester encouraged him to write the final volume of his *Last Lion* trilogy.

Rick Atkinson for permission to use the written excerpts from his answer to my question after his talk about *The Guns of Last Light* at the Politics and Prose bookstore.

An excerpt from the obituary of Ben Coutts is published with the permission if © Telegraph Media Group Limited.

Quotation from "Democratizing the Oxford English Dictionary: The longtime editor of the OED takes readers inside the lexicographical revolution." Reprinted with permission of The Wall Street Journal, Copyright © 2016 Dow Jones & Company, Inc. All Rights Reserved Worldwide License Number 5373800363983.

Quotation from "Review – Books: Anxieties Immune to Reason" Reprinted with permission of The Wall Street Journal, Copyright © 2018 Dow Jones & Company, Inc. All Rights Reserved Worldwide License Number 5373791214166.

"The Secret Life of Richard Watt," Dartmouth Alumni Magazine, March 1963 issue.

For quotes reproduced from the writings of Winston S. Churchill: Reproduced with permission of Curtis Brown, London on behalf of The Estate of Winston S. Churchill © The Estate of Winston S. Churchill

The Fall of France: The Nazi Invasion of 1940, Julian Jackson, Copyright Julian Jackson 2003, Reproduced with permission of the Licensor through PLSclear.

Good Prose: The Art of Nonfiction, Tracy Kidder and Richard Todd, 2013, Penguin Random House

The Maisky Diaries: The Wartime Revelations of Stalin's Ambassador to London, Gabriel Gordotetsky (editor), 2016, Yale University Press.

Perennial Seller: The Art of Making and Marketing Work That Lasts, Ryan Holiday, 2017, Penguin Random House, LLC

Superforecasting: The Art and Science of Prediction, Philip E. Tetlock, 2015, Penguin Random House LLC.

With Wings Like Eagles: The Untold Story of the Battle of Britain, Michael Korda, 2009, HarperCollins Publishers.

The photograph of General Edward Louis Spears with General Charles de Gaulle is licensed from Getty Images. The photographs of Admiral Francois Darlan, Admiral Sir James Somerville, and Paul Reynaud are licensed from Alamy, Inc.

Notes

ABBREVIATIONS USED IN THESE NOTES

ADM   The National Archives, Admiralty Officers' Service Records

BU / RMW   Richard M. Watt Collection, Howard Gotleib Archival Research Center, Boston University, Boston

CHUR / SMVL   Admiral Sir James Somerville's papers at the Churchill Archives Centre, Cambridge

FDR   Franklin D, Roosevelt Library, Hyde Park, New York

Booklet   *1918 and 1940: The Signing of the Armistice in the Forest Glade at Compiegne*, A booklet that is sold in the Armistice Museum

Bullitt   *For the President: Personal and Secret, Correspondence Between Franklin D. Roosevelt and William C. Bullitt*

Secret Life   The Secret Life of Richard Watt, Dartmouth Alumni Magazine, March 1963

The Second World War series, by Winston S. Churchill, is cited as follows:
WSC 1   Volume 1. *The Gathering Storm*
WSC 2   Volume 2. *Their Finest Hour*

P&P RA Video   A video of Rick Atkinson's talk about *The Guns at Last Light* from May 18, 2013 can be viewed on the Politics and Prose YouTube Channel: https://www.youtube.com/watch?v=yb51OSLqZmc

INTRODUCTION

1   **Every author briefly mentioned Churchill's pivotal role**: As I note in Chapter 1: "It's typically addressed in a few paragraphs; occasionally it gets several pages. Andrew Roberts tells the story across two of the 982 pages in his definitive *Churchill: Walking with Destiny*. Paul Reid covers the buildup, the carnage, and the aftermath in six of the 1,053 pages in *Defender of the Realm, 1940-1965*. In addition, in his *Churchill: A Biography*, Roy Jenkins told the story across four of his 912 pages.

1   **... ended with the Royal Navy killing more French seamen than the Germans killed during the entire war**: This statement originally appeared in what historian John Toland termed a "quasi diary" of French

journalist Alfred Fabre-Luce. It is referenced in Toland's Adolf Hitler (p. 849) and in Alexander Werth's France: 1940-1955 (p. 9)

2   ... writing a paper on how to improve forecast accuracy: I sold sales forecasting software for 39 years. If, by chance you're interested in a free copy of my "42 Principles of Forecasting" e-book, email me at bill.whiteside@perfectlytruestory.com

2   a reading by a Pulitzer-Prize-winning historian: P&P RA Video

2   ... a pilgrimage to a remote site outside of Paris: The story of this trip is detailed in "Chapter 22: Compiegne"

2   "the greatest dishonor of all time": Before the Germans presented their armistice terms to the French at Compiegne on June 21, 1940, General Wilhelm Keitel recited a preamble of grievances. It was stated that the armistice agreement to which the French subjected Germany at that same location in 1918 was "the greatest dishonor of all time."

4   Last Lion Trilogy: The Last Lion Trilogy comprises: Volume 1: *Visions of Glory 1874-1935*, Volume 2: *Alone 1932-1940*, and Volume 3: *Defender of the Realm 1940-1965*. The first two volumes were written by William Manchester. The third volume was written by William Manchester and Paul Reid

4   Paul Reid subsequently shared with me: I heard Paul Reid describe his discussion with William Manchester at a conference of the International Churchill Society. When I asked Paul to clarify the details of the conversation, he very kindly provided the details in an email.

5   ... published as a collaboration between Manchester and Reid: Paul Reid devotes the first two-plus pages of his Author's Note at the beginning of *Defender of the Realm, 1940-1965* to a description of his collaboration with William Manchester. It is an especially fascinating account for anyone with an interest in how history is written.

5... audio version of Perennial Seller: The unabridged audio version of Perennial Seller, which is read by its author Ryan Holiday and runs for 7 hours, can be found at audible.com

5   "Who is this thing for?": Holiday, *Perennial Seller*, 45

6   "Take away this pudding, it has no theme": So many "Churchill quotes" are either mis-attributed or manufactured that I default to distrust-but-verify mode. My go-to source for validation of Churchill quotes and stories is the winstonchurchill.org website of the International Churchill Society. According to a statement found at - https://winstonchurchill.org/resources/reference/frequently-asked-questions/personal-life/ - this quote " is probably true, though not attributed"

6   "It's not what a book is, it's what a book does ...: Holiday, *Perennial Seller*, 48

6   "Just as we should ask 'who is this for?' we must also ...: Holiday, *Perennial Seller*, 48

CHAPTER 1: THIS IS NOT THAT BOOK

9   Andrew Roberts tells the story: Roberts, *Churchill: Walking with Destiny*, 573-574.

9   Paul Reid covers the buildup, the carnage, and the aftermath: *Manchester and Reid, Winston Spencer Churchill, Defender of the Realm, 1940-1965*, 105-110.

10 "For as long as heroes are written about ...": Bridges and Kimball (ed.), *Athwart History: Half a Century of Polemics, Animadversions, and Illuminations, A William F. Buckley Jr. Omnibus*, 277.

10 bitter opposition of Britain's senior naval officers: Multiple sources describe the opposition of British naval officers to the planned action against the French Fleet. A good starting point is *The Somerville Papers*, edited by Michael Simpson, pages 88-91.

10 unanimous and boisterous cheers of approval: Colville, *The Fringes of Power*, (Diary entry for July 4, 1940), 184-185.

CHAPTER 2: WHAT DO I DON'T HAVE

16 City Books: As you can tell, I love used bookstores. There used to be several on East Carson St. in Pittsburgh. I had a number of customers in the Pittsburgh area, and our daughter Brittany attended the University of Pittsburgh. Sadly, all of those stores have either closed or moved on. Fortunately, City Books lives on - at its new location: 908 Galveston Ave. in Pittsburgh, as well as at citybookspgh.com. When I checked the current status of City Books, I found an article about the closing of the East Carson St. location. In the photo that accompanied the article, I recognized Chong Ae Gelblum, one of the original co-owners, and my partner in conversation about my list of used books. That was an unexpected delight.

CHAPTER 3: BEN COUTTS' OBITUARY AND THE STATUE WITH THE BLOOD RED HANDS

19 BRITISH SEIZE OF SINK BULK OF FRENCH FLEET: *New York Times*, Friday, July 5, 1940, p. 1.

19 NAVY TAKES OR SINKS FRENCH WARSHIPS: *The Daily Telegraph* (London), Friday, July 5, 1940, p.1. "Takes ..." refers to other ports, mostly in British or British-controlled harbors, where Britain swiftly assumed control of French ships.

20 L'ODIEUSE AGRESSION DE L'ANGLETTERRE: *Le Matin* (Paris), Saturday, July 6, 1940, p.1.

20 BRITAIN SEIZES FRENCH NAVY IN BATTLE: *Lancaster Intelligencer Journal* (Pennsylvania), Friday, July 5, 1940, p.1.

20 "a huge man seldom seen out of kilt": Ben Coutts' obituary appeared in January 3, 2004 edition of *The Telegraph*. It's a fascinating read and can be found at: https://www.telegraph.co.uk/news/obituaries/1450792/Ben-Coutts.htm. I found additional details on his life in his biography *Bothy to Big Ben ... and beyond*.

21 the Laconia was torpedoed by a German U-boat, U-156: Peillard, *The Laconia Affair*, 11.

21 1,800 Italian prisoners of war: Peillard, *The Laconia Affair*, 49.

21 **1,113 who survived the Laconia's sinking**: Peillard, *The Laconia Affair*, 215.

22 **"The French sailors, Coutts remembered ..."**: See Ben Coutts' obituary above.

22 **Francois Darlan ... pressed for a declaration of war**: Shirer, *The Collapse of the Third Republic*, 918

22 **"I've been betrayed by my brothers in arms"**: Ibid.

22 **specifically for the bombing of the British naval base at Gibraltar**: Ibid.

23 **"We have just lost one war. Are we about to start and lose another"**: Collier, *1940: The Avalanche*, 156.

23 **a weak, symbolic bombing run**: Playfair, *The Mediterranean and Middle East, Vol I, The Early Successes Against Italy (to May 1941)*, 142-143.

23 **"England was beaten, and it was only ..."**: Bloch, *Ribbentrop*. 313.

24 **"For the moment it proves the fighting spirit ..."**: Gibson (ed.), *The Ciano Diaries, 1939-1943*, 273.

24 **"served forcibly to underscore ..."**: Sherwood, *Roosevelt and Hopkins, An Intimate History*, 149.

24 **It is with sincere sorrow that I must now announce**: Churchill, Winston, (1940, July 4), *French Fleet*, [Hansard], (Vol. 1043).

25 **I fear the loss of life among the French**: Churchill, Winston, (1940, July 4), *French Fleet*, [Hansard], (Vol. 1049).

25 **I leave the judgement of our action, with confidence**: Churchill, Winston, (1940, July 4), *French Fleet*, [Hansard], (Vol. 1049).

25 **"loud, powerful and unanimous ovation"**: Maisky, *The Maisky Diaries*, 290.

25 **"Churchill lowered his head and tears ran down his cheeks"**: Ibid.

25 **"Churchill has once more shown himself as ..."**: *The Daily Express* (London), Friday, July 5, 1940, p.4.

26 **Only two Britons are honored**: I spent hours researching statues of Britons in Paris and was only able to identify the statues of Winston Churchill and King Edward VII. As with every other statement of fact, I am, of course, open to being corrected with specific information.

26 **The $400,000 cost of the statue**: From the article "Churchill Returns to Paris," BBC News, November 11, 1999. The article notes that the cost of the statue was £250,000. The average exchange rate in 1999 was 1.62 USD to the British Pound.

26 **The statue was desecrated during the night of November 2, 1999**: Finest Hour Magazine, No. 104. Autumn 1999, p. 8.

27 **"no act was ever more necessary"**: Churchill, *The Second World War*, 232.

CHAPTER 4: A MOST DISREPUTABLE SOURCE

30 **My Google search immediately introduced me**: A Google search for "David Irving Holocaust Denial" (without the quote marks) will produce a long list of articles and papers. A BBC article, titled "The true story behind denying the Holocaust" provides a good starting point. It

can be found online at https://www.bbc.com/news/entertainment-arts-38758249.

31   **landmark libel trial in Great Britain**: Likewise, a Google search for "David Irving loses libel suit" (without the quote marks) will produce a long list of articles and papers. The article from *The Guardian* at this link - titled "Irving loses Holocaust libel case" is a good starting point: theguardian.com/books/2000/apr/11/irving.uk.

31   **Denial**: The official website for the movie "Denial" provides an abundance of information about the movie (including a trailer), as well as the stories behind the movie. You can find it here: https://bleecker-streetmedia.com/denial.

31   **her book *Denying the Holocaust***: Deborah Lipstadt's *book Denying the Holocaust: The Growing Assault on Truth and Memory* is available on Amazon.com and at other booksellers. Ms. Lipstadt has other books in which she has written more broadly about Antisemitism and about the Holocaust, as well as a book about the trial of Adolf Eichmann.

31   **That $3 million obligation**: An article from the Jewish Telegraphic Agency titled "Holocaust denier faces bankruptcy" discusses the financial obligations incurred by David Irving in the aftermath of his lawsuit against Debora Lipstadt. You can find it here: https://www.jta.org/2000/05/09/lifestyle/holocaust-denier-faces-bankruptcy.

31   **Evans' Third Reich Trilogy**: *The Coming of the Third Reich, The Third Reich in Power, The Third Reich at War.*

31   **"Not one of his books, speeches or articles, not one paragraph**: This quote is taken from the "Expert Witness Report by Richard J. Evans FBA, Professor of Modern History, University of Cambridge." It can be found here: https://www.hdot.org/evans/#evans_6.html.

CHAPTER 5: THE STORIES BEHIND TOUCHDOWN JESUS

34   **named in memory of Father Auguste Lemonnier**: The origins of the library at Notre Dame are described here: http://archives.nd.edu/library.htm.

34   **475,000 books**: http://archives.nd.edu/about/news/index.php/2014/memorial-library-dedication-1964/.

34   **Notre Dame's student body grew by more than 90%**: ND's enrollment grew from 4,979 to 9,600 students between 1952 and 1987. I could only find these numbers in Wikipedia. Yes, I know. https://en.wikipedia.org/wiki/University_of_Notre_Dame#cite_note-76.

34   **the University's endowment grew almost forty-fold**: O'Brien, *Hesburgh, A Biography*, 1.

34   **all-male school welcomed co-education**: https://50goldenyears.nd.edu/news-and-features/almost-mary-ed-near-merger-ended-with-notre-dame-welcoming-women-50-years-ago/.

34   **his passionate involvement in America's civil rights movement**: Father Hesburgh was a member of the U.S. Commission on Civil Rights. One of the most iconic photos from his life shows him standing next to the Reverend Martin Luther King, arms linked, at a civil rights

crusade in Chicago in June 1964. https://hesburgh.nd.edu/fr-teds-
life/champion-of-civil-rights/civil-rights-commission/.

34   **thousands of Carling Black Label beer cases**: Notre Dame maintains
the "Hesburgh Portal" - aka a website about "Father Hesburgh's Life &
Legacy." The story of the transfer of books from Lemonnier to the
new Memorial Library is told here: https://hesburghpor-
tal.nd.edu/story-administration-library-1.html. "Why Carling Black
Label cases?" is still an unsolved mystery to me.

35   **makeshift roller-coaster-like conveyor**: "Father Hesburgh's Life &
Legacy." The story of the transfer of books from Lemonnier to the
new Memorial Library is told here: https://hesburghpor-
tal.nd.edu/story-administration-library-1.html.

35   **"books of all special fields regardless of age"**: Notre Dame Alumnus
Magazine, Vol. 41, No. 6, Year-End 1963. p. 6.

35   **"book collectors who could be persuaded"**: Ibid.

35   **"and take advantage of the tax angle"**: Ibid.

35   **inspired visions of a grain elevator**: "Father Hesburgh's Life & Legacy." Father Hesburgh mentioned the grain elevator story in a speech
that is described here: https://hesburghportal.nd.edu/story-admin-
istration-library-2.html

35   **the Central Library of the Universidad Nacional Autonoma de Mexico**: Schmitt, *Words of Life*, p. 53.

36   **$8 million budget**: Ibid, p. 30.

36   **$200,000 donation from Mr. and Mrs. Howard V. Phalin**: Ibid, p. 54

36   **Millard Sheets produced a massive work of art**: Ibid.

36   **unveiled and dedicated on May 7, 1964**: Ibid, p. 2.

36   **he jokingly noted was called "Ted's Mahal"**: Notre Dame Alumnus
Magazine, Vol. 42, No. 4, Aug-Sept 1964.

37   **The Word of Life**: Schmitt, *Words of Life*, p. 67.

37   **"I could hardly be called a pillar of the Church"**: Jenkins, *Churchill, A
Biography*, p. 49.

37   **a light that shines in the dark**: The quote, "I could hardly be called a
pillar of the Church" appears early in Roy Jenkins' landmark *Churchill, A Biography*. Jenkins most surely did not have the Book of John in
mind, but I could not help noticing that the title of the 250-page section in which he tells the story of the critical War years (1939-1945)
was titled "The Saviour of His Country and the Light of the World?"
Jenkins, *Churchill, A Biography*, p. 549.

38   **Our father, a former Notre Dame quarterback**: Notre Dame's unde-
feated football team was voted national champions at the end of the
1949 season. *The South Bend Tribune's* recap of ND's 28-7 victory
over the University of Iowa on November 19, 1949 included a paragraph that described the action after ND scored its final touchdown
with 37 seconds to play on a pass from starting quarterback Bob Williams: "In the remaining remnants of time Iowa was still trying to
score but a Drahn pass was intercepted by Quarterback Bill Whiteside
and that about ended the fracas." Like many players of that era our
dad played both offense and defense. Much later in life, when shown
this clipping, he proudly joked that not many players could claim to
have ended a fracas, especially a fracas at Notre Dame.

38   **The incoming class of about 2,000 freshmen included 125 women**: I was there that first year! Also: https://50goldenyears.nd.edu/news-and-features/almost-mary-ed-near-merger-ended-with-notre-dame-welcoming-women-50-years-ago/.

40   **we watched Pitt beat Notre Dame in quadruple overtime**: https://pittnews.com/article/22685/archives/south-bend-slam-pitt-takes-down-irish/.

41   **Spears' first wife, Mary Borden**: Egremont, *Under Two Flags: The Life of Major General Sir Edward Spears*, p. 77

41   **a biography written by Alain Darlan**: Darlan, *L'Amiral Darlan Parle.*

42   **Dewey Decimal System**: Although it is now called the Dewey Decimal Classification System, my mind still defaults to the Dewey Decimal System of my childhood. John P. Comaromi, Associate Professor, School of Librarianship at Western Michigan University in Kalamazoo, Michigan, has written an interesting and widely sourced paper on Melvil Dewey and his system. http://hdl.handle.net/2142/1778.

CHAPTER 6: BOOKEYE

45   **Extraordinary character**: James, *Chips: The Diaries of Sir Henry Channon*, 255-256.

48   **Bookeye** is a product of Digital Library Systems Group (DLSG), a subsidiary of Image Access, Inc. in Boca Raton, FL. You can find more information at www.imageaccess.com.

CHAPTER 7: FDR LIBRARY, HYDE PARK, NY

52   **Prominent visitors included Winston Churchill**: Winston Churchill visited Hyde Park for two days of meetings with FDR during a trip to the U.S. in mid-June 1942.

52   **King George, VI and Queen Elizabeth**: King George VI and Queen Elizabeth visited the U.S. in early June 1939. In addition to the time they spent in New York City and Washington, DC, the Royal couple also spent a relatively informal two days with Franklin and Eleanor Roosevelt at their home in Hyde Park. Details: https://www.fdrlibrary.org/royal-visit.

52   **FDR and Eleanor Roosevelt are buried on the grounds**: https://www.nps.gov/places/burial-site-of-franklin-and-eleanor-roosevelt.htm.

52   **as is Fala, FDR's legendary Scottish Terrier**: https://fdr.blogs.archives.gov/2017/10/12/the-adventures-of-fala-first-dog-the-case-of-the-dog-who-didnt-bark-on-the-boat/.

54   **In this short letter, he [Lord Lothian] mentioned**: Letter, Lord Lothian to Franklin D. Roosevelt, December 21, 1938, Pres's Secry's File, Diplomatic Correspondence, FDR.

54   **Roosevelt wrote this in pencil**: Ibid

55   "All over the world people will remember": Letter, Alain Darlan to El-
      eanor Roosevelt on second anniversary of FDR's death - April 10,
      1947, Pres's Secry's File, Diplomatic Correspondence, FDR.

56   "The French General Staff expects an attack ...": Letter, William C.
      Bullitt, Jr. to Judge R, Walton Moore, April 18, 1940, p. 2, Pres's Se-
      cry's File, Diplomatic Correspondence, FDR.

57   "England will never give up as long as he remains a power ...": Letter,
      Joseph P. Kennedy to Cordell Hull, May 15, 1940, Section 1, Pres's Se-
      cry's File, Diplomatic Correspondence, FDR.

58   "the lady love of each hates the lady love of the other": Letter, Wil-
      liam C. Bullitt, Jr. to Judge R, Walton Moore, April 18, 1940, p. 2,
      Pres's Secry's File, Diplomatic Correspondence, FDR.

59   Erik Larson on his visits to archives: In a June 4, 2015 blog post titled
      "It's All in the Details," Eric Larson begins: "A surprising number of
      readers - meaning more than one - have expressed an interest in how
      I go about organizing the materials I collect while researching my
      books." I - of course - was fascinated by one of my favorite writer's
      accounts of how he organizes his research. https://eriklar-
      sonbooks.com/2015/06/its-all-in-the-details/.

CHAPTER 8: INSCRUTABLY INSCRIBED

No Notes.

CHAPTER 9: MUG SHOTS

67   his secret "Xavier 377" signature: Brown, *The Road to Oran*, 62.

68   Somerville played a largely unsung role: Woodward, *Ramsay at War*,
      53

68   rowing his 16-foot skiff: Macintyre, *Fighting Admiral*, 26 & 144.

69   You are charged with one of the most disagreeable tasks: WSC 2,
      235.

69   "he could pour forth the language of a fisherman": CHUR / SMVL
      8/16, Recollections of Somerville by Commander Edward William
      Boucher Edwards.

73   his bovine blue eyes: Spears, *Assignment to Catastrophe, Volume 2: The
      Fall of France, June 1940*, 17.

CHAPTER 10: WORDS OF EXTINCTION

76   "a biography of each word": Wall Street Journal, review of "The Word
      Detective" by John Simpson, November 4, 2016

77   As nearly as possible the date of its birth or first known appearance:
      Ibid

CHAPTER 11: THE CHURCHILL ARCHIVES CENTRE, UNIVERSITY OF CAMBRIDGE

83 **"Weekly Review of the War" broadcasts**: The BBC presented a weekly 15-minute "War Commentary" by members of Britain's armed services. Admiral Somerville made several broadcasts after being asked to fill in for Major-General Sir Ernest Swinton, who was ill. Admiral Somerville's introduction to his initial broadcast offers a sense of his colloquial approach: "I'm here tonight, at pretty short notice, to take the place of General Swinton, whose illness we all most sincerely regret. I've no idea why I've been chosen for this job. Sailors are proverbially a pretty dumb lot and, by common report, when they do give tongue their language is not always suitable for the microphone."

CHAPTER 12: PERFECTLY ADEQUATE

88 **Christopher Somerville letter**: From his website – christophersomerville.co.uk: "Christopher Somerville is Walking Correspondent of The Times. His long-running 'A Good Walk' series appears every Saturday in the Times Weekend section. He has written some 40 books, many about his travels on foot in various parts of the world, and thousands of articles in all the national newspapers. He has had two collections of poetry published. He loves music, and sometimes tries to play it."

CHAPTER 13: WRITING PRACTICE

89 **Dr. Atul Gawande's 5 Rules**: Dr. Atul Gawande's Harvard Medical School commencement address is available here: http://boutlis.com/files/05-06-09-Five%20rules%20by%20Atul%20Gawande.pdf.

90 **"because it enabled me to fly under the radar."**: From "Atul Gawande Rocks in the O.R.," New York Times, April 3 ,2007.

90 **"We learn new skills by doing. We improve those skills by doing more."**: Tetlock, *Superforecasting*, 178.

91 **99-year-old-family-owned-dairy**: When I tell people that I worked for a dairy in Lancaster County Pennsylvania, the common perception is that I worked for Turkey Hill. I worked for a smaller company - Penn Dairies - whose excellent ice cream was sold under the Pensupreme brand. There is absolutely no correlation here, but Penn Dairies was sold several times and the Pensupreme brand was retired a few years after I left to start my software business.

91 **Demand Solutions**: Demand Solutions is the name of the sales forecasting, supply planning (and much more) software that is developed and supported by Demand Management, Inc, a wholly owned subsidiary of Logility, Inc.

91 **Steve Johnston**: Steve Johnston is entirely responsible for the second two-thirds of my business career. You can get a sense of this

incredibly generous, talented, and interesting man in the tribute that I wrote a short time after Steve passed away: https://www.perfectly-truestory.com/bw-writing/in-tribute-to-steve-johnston-a-software-pioneer-and-a-true-character-1.

93   **Manage What Matters: The Pareto Principle, ABC Analysis and How to Manage by Exception**: If by chance you are interested in a pdf copy of this or any other papers from my past life, just let me know by email. My address is bill.whiteside@perfectlytruestory.com.

93   **In 1889, at the age of 41**: http://statprob.com/encyclopedia/Vilfredo-FederigoSamasoPARETO.html.

94   **80% of horse races are won by 20% of jockeys**: FlatStats analyzed 258,123 horses in 23,343 races for an article titled: "Pareto Principle in Horse Racing." https://www.flatstats.co.uk/blog/turf/80_20_rule_ap-plied_to_horse_racing.html.

94   **80% of all flight delays occur in 18% of major U.S. airports**: When I traveled more extensively for business and flew on a weekly basis, it just seemed obvious that some airports were more prone to flight de-lays than others. I downloaded a table of flight delays from the web-site of the Federal Aviation Administration and ran the math in Excel to generate this calculation and prove my theory.

94   **A year after the State of Colorado legalized marijuana**: I could not re-locate the original source for this stat, but I verified these numbers for a presentation a bit more than a year after Colorado legalized ma-rijuana use.

95   *The Signal and the Noise: Why So Many Predictions Fail – But Some Don't*: by Nate Silver, published by Penguin Press in January 2012

95   **12 Supply Chain Forecasting Lessons from The Signal and the Noise**: Another papers from my past life. Contact me if you would like a copy.

96   **My LinkedIn profile**: LinkedIn is a professional and business-oriented social media platform. I would be happy to connect with anyone who sends me an invitation. My profile address is: https://www.linkedin.com/in/bill-whiteside-lancaster-pa/

96   **Flight 93 memorial in Shanksville, Pennsylvania**: I am normally a slow writer, and I tend to have an affinity for long titles. This piece – simply titled "Shanksville, PA" – flowed quickly after I accidentally found myself near the original homespun memorial to a group of he-roes from September 11, 2001. https://www.perfectly-truestory.com/bw-writing/shanksville-pa

96   **my encounter with Rollerblades, angels, and cow selfies**: "The An-gels of Dairy Road" is one of the best – and without doubt the most uplifting – pieces that I have ever written. https://www.perfectly-truestory.com/bw-writing/the-angels-of-dairy-road

96   **Honor Flight**: From honorflight.org: "The Honor Flight Network is a national network of independent Hubs working together to honor our nation's veterans with an all-expenses paid trip to the memorials in Washington, D.C., a trip many of our veterans may not otherwise be able to take."

101 **"These German pilots all became available"**: WSC 2, 182.

101　**The Royal Air Force estimates that**: The Secretary of State for Air (Mr. Philip Noel-Baker, (1947, May 14), *Battle of Britain (Enemy Losses)*, [Hansard], (Vol. 1483}. As the Secretary of State for Air reported to the House of Commons, the R.A.F. estimated that "2,692 enemy aircraft had been destroyed." He added that "German records show that, in fact, 2,376 of their aircraft had been put out of action; of these, 1,733 were destroyed and 642 were damaged."

CHAPTER 14: KEEPING TRACK & KEEPING SCORE

106　**Scrivener**: James Fallows, Seth Mnookin, and legions of other established authors swear by Scriver. I'm so conformable with Microsoft Office that Scrivener was not a good enough fit for me to make a switch. I've read nothing but good things about Scrivener, and the software's fans are quite passionate. You can learn more at www.literatureandlatte.com/scrivener/overview.

CHAPTER 15: TOUT LE MONDE SAIT ... (*EVERYBODY KNOWS ...*)

113　**"Two main reasons have led me to write this book"**: Darlan, *L'Amiral Darlan Parle*, 7. The original French text from which this moderately mangled English translation was generated by Google Translate appears on page 7 of *L'Amiral Darlan Parle* by Alain Darlan. The original French text reads : « Deux raisons principales m'ont conduit a ecrire ce livre, par lequel se fait enfin entendre, dix ans apres sa disparition tragique, le voix de Francois Darlan, Amiral de la Flotte et Vice-President du Conseil ... mon pere. »

CHAPTER 16: THREE LOATHSOME FIGURES

120　**von Brickendrop**: Evans, *The Third Reich*, 630.
120　**Ribbentrop sharply kicked his heels**: Ibid.
120　**"the most brainless boy in his class"**: Bloch, *Ribbentrop, A Biography*, 5.
120　**"pushiness and vanity"**: Ibid.
120　**"One could not talk to Ribbentrop"**: von Ribbentrop, *The Ribbentrop Memoirs*, x.
120　**"a shrill bully"**: Ibid, xi.
120　**"a combination of vanity, stupidity and superficiality"**: Henderson, Failure of a Mission, 109.
120　**"there is no hell in Dante's inferno"**: Ibid
120　**"I honestly hated him."**: von Ribbentrop, *The Ribbentrop Memoirs*, x.
120　**"Germany's No. 1 parrot"**: Ibid.
120　**"He is such an imbecile that he is a freak of nature."**: Ibid.
120　**"a dangerous fool"**: Schmidt, *Hitler's Interpreter*, 33.
120　**"If Hitler was displeased with him"**: Ibid.
121　**adopted him in 1925**: Shirer, *The Nightmare Years: 1930-1940*, 196

121 "Of all my sons in law": Kelly, *22 Cells in Nuremberg*, 95

121 five sons, one of whom they named Adolf: Bloch, Ribbentrop, A Biography, 14-15.

121 Ribbentrop is the only member of the Nazi party: Ibid, 86.

121 "was not accompanied by the slightest comprehension": Shirer, *The Nightmare Years: 1930-1940*, 196.

122 "I often saw him keep at it so long": von Ribbentrop, *The Ribbentrop Memoirs*, xi.

122 his son Rudolph had been rejected for admission to Eton: Bloch, *Ribbentrop: A Biography*, 101.

122 convinced the German Foreign Minister: Ibid, 261.

122 Ribbentrop refused to meet with the British Ambassador: Schmidt, *Hitler's Interpreter*, 157.

123 Ribbentrop quietly replied: Ibid, 158.

123 "If we lose this war": Ibid

123 "That was the last time I saw Herr von Ribbentrop before he was hanged.": WSC 1, 272.

123 Wikipedia entry for Joachim von Ribbentrop": https://en.wikipedia.org/wiki/Joachim_von_Ribbentrop

123 any of the other nine German war criminals: The nine other men who followed Ribbentrop to the Gallows on October 16, 1946 were: Hans Frank, Wilhelm Frick, Alfred Jodl, Ernst Kaltenbrunner, Wilhelm Keitel, Alfred Rosenberg, Fritz Sauckel, Arthur Seyss-Inquart, and Julius Streicher. The ten men were hanged individually over roughly a two-hour period. Hermann Goering, who was originally scheduled to be the first man to hang, cheated the hangman by biting into a concealed potassium cyanide capsule on the eve of the scheduled executions.

124 American emissary Sumner Welles later noted: Welles, *The Time for Decision*, 122.

124 "Tell Paul that we must give up": Bois, *Truth on the Tragedy of France*, 355.

125 "short, homely, plain, dark": *Time Magazine*, August 5, 1940, 23.

125 "chattered like a magpie": Sheean, *Between Thunder and the Sun*, 114.

125 "untidy" and "devoid of charm": Spears: *Assignment to Catastrophe, Vol. I, Prelude to Dunkirk, June 1939 - May 1940*, 90-91.

125 "behaved at times like a sovereign": Sheean, *Between Thunder and the Sun*, 107.

125 "generals, high officers, members of the": Ibid, 110.

125 "Wait a moment. I think I know where it might be.": Barber, *The Week France Fell*, 129.

125 "Chut. It was in Madame de Portes' bed.": Ibid.

125 "Ah, you don't know what a man ...": Ibid, 27.

126 "Paul Reynaud returned to Tours": Ibid, 146.

126 they also provisionally selected Reynaud: Ibid, 297.

126 Spanish authorities insisted on searching: Ibid.

126 "It's going to be most difficult to prove": Ibid, 298.

127 "The people of France deserve better": Bullitt, 453, June 6, 1940 letter from Bullitt to FDR.

127 Reynaud lost control: Barber, The Week France Fell, 299.

128 **"to throw warm bodies at"**: Williams, *Pétain: How the Hero of France Became a Convicted Traitor and Changed the Course of History*, 83.

129 **reduced the French army to impotence**: Watt, *The Kings Depart*, 68.

129 **"They call me only in catastrophes"**: Watt, *Dare Call It Treason*, 214.

129 **He mounted the hood of his car**: Watt, *Dare Call It Treason*, 222.

129 **We fight because**: Ibid, 230.

129 **554 men were condemned to death**: Smith, *England's Last War Against France: Fighting Vichy 1940-1942*, 20.

131 **if a large part of France was occupied**: Eden, *The Reckoning*, 128.

131 **"glacial and morose"**; Spears, *Assignment to Catastrophe, Vol. I, Prelude to Dunkirk, June 1939 - May 1940*, 316.

131 **"his serene acceptance of the march of adverse events"**: Shirer, *The Collapse of the Third Republic*, 749.

131 **"He looks buoyant this morning"**: Eden, *The Reckoning*, 135.

132 **"a vain, doddering old man"**: Sevareid, *Not So Wild a Dream*, 153.

132 **"I give to France the gift of my person"**: Shirer, *The Collapse of the Third Republic*, 854.

132 **He acquiesced to German demands**: Williams, *Pétain: How the Hero of France Became a Convicted Traitor and Changed the Course of History*, 220.

132 **Pétain is believed to be solely responsible**: Ibid, 175

132 **He acquiesced to the arrest**: Ibid

133 **"You're a general!"**: de Gaulle, *The Complete War Memoirs of Charles de Gaulle*, 64.

133 **Offers of asylum for the Marshal**: Williams, *Pétain: How the Hero of France Became a Convicted Traitor and Changed the Course of History*, 264.

133 **De Gaulle commuted the Marshal's sentence**: Watt, *Dare Call It Treason*, 297.

CHAPTER 17: JOURNEY TO THE EDGE OF WORD

135 **Of all the practical skills**: La Salle College High School, 1970 Blue and Gold Yearbook, p. 47.

135 **the A, S, D, L and C keys are blank**: I took a picture and preserved it on my website to prove this. https://www.perfectly-truestory.com/hows-the-book-going.

136 **had once "blown up" and old contact management program**: Sidekick, from Starfish Software, not to be confused with Borland Sidekick, a package of utilities that was better known and more widely used.

136 **A Word file is fully saturated when**: I found this information on a Microsoft site: https://docs.microsoft.com/en-us/office/troubleshoot/word/operating-parameter-limitation.

137 **There are 783,137 words in the King James version of the Bible**: I found this on a site called wordcounter.net: https://word-counter.net/blog/2015/12/08/10975_how-many-words-bible.html#.

137 **587,387 words in Tolstoy's *War and Peace*:** wordcounter.net again: https://wordcounter.net/blog/2016/10/28/102640_how-many-words-is-war-and-peace.html#.

CHAPTER 18: RICK ATKINSON – OUTLINES AND FINE BRUSHSTROKES

141 **"just over the horizon, another continent waited.":** Atkinson, *An Army at Dawn*, 541.

142 **"I'm an inveterate outliner ... and I go through ...":** From a transcript of an interview with Rick Atkinson on the C-SPAN program "Booknotes" which first aired on November 11, 2002

144 **"the army didn't really examine eyes, it just counted them.":** P&P RA Video. Quoted with permission from Rick Atkinson.

144 **His talk can be viewed on the Politics and Prose YouTube channel:** Ibid.

145 **Rick Atkinson's reply to my question:** Ibid.

CHAPTER 19: I WENT TO SCHOOL ON LAURA HILLENBRAND TOO

150 **"just studying all the writerly decisions she made":** "The Unbreakable Laura Hillenbrand," by Dorian Karchmar, *New York Times Magazine*, December 18, 2014, p. 36.

150 **"a model to aspire to" ... "I think she is the best.":** Ibid.

CHAPTER 20: EVERY SIDE OF THE STORY

154 **"the fundamental elements of a story's structure":** Kidder and Todd, *Good Prose: The Art of Nonfiction*, 40.

154 **"how do you distinguish between this that you use, and this that you don't use":** P&P RA Video.

CHAPTER 21: OH NO! I ALREADY READ THIS

157 **"I am incapable of fixing anything that isn't made of words.":** Kidder and Todd, *Good Prose: The Art of Nonfiction*, 166.

161 **"facts to love":** P&P RA Video.

CHAPTER 22: COMPIEGNE

164 **The Compagnie Internationale des Wagons-Lits:** Much of the history of the company, along with stories about the Orient Express can be found on the Wagon-Lits Diffusion website: https://www.wagons-lits-diffusion.com/en/pages/un-peu-d-histoire/orient-express-bis.html.

164   **Wagon-lit #2419D**: Booklet - *1918 and 1940: The Signing of the Armistice in the Forest Glade of Compiegne*, p. 5, (a booklet that is sold at the armistice site).

165   **"What do you want, gentlemen?"**: *Time Magazine*, July 1, 1940, p. 20.

165   **Source for dialogue**: Ibid, p. 20-21

166   **donated to France's Musee de l'Armee**: "Hitler in war, Merkel in peace: A train car for history," AP article, by Thomas Adamson, November 7, 2018. https://apnews.com/article/forests-world-war-i-germany-international-news-france-45ed2aad6c7a4261a92339db16fd3a79.

166   **Arthur Henry Fleming, an American lumber magnate**: "A.H. Fleming Dies; Aided Education." Obituary for Arthur H. Fleming, New York Times, August 12, 1940, p. 15.

167   **Marshal Foch and General Weygand were among**: Booklet, 16.

167   **Participants in the ceremonial unveiling**: Ibid, 18.

167   **67 signatures**: I counted the signatures on a PDF copy of the "Treaty of Peace with Germany (Treaty of Versailles)" that is available on the U.S. Library of Congress website: https://tile.loc.gov/storage-services/service/ll/lltreaties//lltreaties-ustbv002/lltreaties-ustbv002.pdf.

167   **"It is not a peace treaty. It is a twenty-year armistice"**: Agar, *Britain Alone: June 1940-June 1941*, 26

168   **General Maxime Weygand, who sat across**: Shirer, *The Collapse of the Third Republic*, 871.

169   **Hitler and his generals had declined France's plea**: Ibid, 864.

169   **rolled over rusty tracks**: Ibid, 871.

170   **"springy step," etc.**: Shirer, *Berlin Diary*, 420.

170   **"afire with scorn, anger, hate"**: Ibid, 422.

171   **"burning contempt for this place"**: Ibid.

172   **Keitel, who would be hanged at Nuremburg five years later**: Gilbert, *Nuremburg Diary*, 393

172   **Finally, at 8:15 that night**: Shirer, *The Collapse of the Third Republic*, 871.

173   **Marshal Foch's carriage was taken to Germany**: https://www.history.co.uk/article/the-compi%25C3%25A8gne-wagon-one-train-carriage-two-peace-treaties.

173   **dissembled into packing cases**: Booklet, 17.

173   **temporarily encased in wood for protection**: Ibid, 23

173   **conflicting stories about precisely how**: "Hitler in war, Merkel in peace: A train car for history," AP article, by Thomas Adamson, November 7, 2018. https://apnews.com/article/forests-world-war-i-germany-international-news-france-45ed2aad6c7a4261a92339db16fd3a79.

176   **"scorn, anger, hate, revenge, triumph"**: Shirer, *Berlin Diary*, 422.

176   **an exact replica of wagon-lit #2419**: Booklet, 29.

178   **Joan of Arc had been captured at Compiegne in 1430**: https://www.jeanne-darc.info/location/siege-of-compiegne/.

178   **rounds of golf had been played there during the 1900 Paris Olympics**: http://www.thegolfballfactory.com/the-golf-course/hole2/olympic-golf.htm.

178 **the Duke's son, Jean de Noailles:** Story of the Chateau: David Brown, *The Road to Oran*, p. 8; Jean de Noailles: https://castlesandcoffee-houses.com/2014/06/10/jean-de-noailles-a-hero-of-the-french-re-sistance/

CHAPTER 23: ELEVEN MEN WITH WHOM IT WOULD BE AGREEABLE TO DRINK A PINT

181 **Historian Andrew Roberts has written that Churchill and Smith:** Roberts, *Churchill: Walking with Destiny*, 150.

182 **Sir Martin Gilbert wrote that after Churchill received news:** Gilbert, *Road to Victory: Winston S. Churchill, 1941-1945*, 1341.

183 **took the opportunity to sit in the observer's seat:** CHUR / SMVL 14/3, Correspondence between Commander John Somerville and Martin Stephen about Martin Stephen's book *The Fighting Admirals*. Recollections of Somerville by Commander Edward William Boucher Edwards.

183 **have to go down each stair carefully instead of:** Macintyre, *Fighting Admiral: The Life of Admiral of the Fleet Sir James Somerville*, 83.

183 **admiral rowing his skiff around his flagship:** Ibid, 144.

183 **Invalided out of the service:** CHUR / SMVL 6/4, Correspondence with the Admiralty about Somerville's Request to be Restored to the Active List.

183 **"with only vague authority behind him":** Macintyre, *Fighting Admiral: The Life of Admiral of the Fleet Sir James Somerville*, 83

183 **"the foster-father of naval radar":** Ibid.

183 **"Inspector of Anti-Aircraft Weapons and Devices":** Pawle, *The Secret War: 1935-1945*, 31.

183 **"Departments of Wheezers and Dodgers":** Ibid, 39.

184 **played a major supporting role in the evacuation:** Macintyre, *Fighting Admiral: The Life of Admiral of the Fleet Sir James Somerville*, 52.

184 **helped sink the German battleship Bismarck:** Grenfell, *The Bismarck Episode*, 160.

184 **"What, twice a knight at your age?":** Macintyre, *Fighting Admiral: The Life of Admiral of the Fleet Sir James Somerville*, 161.

184 **Promotion to Admiral of the Fleet:** Ibid, 258.

184 **"this filthy business":** CHUR / SMVL 3/22, , Letters to His Wife, Written from Force H, July 1940 - Jan 1941.

184 **"bitter sadness and disgust":** Simpson (ed.), *The Somerville Papers*, 111. The captain and other officers of the Dunkerque sent Somerville a scathing letter on behalf of the nine officers and 200 men who died aboard the French ship.

185 **he simply could not hold back his loathing of Joachim von Ribben-trop:** Steed (ed.), *Hitler's Interpreter*, 11. In his Editor's Preface. R.H.Steed mentioned Hitler and Ribbentrop as two people Schmidt considered "the real enemies of mankind." Schmidt's disdain for Ribbentrop is clear throughout the book.

186 **"Everybody here is in despair at the prospect.":** Colville, *The Fringes of Power*, 122.

186 "What was constant was the respect, admiration and affection": Ibid, 281.

186 that a fighter pilot had greater excitement: Ibid, 412-413.

186 discouraged from keeping diaries: Roberts, *Masters and Commanders*, XXXIV.

189 sailed the North Atlantic with France's Admiral Bruno Marcel Gensoul: Lasterle, "La tragique parenthese de Mers-el-Kébir" (article), 81.

189 France's *Legion d'Honneur*: ADM; Letter from Ambassador Ronald H Campbell to Lord Halifax, April 30, 1940.

189 "He is the noblest Englishman, almost a saint": Life Magazine, February 10, 1941, p. 73.

190 both Chamberlain and King George VI preferred Halifax: Roberts, *Churchill: Walking With Destiny*, 502.

190 it would not be feasible for him to lead the House of Commons: Jenkins, *Churchill*,583.

190 Ambassador to the United States in December 1940: Ibid, 610.

190 "the Navy's here!": Frischauer and Jackson, *The Altmark Affair*, 237.

190 "That was big of Halifax": Marder, *From the Dardanelles to Oran*, 139.

191 born with a withered left arm: Birkenhead, *Halifax: The Life of Lord Halifax*, 23.

191 One of his sons was killed in the war: Ibid, 543

191 "If Darlan had chosen to fight in June 1940": Lacouture, *De Gaulle: The Rebel, 1890-1944*, 231.

192 traced back several generations: Melton, *Darlan: Admiral and Statesman of France*, 5.

192 "the British lion seems to grow wings": Werth: *France: 1940-1955*, 81.

192 "a bad man with a narrow outlook and a shifty eye": Atkinson, *An Army at Dawn, The War in North Africa – 1942-1943*, 95.

192 multiple solemn assurances from Darlan: Lamb, *Churchill as War Leader*, 63-68.

192 crippled the French Navy's communications capabilities: Brown, *The Road to Oran: Anglo-French Naval Relations, Sept 1939 – July 1940*, 140.

192 relocating the Admiralty: Ibid.

193 his Daily Express supported Neville Chamberlain's policy of appeasement: Cockett, *My Dear Max: The Letters of Brendan Bracken to Lord Beaverbrook, 1925-1958*, 21-22.

193 the Ministry of Aircraft Production: Ibid, 23

193 hand-written note asking Churchill to reconsider: Chisolm and Davie, *Lord Beaverbrook: A Life*, 375.

193 "Beaverbrook knew little or nothing about manufacturing airplanes": Korda, *With Wings Like Eagles: The History of the Battle of Britain*, 161.

193 "Organisation is the enemy of improvisation.": Taylor, *Beaverbrook*, 421.

194 increased monthly production of new Spitfires and Hurricanes: Calder, *The People's War: Britain, 1939-1945*, 146.

194 He also returned almost as many: Holland, *The Battle of Britain: Five Months That Changed History, May-October 1940*, 323.

194 built an organization – largely staffed by civilians: Calder, *The People's War: Britain, 1939-1945*, 148.

194 the press baron had even cancelled: Roberts, *Churchill: Walking With Destiny*, 421.

194 Beaverbrook firmly reinforced Churchill's commitment: Chisolm and Davie, *Lord Beaverbrook: A Life*, 379.

195 ignoring directions – but not firm orders: Bullitt, 458-459, June 9, 1940 telegram from Cordell Hull to Bullitt. P. 465, Draft of June 11, 1940 telegram from FDR to Bullitt. It is unclear if this telegram was ever sent.

195 asked to fill the governing void: Ibid, 462, June 11, 1940 telegram from Bullitt to FDR.

195 coordinate the inevitable transfer of control: Ibid, June 11, 1940 telegram from Bullitt to Cordell Hull.

195 the most brilliant student in his class: Ibid, xxxvii.

195 sometimes caustic member: Ibid, 13.

195 Bullitt wed Louis Bryant: Ibid, 15

195 Warren Beatty played John Reed in the movie "Reds": "Reds" page on the IMDb website: https://www.imdb.com/title/tt0082979/.

195 a psychological profile of President Wilson – with his co-author Sigmund Freud: Bullitt, 17. Their book – *Thomas Woodrow Wilson: A Psychological Study* – was published shortly after Bullitt's death in 1967. Freud had died 28 years before.

196 first American Ambassador to the Soviet Union: Ibid, 58.

196 appointed U.S. Ambassador to France in 1936: Ibid, 167.

196 spent weekends at a centuries-old chateau: Ibid, 217.

196 one joked of his wish that Bullitt: Brownell and Billings, *So Close to Greatness*, 207.

196 "they call me only in catastrophes": Watt, Dare Call It Treason, 214.

197 "right honorable member for Paris": Spears, *Assignment to Catastrophe: Vol. II, The Fall of France, June 1940*, 294.

197 "A man in his early forties": Spears, *Assignment to Catastrophe: Vol. I, Prelude to Dunkirk, June 1939 - May 1940*, 92.

197 Spears helped smuggle Charles de Gaulle: Ibid, 319.

198 the German Anschluss in Austria: Shirer, *This is Berlin*, 11, Transcript of a March 12, 1938 radio broadcast.

198 Hitler's furious harangues: Shirer, *The Nightmare Years: 1930-1940*, 116.

198 at Munich: Shirer, *This is Berlin*, 32, Transcript of a September 29, 1938 radio broadcast.

198 ritual staging of the armistice signing at Compiegne: Shirer, *Berlin Diary*, 414.

CHAPTER 24: JUST WHO DO YOU THINK YOU ARE?

201 "distorted sense of reality": Kidder and Todd, *Good Prose*, 168.

201 "it's as if you are required to think your work is more important": Ibid.

CHAPTER 25: MY ALMOST FIRST BOOK

207 **Art Sobczak**: You can learn more about Art Sobczak's books, newsletter, podcasts, training, and speaking at his website: www.smartcalling.com.

208 **"Publishers are in the business of printing books"**: I recalled this quote in fairly good detail. Art Sobczak was kind enough to confirm the specific wording in an email.

209 **White(side) papers**: If you'd like a copy of any of my papers: "12 Supply Chain Forecasting Lessons fom the Signal and the Noise," "Manage What Matters: The Pareto Principle, ABC Analysis, and How to Manage by Exception," or "42 Principles of Forecasting," just email me at bill.whiteside@perfectlytruestory.com

CHAPTER 26: PLATFORM

213 **"a platform is the combination of the tools, relationships, access"**: Holiday, *Perennial Seller*, 179-180.

214 **"the single most important and effective way to communicate"**: Ibid, 185.

215 **My brother-in-law's brother, who designs websites for a living**: John Oppenheimer at One Sky Media does great work at affordable prices: 1skymedia.com.

216 **www.perfectlytruestory.com**: In addition to progress updates on my book, my www.perfectlytruestory.com website also provides a number of articles that I have written, as well an archive of my monthly newsletters. Even though I sold software for thirty years, I'm not very technical. After first gathering the pictures and text that I had in mind, and laying it out in PowerPoint, I was able to build my own site on squarespace.com. I recommend them highly. If you intend to build a site of your own, be sure to do your homework, and prepare the material that you intend to post in advance.

CHAPTER 27: I'M NOW THAT GUY

217 **Between Hope and Fear**: *Between Hope and Fear: A History of Vaccines and Human Immunity* by Michael Kinch, published in paperback by Pegasus Books, can be found on Amazon.com and at other booksellers.

217 **"far better documented ... especially clear ... masterly exposition"**: Wall Street Journal, August 18-19, 2018, William F, Bynum review of *Between Hope and Fear* by Michael Kinch.

217 **"This is a fine book, marred only by a few"**: Ibid

217 **James Fallows**: A great way to catch up on James Fallows and his writing is to visit: www.theatlantic.com/author/james-fallows/.

218 **"given the choice between war and dishonor"**: This Churchill quote appears to have credence; I did not find it debunked. However, I've

not been able to confirm the specific source or venue for this quote, other than it was made in response to Neville Chamberlain's partici- pation in the Munich agreement.

CHAPTER 28: TOO DAMN INTERESTING

220 "I kept a diary during the war years": Colville, *Footprints in Time*, 67.
220 "with affection and penitence": Colville, *The Fringes of Power*, Dedica- tion page.
220 "I thought the Churchill girl rather supercilious": Ibid,120
220 "her views are as ill-judged as they are decisive": Ibid, 173
221 "You know I can stop you": Ibid, 411
221 "the short, sharp battle of the fighter pilot": Ibid
222 "I am becoming aware of how little we are worth": Ciano, The Ciano Diaries, 119
222 "Either he is under hallucinations, or he really is a genius": Ibid, 154.
222 "that pack of presumptuous vulgarians": Ibid, 212.
222 "base cowardice": Ibid, 583
222 "He is the exaggerated echo of Hitler": Ibid, 154
222 Edda unsuccessfully attempted to barter: Ibid, v
223 tied the seated Ciano to a chair and shot him in the back: *Time Maga- zine*, July 10, 1944, p. 36.
224 Originally a foreign correspondent for: Shirer, *The Nightmare Years: 1930-1940*, 274.
224 He was in Vienna on the day Germany annexed Austria: Ibid, 291
224 Nazi rallies in Nuremberg: Ibid, 127
224 was allowed to accompany German forces into France: Ibid, 166
224 "I saw his face light up successfully with hate": Shirer, *The Collapse of the Third Republic*, 879.
225 He commanded a small army of researchers: Reynolds, *In Command of History*, 89.
225 dealt with government secrecy laws: Ibid, 30
225 British tax code that threatened to take 97.5 per cent: Ibid, 10
225 sensitive to the feelings and reputations: Ibid, xxii
226 married for 50 years to Mary Borden: Mary Borden and General Spears were married on March 30, 1918. They remained married until her death on December 2, 1968.
226 American-born author: Egremont, *Under Two Flags*, 18.
226 inherited wealth: Ibid.
226 founded and helped run a field hospital: Borden, *Journey Down a Blind Alley*, 6.
226 roving ambulance corps: Ibid, 243.
226 affair with his secretary for decades: Egremont, *Under Two Flags*, 132.
226 married her ... on year after his wife's death: Ibid, 305.
227 Spears asked his doctor to recommend: Ibid, 273.
227 "had a streak of metallic ruthlessness": Colville, *Winston Churchill and His Inner Circle*, 257.
227 "If he had the word SHIT written on his forehead": Hart-Davis, *The Power of Chance*, 67-68, Rupert Hart-Davis, who became a publisher

later in life, later described Spears as "the greatest living shit" after a falling out that involved Hart-Davis' publication of Duff Cooper's autobiography.

227 **Story of Spears' dog and the housekeeper who refused to fetch his whip**: Egremont, *Under Two Flags*, 132.

CHAPTER 29: EVERYBODY KNOWS A SALESMAN CAN'T WRITE A BOOK

230 **"My work is finished. Your work begins."**: Watt, *The King's Depart*, 70.

230 **their train was slowed to a crawl**: Ibid, 402.

230 **reluctance to accept the treaty's *schmachparagraphen***: Ibid, 479.

231 **I learned that Richard M. Watt was a Dartmouth grad**: Obituary: https://www.amazon.com/Richard-M-Watt/e/B001HCVHZ2/ref=aufs_dp_fta_dsk.

231 **His author's page on Amazon.com**: https://www.amazon.com/Richard-M-Watt/e/B001HCVHZ2/ref=dp_byline_cont_pop_book_1.

235 **Evan Hill was not a professor; he was a writer**: *Secret Life*, 34.

235 **a story of his that appeared in a 1971 issue of Sports Illustrated**: Richard M. Watt's story "But You Never Were a Boar" was published in the November 22, 1971 issue of *Sports Illustrated*. It can be found online.

235 **Letter to Evan Hill**: Ibid.

236 **"It is even more exciting than your explanation"**: BU / RMW, Letter from Evan Hill to Richard Watt, August 27, 1959.

236 **Don Murray**: I did not initially understand – but gradually came to appreciate, thanks to my correspondence with Lin Watt - how Don Murray's influence extended well beyond his friendship with Dick Watt. He was a Pulitzer Prize-winning journalist, the author of 18 books, and a widely revered writing coach.

237 **"Write a book. There's no future in writing magazine articles."**: *Secret Life*, 34

237 **"but took not a single course in writing"**: Ibid, 33.

237 **He visited the library at West Point**: Ibid, 34.

237 **"Dick bought a paperback French grammar"**: Ibid

238 **a receipt for $67.50 for the translation**: BU / RMW. This receipt is in the collection.

238 **Herb Jaffe**: After a successful run as a literary agent, Herb Jaffe jumped to the movie business, and enjoyed a successful second career as an independent film producer.

238 **"You are now a professional writer; we've had our first rejection"**: BU / RMW, Letter from Herb Jaffe to Richard Watt, February, 27, 1961.

239 **"revealed the holes in his writing"**: *Secret Life*, 34.

239 **"I could never do all my research first"**: Ibid.

239 **"he'd mark that up and rewrite it, and rewrite that"**: Ibid.

239 **Watt combed the world for source materials**: Ibid.

240 **"I cannot think of any particular reason why you should help me"**: BU / RMW, Mr. Watt ended letters to multiple authors with this phrase.

240 **Questions to General Spears**: BU / RMW, Letter from Richard Watt to "Sir Edward" Spears, August 4, 1960.

241 **brutally frank critiques**: BU / RMW, The archives include multiple letters from Simon & Schuster with copious suggestions for edits.

241 **Korda agreed that Simon and Schuster would**: BU / RMW, Letter from Michael Korda to Richard Watt, Undated.

241 **"provide a protective cover against any possible attacks"**: BU / RMW, Letter from Michael Korda to Richard Watt, January 23, 1962.

241 **Colonel John Elting**: After retiring from the military in 1968, Colonel Elting "tried to be a historian." He succeeded, eventually writing 16 books.

242 **"Watt has done superbly well"**: Book review titled "Mutiny was the Order of the Day" by Alistair Horne, *New York Times*, Sunday, April 7, 1963, p. 31.

242 **"Watt skillfully evokes the eerie, secret struggle"**: *Time Magazine*, May 17, 1963, p. 126.

242 **"I found it fascinating. Once you get into it"**: BU / RMW, Letter from William L. Shirer to Michael Korda

243 **"an original and valuable work of history"**: Ibid, Letter from Michael Korda to Richard M. Watt.

243 **"Just think, if you do well enough"**: Ibd

243 **"Or if you want to talk about a third book"**: Ibid, Letter from Editor at Prentice-Hall to Richard M. Watt

244 **General Spears' minute corrections to Watt's manuscript**: Ibid, Letter from Richard Watt to his British publisher - Chatto & Windus, March 18, 1963.

244 **"You have in your first venture into authorship"**: Ibid, Letter from Sir Edward Louis Spears to Richard Watt, April 4, 1963.

244 **"You know far more about the events ... than I did"**: Ibid, Letter from Sir Edward Louis Spears to Richard Watt, September 21, 1962.

245 **"the best person to write the story"**: Ibid.

245 **"I was right to ask you to write the story of that period"**: Spears, *Assignment to Catastrophe, Volume 2: The Fall of France, June 1940*, 90.

245 **"I did not feel that I could write a story of which Pétain would be the hero."**: BU / RMW, Letter from Sir Edward Louis Spears to Richard Watt, September 21, 1962.

245 **"I have come to the conclusion that the time is ripe"**: Ibid, Letter from Sir Edward Louis Spears to Richard Watt, October 4, 1962.

246 **"There are golf-widows and fishing-widows and poker-widows"**: Ibid, Letter from Michael Korda to Richard Watt, May 1, 1962.

246 **"Everybody knows a salesman can't write a book, and I wasn't"**: *Secret Life*, 34.

EPILOGUE

249 **Chartwell Booksellers**: Chartwell Booksellers is located in the lobby of
     the Park Avenue Plaza Building, between Park and Madison Avenues
     in New York City. Their street address is 55 East 52nd Street, NY, NY
     10055. They have a great website at chartwellbooksellers.com. From
     their site: "Chartwell Booksellers is the only standing bookshop in the
     world devoted to the writings of Sir Winston Churchill.... Chartwell
     offers the largest selection anywhere of rare Churchill first editions,
     books about Winston Churchill and newly published works." They
     also deal in "autographed Churchilliana, including signed books, let-
     ters, documents and all manner of paper ephemera." Barry Singer, the
     owner of Chartwell Booksellers, is also the author of *The Art of Being
     Winston Churchill*, a fascinating study of Churchill's lifestyle, that is
     generously seeded with rare photographs.

Sources & Bibliography

Archival Material

Franklin D. Roosevelt Presidential Library
Hyde Park, NY
      Eleanor Roosevelt Papers
      Franklin D. Roosevelt Papers
      Press Secretary Papers

Churchill Archive Centre, Churchill College, University of Cambridge
Cambridge, U.K.
      Admiral Sir Dudley Pound Papers
      Admiral Sir James Somerville Papers
      John Colville Papers
      Major-General Sir Edward Spears Papers
      Winston Churchill Papers

Howard Gotlieb Archival Research Center, Boston University
Boston, MA
      Richard M. Watt Papers

Books: Writing and Marketing

Brown, Daniel James. *The Boys in the Boat: Nine Americans and Their Epic Quest for Gold at the 1936 Berlin Olympics*. New York: Penguin Books, 2014.
Hart, Jack. *Story Craft*. Chicago: The University of Chicago Press, 2011.
Hillenbrand, Laura. *Seabiscuit: An American Legend*. New York: Ballantine Books, 2002.
Holiday, Ryan. *Perennial Seller*. New York: Portfolio/Penguin, 2017.
Jelen, Carol and McCallister, Michael. *Build Your Author Platform*. Dallas: BenBella Books, 2014.
Kidder, Tracy and Todd, Richard. *Good Prose: The Art of Nonfiction*. New York: Random House Trade Paperbacks, 2013.
King, Stephen. *On Writing: A Memoir of the Craft*. New York: Scribner, 2000.
McPhee, John. *Draft No. 4*. New York: Farrar, Straus and Giroux, 2017.
Tuchman, Barbara. *Practicing History*. New York: Ballantine Books, 1981.

Books: History and People

Agar, Herbert. *The Darkest Year: Britain Alone, June 1940-June 1941*. London: The Bodley Head, 1972.

Amery, Leo. *My Political Life: The Unforgiving Years, 1929 – 1940*. London: Hutchinson, 1955.

Atkinson, Rick. *An Army at Dawn, The War in North Africa - 1942-1943*. New York: Henry Holt and Company, 2002.

--------. *The Day of Battle: The War in Sicily and Italy, 1943-1944*. New York: Henry Holt and Company, 2005.

Barber, Noel. *The Week France Fell*. New York: Stein and Day, 1976.

Bell, P.M.H. *A Certain Eventuality: Britain and the Fall of France*. Westmead: Saxon House, 1974.

Benoist-Mechin, Jacques. *Sixty Days that Shook the West*. New York: G.P. Putnam's Sons, 1963.

Birkenhead, Earl of. *Halifax*. Boston: Houghton Mifflin Company, 1966.

Black, Conrad. *Franklin Delano Roosevelt*. New York: Public Affairs, 2003.

Bloch, Michael. *Ribbentrop, A Biography*. New York: Crown Publishers, Inc., 1992.

Bois, Elie. *Truth on the tragedy of France*. London: Hodder and Stoughton, 1941.

Bond, Brian. *Britain, France, and Belgium: 1939-1940*. London: Brassey's, 1975.

Bonham-Carter, Violet. *Winston Churchill: An Intimate Portrait*. New York: Harcourt, Brace & World, 1965

Boothby, Robert. *I fight to Live*. London: Victor Gollancz, 1947.

--------. *Recollections of a Rebel*. London: Hutchinson, 1975

Borden, Mary. *Journey down a Blind Alley*. New York: Harper & Brothers, 1946.

Brown, David. *The Road to Oran: Anglo-French Naval Relations, September 1939 - July 1940*. London: Frank Cass, 2004.

--------. *The Royal Navy and the Mediterranean: Vol. III November 1940-December1941*. London: Taylor & Francis, 2013.

Brownell, Will. *So Close to Greatness: The Biography of William C. Bullitt*. New York: Macmillan Publishing Company, 1987.

Buckley, William F., *Athwart History: Half a Century of Polemics, Animadversions, and Illuminations*. New York: Encounter Books, 2010.

Bullitt, Orville (Ed.). *For the President, Personal and Secret - Correspondence Between Franklin D. Roosevelt and William C. Bullitt*. Boston: Houghton Mifflin Company, 1972.

Calder, Angus. *The People's War: Britain 1939-45*. New York: Pantheon Books, 1969.

Chisholm, Anne and Michael Davie. *Lord Beaverbrook: A Life*. New York: Alfred A. Knopf, 1993.

Churchill, Winston. *Great Contemporaries*. London: Thornton Butterworth Ltd, 1937.

--------. *The Second World War: The Gathering Storm*. Boston: Houghton Mifflin Company, 1948.

--------. *The Second World War: Their Finest Hour*. Boston: Houghton Mifflin Company, 1948.

Churchill, Winston. *Never Give In – The Best of Winston Churchill's Speeches.* New York: Hyperion, 2003.

Ciano, Count Galeazzo and Hugh Gibson (Ed.). *The Ciano Diaries, 1939-1943.* New York: Howard Fertig, 1973.

Cockett, Richard. *My Dear Max: The Letters of Brendan Bracken to Lord Beaverbrook, 1925-1958.* London: The Historian's Press, 1990.

Collier, Richard. *1940, The Avalanche.* New York: The Dial Press, 1979.

Colville, John. *Footprints in Time.* London: Collins, 1976.

--------. *The Churchillians.* London: Weidenfeld and Nicolson, 1981.

--------. *The Fringes of Power.* Guilford, CT: The Lyons Press, 1985.

--------. *Winston Churchill and His Inner Circle.* New York: Wyndham Books, 1981

Cooper, Duff. *Old Men Forget: The Autobiography of Duff Cooper.* London: Rupert Hart-Davis, 1953.

Coutau-Begarie. Herve and Claude Huan. *Lettres et notes de l'Amiral Darlan.* Paris: Economica, 1953.

Coutts, Ben. *Bothy to Big Ben ... and beyond.* Oxford: Mercat Press, 1998.

Cunningham, Admiral Andrew Browne. *A Sailor's Odyssey: The Autobiography of Admiral of the Fleet, Viscount Cunningham or Hyndhope.* London: Hutchinson & Co., Ltd, 1951.

Darlan, Alain. *L'Amiral Darlan Parle.* Paris: Amiot – Dumont, 1952.

De Gaulle, Charles. *The Complete War Memoirs of Charles de Gaulle.* New York: Simon & Schuster, 1955.

De Montmorency, Alec. *The Enigma of Admiral Darlan.* New York: E.P. Dutton, 1943.

Eade, Charles. *Churchill – By His Contemporaries.* London: The Reprint Society, 1953.

--------. *Secret Sessions of the Right Hon. Winston S. Churchill.* London: Cassel & Co, 1946.

Eden, Anthony. *The Memoirs of Sir Anthony Eden, Vol 1: Facing the Dictators.* London: Cassell & Co, 1962.

--------. *The Memoirs of Sir Anthony Eden, Vol 2: The Reckoning.* London: Cassell & Co, 1965.

Egremont, Max. *Under Two Flags: The Life of General Sir Edward Spears.* London: Weidenfeld & Nicolson. 1997.

Evans, Richard J., *The Third Reich in Power, 1933-1939.* New York: The Penguin Press. 2005.

Francois-Poncet, Andre. *The Fateful Years: Memoirs of a French Ambassador in Berlin, 1931-1938.* New York: Harcourt, Brace and Company, 1949.

Frischauer, William and Robert Jackson. *The Altmark Affair.* New York: The MacMillan Company, 1955.

Gates, Eleanor. *End of the Affair: The Collapse of the Anglo-French Alliance, 1939-40*, Berkeley: University of California Press, 1940.

Gilbert, G.M., *Nuremberg Diary.* Boston: De Capo Press, 1995.

Gilbert, Martin. *Road to Victory. Winston S. Churchill 1941-1945.* Toronto: Stoddart, 1986.

--------. *Winston Churchill, The Wilderness Years.* Boston: Houghton Mifflin Company, 1982.

Grenfell, Russell. *The Bismarck Episode.* New York: The MacMillan Company, 1949.

Halifax, Lord. *Fullness of Days*. New York: Dodd, Mead & Company, 1957.

Hart-Davis, Rupert. *The Power of Chance*. London: Trafalgar Square, 1992.

Henderson, Sir Nevile. *Failure of a Mission: by the British Ambassador to Berlin 1937-1939*. New York: G.P. Putnam's Sons, 1940

--------. *Water Under the Bridges*. London, Hodder & Stoughton, 1945.

Holland, James. *The Battle of Britain: Five Months that Changed History. May-October 1940*. New York: St. Martin's Press, 2010.

Horne, Alistair. *Seven Ages of Paris*. New York: Alfred A. Knopf, 2003.

--------. *To Lose a Battle: France 1940*. Boston: Little Brown and Company. 1969.

Hull, Cordell. *The Memoirs of Cordell Hull (Volume 1)*. New York: The Macmillan Company, 1948.

Jackson, Julian. *The Fall of France: May-June 1940*. Oxford: Arthur Barker Limited, 1975

James, Robert Rhodes. *Chips: The Diaries of Sir Henry Channon*. London: Weidenfeld and Nicolson, 1967.

Jeanneny, Jean-Noel. *Jules Jeanneny : Journal Politique : Septembre 1939 – Julliet 1942*. Paris : Librarie Armand Colin. 1972.

Jenkins, Roy. *Churchill, A Biography*. New York: Farrar, Straus and Giroux, 2001.

Kelly, Douglas M., *22 Cells in Nuremberg*. New York. Greenberg: Publisher, 1947

Korda, Michael. *With Wings Like Eagles: The History of the Battle of Britain*. New York: Harper Perennial, 2009.

Lacouture, Jean. *De Gaulle, The Rebel, 1890-1944*. New York: W.W. Norton & Company, 1990.

Lamb, Richard. *Churchill as War Leader*. New York: Carroll & Graf Publishers, 1991.

Larson, Erik. *The Splendid and the Vile*. New York: Crown. 2020.

Liebling, A.J., *Liebling's War: World War II Dispatches of A.J. Liebling*. New York: The Library of America, 2011.

Lukacs, John. *Five Days in London. May 1940*. New Haven: Yale University Press, 1999.

--------. *Remembered Past, John Lukacs on History, Historians and Historical Knowledge, A Reader*. Wilmington: ISI Books, 2005.

--------. *The Duel*. New Haven: Yale University Press, 1990.

Macintyre, Donald. *Fighting Admiral – The Life and Battles of Admiral of the Fleet Sir James Somerville*. London: Evans Brothers Limited, 1961.

Maisky, Ivan. *Memoirs of a Soviet Ambassador, The War: 1939-43*. New York: Charles Scribner's Sons, 1967.

Manchester, William and Paul Reid. *The Last Lion: Winston Spencer Churchill, Defender of the Realm, 1940-1965*. Boston: Little, Brown and Company, 2012.

Marder, Arthur. *From the Dardanelles to Oran: Studies of the Royal Navy in War and Peace, 1915-1940*. London: Oxford University Press, 1974.

Maurois, Andre. *Tragedy in France*. New York: Harper & Brothers, 1940.

--------. *Why France Fell*, London: John Lane, 1940.

Meacham, Jon, *Franklin and Winston: An Intimate Portrait of an Epic Friendship*. New York: Random House Trade Paperbacks, 2004.

Melton, George. *Darlan: Ambassador and Statesman of France.* Westport, CT: Praeger, 1998.

Moran, Lord. *Churchill at War 1940-45.* New York: Carroll & Graf Publishers, 2002.

Murphy, Robert. *Diplomat Among Warriors.* New York: Doubleday & Company, 1964.

O'Brien, Michael. *Hesburgh, A Biography.* Washington, DC: The Catholic University of America Press, 1998.

Olson, Lynne. *Citizens of London.* New York: Random House, 2010.

--------. *Troublesome Young Men.* New York. Farrar, Strauss and Giroux, 2007.

Orwell, George and Peter Davison (ed.). *George Orwell Diaries,* New York: Liveright Publishing Corporation, 2012.

Packwood, Allen. *How Churchill Waged War.* Yorkshire: Frontline Books, 2018.

Panter-Downes, Mollie. *London War Notes, 1939-1945.* New York: Farrar, Straus and Giroux, 1971.

Pawle, Gerald. *The Secret War: 1939-45.* New York: William Sloan Associates, Inc., 1957.

Peillard, Leonce. *The Laconia Affair.* New York: G.P. Putnam's Sons. 1963.

Playfair, Major General I.S.O., *The Mediterranean and Middle East, Vol I, The Early Successes Against Italy (to May 1941).* London: Her Majesty's Stationery Office, 1954.

Porch, Douglas. *The Path to Victory.* New York: Farrar, Straus and Giroux, 2004.

Ribbentrop, Joachim von. *The Ribbentrop Memoirs.* London: Weidenfeld & Nicolson, 1954.

Roberts, Andrew. *Churchill, Walking with Destiny.* New York: Viking, 2018.

--------. *Masters and Commanders.* New York: HarperCollins, 2009.

--------. *The Holy Fox,* London: Weidenfeld and Nicolson, 1991.

Roskill, Stephen. *The War at Sea: 1939-1945: Volume 1: The Defensive.* London: Her Majesty's Stationery Office, 1954.

Schmidt, Dr. Paul. *Hitler's Interpreter.* London: William Heinemann Ltd, 1951.

Schmidt, Bill. *Words of Life.* South Bend, Indiana: University of Notre Dame Press, 2013.

Sebag-Montefiore, Hugh. *Dunkirk: Fight to the Last Man.* Cambridge, Massachusetts: Harvard University Books, 2006.

Seldes, George: *Witness to a Century.* New York: Ballantine Books, 1987

Sevareid, Eric. *Not So Wild a Dream.* New York: Alfred A. Knopf, 1947.

Sheean, Vincent. *Between the Thunder and the Sun.* London: Random House, p. 1943.

Sherwood, Robert. *Roosevelt and Hopkins: An Intimate History.* New York: Harper and Brothers, 1948.

Shirer, William H., *"This is Berlin". Radio Broadcasts form Nazi Germany.* Woodstock, NY: The Overlook Press, 1999.

--------. *The Collapse of the Third Republic.* New York, Simon & Schuster, 1969.

--------. *The Nightmare Years: 1930-1940.* Boston: Little, Brown and Company, 1984.

--------. *Berlin Diary.* New York: Knopf. 1941.

--------. *The Rise and Fall of the Third Reich*. New York: Simon & Schuster, 1960.

Silver, Nate. *The Signal and the Noise: Why So Many Predictions Fail – But Some Don't*. New York: The Penguin Press. 2012.

Simpson, Michael (ed.). *The Somerville Papers: Selections from Private and Official Correspondence*. Aldershot: Navy Records Society, 1995.

Smith, Dennis Mack. *Mussolini*. New York: Knopf, 1982.

Somerville, Christopher. *Our War: How the British Commonwealth Fought the Second World War*. London: Weidenfeld & Nicolson, 1998.

Spears, Major-General Sir Edward. *Assignment to Catastrophe: Vol. I. Prelude to Dunkirk, June 1939 – May 1940*. New York: A.A. Wyn, Inc. 1954.

--------. *Assignment to Catastrophe: Vol. II. The Fall of France, June 1940*. New York: A.A. Wyn, Inc. 1955.

--------. *The Picnic Basket*. New York: W.W. Norton & Company, 1967.

--------. *Two Men Who Saved France: Pétain and de Gaulle*. New York: Stein and Day, 1966.

Taylor, A.J.P., *Beaverbrook*. New York: Simon & Schuster, 1972.

Thompson, Inspector Walter Henry. *Assignment: Churchill*. New York: Farrar, Straus and Young, 1955.

Toland, John. *Adolf Hitler*. New York: Ballantine Books, 1976.

Tute, Warren. *The Deadly Stroke*. New York: Coward, McCann & Geoghegan, Inc. 1973.

`Watt. Richard M, *Dare Call It Treason*. New York: Simon & Schuster, 1963.

--------. *The King's Depart: The Tragedy of Germany: Versailles and the German Revolution*. New York: Simon & Schuster, 1968.

Welles, Sumner. *The Time for Decision*. New York: Harper & Brothers, 1944.

Werth, Alexander. *France: 1940-1955*. New York: Henry Holt and Company, 1956.

--------. *The Last Days of Paris, A Journalist's Diary*. London: Hamish Hamilton, 1940.

--------. *The Twilight of France, 1933-1940. A Journalist's Chronicle*. New York, Harper Brothers, 1942.

Wilson, Charles. Pétain: How the Hero of France Became a Convicted Traitor and Changed the Course of History. New York: Palgrave Macmillan, 2005.

Magazines, Journals, Newspapers and Other

Life Magazine
Look Magazine
The New Yorker
Time Magazine
Lancaster Intelligencer Journal (Pennsylvania)
Le Matin (Paris)
The Daily Telegraph (Paris)
The Journal of Military History. "Could Admiral Gensoul have averted the tragedy of Mers el-Kébir?", by Philippe Lasterle; Vol. 67, No. 3; July 2003; pp. 835-844.

About the Author

After selling software for thirty years, I abandoned that career to finish writing a book that I started researching to keep my mind engaged during my time on the road. I was intrigued by an incident from early in Winston Churchill's first term as Britain's prime minister. As I dug into the story from multiple angles, my diversion evolved into an obsession. The more I learned, the more it became a book I just had to write. This is the story of how I learned to research and write that book.

I grew up in the Philadelphia suburbs, the oldest of six kids, and graduated from the University of Notre Dame with a degree in Management. My wife Barbara and I have lived in Lancaster County, Pennsylvania for more than 35 years, and have been blessed with a son (Billy) and a daughter (Brittany).

Index

CPSIA information can be obtained
at www.ICGtesting.com
Printed in the USA
LVHW041351240623
750696LV00001B/73

9 798986 660714